19-25

University of Pittsburgh

**Studies
in
Comparative
Education**

UNIVERSITY OF PITTSBURGH
STUDIES IN COMPARATIVE EDUCATION

Khrushchev and the Central Committee Speak on Education
George S. Counts   1959, paper, $1.50

Society and Education in Brazil
Robert J. Havighurst and J. Roberto Moreira
                                                      1965, paper, $2.50

Scottish and English Schools: Survey of the Past Fifty Years
G. S. Osborne   1967, $8.00

Examinations: An Account of Their Evolution as
Administrative Devices in England
Robert J. Montgomery   1968, $6.95

Nepal in Transition: Educational Innovation
H. B. Reed and Mary Jane Reed   1968, $5.95

**Society
and Education
in Brazil**

SOCIETY AND EDUCATION IN BRAZIL

Robert J. Havighurst
Professor of Education
The University of Chicago

J. Roberto Moreira
Late Director of the National Department of Education,
Ministry of Education, Brazil

University of Pittsburgh Press

To Anísio Teixeira

Preface

THIS book has two purposes.

One is to show how education works in the development of a modern society. In Brazil we see a country moving with tremendous speed and momentum out of a colonial past into an industrial democratic future. Education is being used as an agent for this transformation, deliberately and consciously. At the same time, the social and economic forces at work in the society are shaping education.

The second purpose is to interpret Brazil to the English-speaking world, which will have to reckon with her as the coming power-center of economic and political affairs in South America. With her land mass, her known and her probable natural resources, and with a population potential that could bring her up to 150 million by the year 2,000, Brazil is the colossus of South America.

This kind of study of education as a major factor in the growth of a society requires attention to the basic social institutions of the family, church, state, and the economy. As these institutions evolve through time they change their own educational activities, and they make increasing demands on the formal institutions of education—the schools and the universities.

The twentieth century is the setting for this book, with more than half of the pages devoted to Brazil since 1945. However, a historical section of three chapters portrays the evolution of Brazilian society through two-and-a-half centuries of colonial exploitation and a century of imperial independence into a modern republic, and the part education played in these events.

Standard Brazilian sources have been used for the social and political history, and for contemporary socioeconomic and educational data, as well as the works of several foreign historians, economists, and sociologists who have made a special study of Brazil. Some of the data have been collected personally by the authors, who have also drawn on their personal experience with education and society in Brazil.

In one sense, this book had its beginning in 1956 when Dr. Moreira was Program Director and I was Co-director of the

Brazilian Government Center for Educational Research. More specifically, it began to take form in 1959 when Dr. Moreira was at the University of Chicago as Visiting Professor of Education. During his stay there he conducted a seminar in Brazilian society and education and prepared a manuscript, which I agreed to translate, on that subject. Dr. Moreira later revised his manuscript and published it in Brazil in 1960 under the title *Educação e Desenvolvimento no Brasil*. In the meantime I translated the manuscript, with the help of Julian Steen of Chicago. The first four chapters of this book, except for some adaptations and additions, are from that translation.

Because of the rapid changes taking place in Brazil, I decided to add material covering events through the end of 1963. I did this work while in Rio de Janeiro as a Fulbright Visiting Professor at the Brazilian Government Center for Educational Research. Dr. Moreira, at that time Director of the National Department of Education in the Brazilian Ministry of Education, was available for consulting.

Both Dr. Moreira and I are grateful to the Center and to its director Anísio Teixeira. While there we were given use of the Center's library and time to do the research which ultimately led to this book.

It has seemed best to preserve some of the Portuguese words in the text, where an English translation is not easily made. These words are collected and explained in the Glossary. Unless a specific translation is indicated, the translations of the foreign references are those of the authors.

Robert J. Havighurst

1964

Contents

Illustrations

Tables

**Society
and Education
in Brazil**

1

The
Land
and the People
of Brazil

WHEN ex-President Theodore Roosevelt in 1913 led an expedition to explore an unknown tributary of the Amazon river in Brazil, he called the attention of his countrymen to a land that was largely unknown to them. With an incomplete picture of the southern part of their hemisphere, of the nature of the land and the people, North Americans were then ready to believe fantastic stories about the tropical primitiveness of Brazil. And even today they are often likely to think of Brazil in terms of the jungles of the Amazon region rather than of a modern city like São Paulo—as large as Chicago and growing more rapidly, carefully designed around a central city where tall buildings reach through the mists of a July morning toward the blue sky with warm color and curving movement, making the stainless steel and glass of New York City seem cold and constrained by comparison. Bringing their gaze down from the skyscrapers of São Paulo to the Praça da República (Plaza of the Republic), North Americans would see Brazilians sunning themselves on the park benches, or busily shopping for crystal ware or leather goods in the modern shops, or buying airline tickets to Paris or New York on Air France, Varig, Lufthansa, Pan-American, or SAS, or lining up at lunch counters for their *cafèzinho*.

North Americans might read in the London or New York newspapers about the Latin American common market, in which Brazil is the principal economic force, or about Brazil's leadership of Latin American nations in matters of international relations, yet the association of tropical forests blanketing the Amazon basin and of jungle tribes of savage Indians persists out of proportion. Actually both images, of the primitive tropical

1

and of the modern, are true of the real Brazil, whose size and complexity make it a country of which many contrasting statements may be true. It is the largest Latin American country, and larger than the United States, except for Alaska. It is the most powerful country in the western hemisphere, after the United States. Yet Brazil is also one of the poor countries of the world, in terms of per capita income, and much of the country's wealth of natural resources is unexploited and unexplored.

TABLE 1

Literacy* of Children and Youth, 1950

	% Literate Age	
Region and state	9-10	16-17
North		
Amazonas	19.4	43.6
Pará	27.0	54.2
Northeast		
Maranhão	13.1	28.6
Piauí	10.0	28.9
Ceará	13.4	34.9
Rio Grande do Norte	18.1	38.5
Paraíba	15.9	34.9
Pernambuco	15.7	35.7
Alagoas	12.1	27.2
East		
Sergipe	24.3	40.9
Bahia	16.7	33.7
Minas Gerais	29.6	47.1
Espírito Santo	31.1	50.8
Rio de Janeiro	37.1	60.7
Guanabara	79.2	89.0
South		
São Paulo	58.7	73.1
City of São Paulo	85.5	93.0
Paraná	38.1	57.6
Santa Catarina	58.1	73.8
Rio Grande do Sul	49.6	71.1
Central West		
Mato Grosso	32.2	56.9
Goiás	15.9	36.9

* The ability to read and write a simple letter.

Source: Giorgio Mortara, "Estudos Demograficos do Laboratorio de Estatística de IBGE, 1956," *Revista Brasileira de Estudos Pedagógicos*, XXXVI (1956), 180-88.

A country of extremes of wealth and poverty, of humid jungles and of dry plains, with sizeable mountains and a long coast line, Brazil has produced a variegated society. Such a society demands a variegated educational system, for the educational system of a country is a kind of mirror in which the major features of the society are reflected, and through which these features are reflected into the lives of the oncoming generation. The most modern schools and universities will be found in the most modern parts of this complex country. And likewise, the poorest schools and the greatest degree of illiteracy will be found in the poorest and least modern parts of the country. (Table 1 shows how illiteracy and school attendance are related to the various geographical regions of the country.)

Geography and Education in Brazil

Brazil is the largest Latin American country, occupying half of the total area of South America. It touches all of the South American countries except Chile and Ecuador, filling a perimeter of 14,373 miles of which 4,604 miles make up the Atlantic coastline. A modern airplane flying at a speed of 300–320 miles per hour would require 46–47 hours to fly completely around the country. To fly across the Brazilian territory from the extreme south to the extreme north, this plane would need approximately eight hours of continuous flight, and the same amount of time would be necessary for an east-west transit. This does not indicate, however, that the shape of Brazil is square. It is much larger in the north than in the south. Its outline on the map suggests a quarter of beef.

The equator passes through the north of Brazil a little above the Amazon river, and the Tropic of Capricorn crosses the country close to the city of São Paulo. Thus Brazil is a tropical country. Of all of its territorial extent only 8 to 9 per cent lies below the Tropic of Capricorn.

It would be a mistake, however, to suppose that more than 90 per cent of the Brazilian territory has a typically tropical climate: warm and humid or hot and dry. There are such regions. There is Amazonia, which has heat and humidity during practically all of the year; and there is the Northeast, which is characterized generally by dry heat throughout the year. In both of these regions the mean maximum daily temperature varies through the year from 75° F. to a little more than 100° F. Whereas in Amazonia it rains almost daily, in the Northeast it seldom rains, and there is a large area, called the Polygon of Drought, where there is rain during only three months of the year. Sometimes rain does not come at all in the Polygon of Drought and twelve months or more may pass without any, as was the case in 1958.

FIGURE 1

REGIONS

In a number of states, however, including Goiás, Minas Gerais, Espírito Santo, Rio de Janeiro, and the larger part of São Paulo, there are extensive areas of moderate climate, neither dry nor humid, with a temperature which varies during the year between 50° and 90° F. The region in which Brasília, the new capital of Brazil, is situated has a most agreeable climate, with regular rains during four months of the year and a low humidity during the rest of the year. The temperature there varies between 60° F. and 80° F., giving the city spring and autumn only, never winter or summer.

Only three states in the South—Paraná, Santa Catarina and Rio Grande do Sul—and a part of São Paulo have the four seasons distinguished as such. These states have an area equivalent to a little more than 8 per cent of the total area of Brazil. Spring comes there from September to December, and the fields and the forests flourish during those months. Summer is the season of fruits, commencing in December and continuing until March, followed by autumn, from March until June, and winter, from June to September. At that time, the temperature can descend quite low, reaching 25° F. in some places. During June and July there are almost daily frosts, and some of the higher places are acquainted with snow.

This general sketch of the Brazilian climate indicates only its salient characteristics. Naturally, in this large tropical area there are mountainous regions in which the climate is agreeable. For example, in the region of Rio de Janeiro, where it is never cold and may be unusually warm in the months of December, January, and February, it is possible to find, only 70 or 80 kilometers away in Petropolis, Nova Friburgo, and Teresópolis a springlike climate during the summer, and a winter which the *Cariocas* (the native inhabitants of Rio) consider to be very cold (48° to 60° F.). Even in the Northeast, close to the equator, there are areas of pleasant climate, such as the Plateau of Borborema.

Constantly warm and humid, typically tropical, in the sense that North Americans understand a tropical climate, is the Amazon region, or more specifically the basin of the Amazon river, with 4,788,374 square kilometers, which makes up more than 53 per cent of the Brazilian territory.

The topography of Brazil shows some striking resemblance to that of the United States, if one keeps in mind the fact that the boundary of Brazil stops in the forest east of the Andes, whereas the United States reaches across the Rocky Mountains to the

Pacific Ocean. There is a range of fairly low mountains in the east of Brazil, rising up from the seacoast in the Serra do Mar, with the highest peaks reaching almost 9,000 feet and sloping down gradually to the river valleys of central Brazil—the Paraná and the Amazon. These valleys get rain all or most of the year. Thus Brazil is mostly a low, well-watered land, with 57 per cent of its area between 700 and 3,000 feet above sea level, and only 3 per cent above 3,000 feet.

One of the educational consequences of the geography of Brazil is that the traditional system of centralized educational administration, with centers of power in the national capital and the state capitals, must contend with a widely extended population, with far-flung lines of communication and very weak systems of control and coordination. Thus the mails may take weeks to deliver a letter from the national capital to a municipal center a thousand miles away, and rural villages may be days or even weeks away by mail from a state capital.

Politically, Brazil has adopted a solution similar to that of the United States, being organized into a federation of twenty-two semi-autonomous states and four territories. In education, this might be expected to result in decentralization, but that is not entirely the case. Although the primary schools and the institutions for the training of primary school teachers are controlled by the states, the secondary schools and higher institutions are subject to federal law and are under the control of the Ministry of Education and Culture, which is a part of the Executive Branch of the Federal Government. The Basic Education Law of 1961 aims toward greater decentralization, giving the states more autonomy.

A brief look at the climatic situation of Brazil indicates that only a decentralized system of educational administration could make the schools sensitive to the needs and adapted to the conditions of the various regions. In the northern region, which includes the states of Amazonas, Acre, and Pará and the territories of Rondônia, Rio Branco, and Amapá, it is difficult for the schools to function from January to May, when the rains are intense and the monthly precipitation always exceeds 250 millimeters (10 inches). In the rural and lightly populated areas, during this season it is practically impossible for a child to go to school if he has to go farther than one kilometer. Even in the urban areas, school attendance is considerably reduced during this season. In addition, in the months of November and December the heat is intense, the mean daily maximum temperature reaching 95° F., which makes school work inefficient because of the physiologic effects of the high temperature.

Consequently, in all of this region school achievement is very low because out of the entire year only five months have climatic conditions favorable for good work in the school room. Hence, the school year should be organized in such a way as to permit the most intensive school activities during these five months, and making the long vacations coincide with the warmer months, while the school day or even the school week might be reduced in the months of heavy rain.

Only in the south of Brazil and in certain parts of the Eastern and midwestern regions is it possible to have a school year similar to that of the United States and of the European countries, because only in these regions are the four seasons well defined and equally distributed over the year.

In the Northeast, where there are long periods without rain, between September and January the rural areas fall into a phase of stagnation, when productive activity ceases almost completely, food is scarce, and water disappears. If it were possible to install schools in places where water can be stored for the dry period, and if adequate food could be provided for school children during this period as well as adequate health service, the dry months would be good for school activities, since nothing else could interfere with them. However, without nutritional assistance and health services pupils can accomplish very little in school during this season.

Besides determining the time of the year when it is best to hold school, the climatic conditions of Brazil also impose a great variety upon school architecture. It would be impossible to expect a standardization of school buildings. Some of the Brazilian architects who have been studying the problem have reached the conclusion that the building materials employed in a given region for the construction of houses generally suggest the best solutions for the building of schools which are suitable to climatic conditions.

Physiography

Brazil is a country of physiographic contrasts. Grand wide rivers cut the country. Best known is the Amazon with its great tributaries; but there are also the Tocantins, the São Francisco, and the Paraná. As we have pointed out, the Northeast suffers from a lack of water. There the rivers, though quite extensive during a part of the year, dry up for a long period of five or more months. This Polygon of Drought has an area of 950,000 square kilometers, which is sufficient to include the area of several European countries.

The Amazon and its tributaries water and nourish more than half of Brazil, forming an area covered with tropical forest almost impenetrable because the great trees with their interlacing branches and climbing vines maintain a moist and muddy forest floor. In this region, the means of communication are the rivers, which are navigable by large ships. Transatlantic cargo vessels can go to the heart of the continent, as far as Manaus, 1,500 miles from the ocean. Tabatinga, where the Amazon enters Brazil from the Andean forest, is only 250 feet above sea level, and the sea is 1,700 miles distant. Manaus is the capital of the state of Amazonas and the principal city of the Amazonian interior, with some 200,000 inhabitants. In addition to river navigation, the other means of travel is the airplane, which places the entire Amazonian area some six to ten hours distant from any other part of Brazil.

The São Francisco is called the "River of Brazilian Unity," for it traverses the interior of Brazil from south to north linking the Northeast with the area near Rio de Janeiro and São Paulo. When the droughts make life uncertain, this river has long been a highway of migration for the excess population of the Northeast to the better watered lands of the South and the area of greatest economic development. Not far from the mouth of the São Francisco river, in the Northeast, lie the falls of Paulo Afonso, which are among the greatest in the world in terms of volume and hydro-electric potential. These falls are gradually being harnessed for the generation of electrical energy, and they represent a great hope for the people who live in the Polygon of Drought. All of this area is economically poor because the land produces little. Industrialization and the extraction and transformation of the mineral riches of the region, which will be permitted by the energy of Paulo Afonso, may help to cure the poverty of the people of the Northeast.

The Tocantins river also flows from south to north, for the most part parallel and to the west of the São Francisco river, and enters the Atlantic Ocean close to the mouth of the Amazon. However, in contrast to the São Francisco which is almost entirely navigable, the Tocantins has many falls and rapids and therefore fails to serve as a means of communication with the interior of Brazil. Its hydro-electric potential, however, is very great and leads to the expectation that with the growth of the new capital, Brasília, and with the economic development of the Central West of Brazil, this hydroelectric potential will be put to use.

The other great Brazilian river, the Paraná, flows in the opposite direction from the São Francisco and the Tocantins, from north to south. The Paraná joins with the Paraguay and the Uruguay rivers to form the great Rio de la Plata which bathes the shores of Uruguay and Argentina and serves the great cities and ports of Montevideo and Buenos Aires. The sources of the Paraná are close to those of the São Francisco and the Tocantins. It was because of this that the Paulistas (pioneers from the state of São Paulo) were able to penetrate into the interior of Brazil during the eighteenth century. By traveling on tributaries of the Paraná, which rise very close to the sea in the state of São Paulo and flow to the west, the Paulistas were able to reach the Paraná and to travel both to the north and to the south, exploring the land of the Central Southwest, which is today highly productive. Later traversing the inland plateau and traveling by means of the São Francisco and the Tocantins, the Paulistas continued the conquest of the still underdeveloped Central West of Brazil.

In their travels, the Paulistas met on the São Francisco river the backwoodsmen from Bahia, to the northeast, who were bent on the same work of conquest and exploration. Thus, the rivers permitted the Brazilians of the seventeenth and eighteenth centuries to take possession of a vast area of land, abundant in vegetable and mineral riches—land which is only now beginning to be definitively explored and occupied. The same rivers in the present century promise to provide electrical energy sufficient for the total industrialization of the country, even when it comes to possess a population of two or three hundred millions. Naturally this will not come to pass very rapidly. The Brazilians are just beginning to develop this hydroelectric potential. However, the great hydroelectric plants at Tres Marias and Furnas in the state of Minas Gerais are already producing energy.

The picture of Brazil as a land entirely covered with immense tropical forests is far from the truth. With the exception of the Amazon basin, which is about half of the country, Brazil does not possess much primeval forest. Man has been able to work a large

FIGURE 2

MAJOR RIVERS

part of the Brazilian territory, although perhaps not in the wisest manner. Consequently, one finds today large desolate areas denuded of ancient forest, as, for example, the so-called Forest Zone of Minas Gerais, where the low second growth forest, much less rich and exuberant, grows on land which because of primitive methods of cultivation has lost its fertility and has been abandoned. In the South a great region of gently undulating plains is covered with a nutritive grass, excellent for the feeding of cattle. There live the Brazilian Gauchos or cowboys, quite similar to their Argentine brothers, although descended from the Paulistas, who came south from the state of São Paulo to develop this territory in the nineteenth century.

Characteristic of the Northeast are the dry lands, where the rains fall only during three or four months of the year and sometimes fail completely. The vegetation, wise as a man, has adapted itself to a condition of scarcity of water. It does not die during the drought but enters into a state of latency, much as the North American vegetation during the winter when the snow and frost give the impression of a grey desert. The vegetation which in the Brazilian Northeast has a dominantly yellow tinge, bears fruit and seeds enveloped in thick starchy hulls, which enable them to survive and facilitate their germination when the rains come. The dried-out trees, some gnarled and twisted, some straight and bare, are brought to life by the rains, and within a few days cover themselves with green, and soon thereafter come into flower. Beneath the trees, which are arranged sparsely and almost regularly over the land, the rains bring into life tufts of grass interlaced with thorny creepers. Above the creeping vegetation and among the larger trees are small shrub-like palms. As soon as the rains stop and the water disappears, everything commences to die once more, and after about two months gives the impression of a devastated land. Nevertheless, man lives there, unprovided with technology and the resources of modern civilization. He lives and thus proves that nature is not completely hostile to him, in spite of the many hardships it imposes.

The soil of the Northeast is not poor, for during the rainy periods the man of the interior contrives to grow all kinds of cereals and vegetables. The wild fruits are also abundant and rich in nutritional value, but underneath the cover of fertile soil at no more than fifty centimeters (half a yard) of depth lies an impermeable layer, which does not allow the soil to conserve moisture for any length of time. All of the Northeast is cut by chains of low mountains, which form plateaus, with natural reservoirs where moisture is conserved and creates oases of constant vegetation.

Brazil is not a land of high mountains. In the North, in the South, and in the center, chains and ranges of low mountains vary in height from a few hundred to twenty-five hundred meters. The highest points are in the South near Rio de Janeiro, and in the extreme North in the ranges which separate Brazil from Venezuela and from the Guianas. But these mountains never reach the grandeur or the height of an Aconcágua or an Ilimani in the Cordillera of the Andes. There are no active volcanoes in any part of the country and no earthquakes. In spite of the fact that the chains of mountains are not high in Brazil, they presented great difficulties to the conquest of the interior. One range, which runs from the South in the state of Santa Catarina almost to the Northeast in the state of Bahia, a few kilometers inland from the coast, was a major obstacle to the exploration and settlement of the interior.

Covered with aggressive forests, inhabited by snakes and wild animals, abounding in steep rises and deep canyons with wet vertical walls, these mountains were conquered by man at great cost. Nevertheless, the mountains were crossed by the men of São Paulo, the Northeast, and Bahia with no tools other than primitive muskets, machetes, and courage. Although the interior was thus conquered, it could not be occupied by a numerous population. Consequently, a demographic map of Brazil, even at the present time, shows a black ribbon of dense population along the coastline from the mouth of the Amazon to the extreme south, with some 50 to 100 kilometers of width and a population density of more than 60 inhabitants per square kilometer. Behind this a broader band reaches a thousand kilometers of width in the South, the Center, and the Northeast, where the population density is 15 to 60 inhabitants per square kilometer. Farther west is a more sparsely populated area, as yet not very large, with a density of 2 to 15 inhabitants per square kilometer, and finally, farther inland to the northwest and the central west, lies the great Amazon region with more than 4 million square kilometers, and with a population density of less than 2 persons per square kilometer. The difficulties placed in the way of the construction of highways by the mountains and tropical forests and the great swamps explain the slow and gradual process of occupation of the interior of the country.

TABLE 2

Regional Differences in Income, School Enrollment, and Literacy

Region	Per capita income, 1958 Cr$ *	US$ 1957	Value of factory production per worker, 1955 (1,000 Cr$)	Primary school enrollment, % of pop. aged 6-10, 1958	Literacy % of pop. aged 5+, 1950	Total school enrollment, % of pop., 1958
Northeast	6,595	95	139	48	25	6.5
North	10,583	136	137	69	40	10.2
Central West	11,974	150	199	80	33	11.2
East	17,028	274	240	72	42	11.3
South	24,500	321	242	96	57	14.6

* Cruzeiros

The uneven distribution of population has educational consequences. About 96 per cent of the people live in large and small demographic concentrations distributed all over the country, but occupying no more than one-eighth of its area. This might be called the social space of Brazil. The other 4 per cent are dispersed over the remaining seven-eights of the country. The children of these 4 per cent cannot attend the ordinary school. Either they receive no instruction, or they must go to a boarding school, or they must have an itinerant teacher, or they must be taught by radio.

Regional Variations

Geographers generally divide the country into psysiographic regions which have substantially different social and economic characteristics. (Table 2 summarizes some of these regional differences.) These physiographic regions are the following:

1. The North, which includes the states of Amazonas, Acre, and Pará, and the federal territories of Rondônia, Rio Branco, and Amapá. This is the largest of the regions, formed mainly by the basin of the Amazon river, covered with tropical forest, almost flooded by the great tributaries and subtributaries of the river-sea, as the Brazilians call the Amazon. The region also includes some pasture land in the territory of Rio Branco and in the east of Pará, principally in the great island of Marajó. It is rich in minerals, and these are just beginning to be exploited. Amapá obtains considerable revenue from the

FIGURE 3

DEMOGRAPHIC DENSITY

Inhabitants per Square Kilometer   less than 1 ⬭   1 to 10 ⬭

10 to 50· ⬭   more than 50 ⬭

exportation of manganese. Recent explorations indicate that the region possesses one of the major oil-bearing strata of the world, which is already being successfully opened up by a few pioneer drillings. This area is very sparsely populated with hardly 2 inhabitants per square kilometer, which means that extensive areas of thousands of square kilometers are entirely unpopulated. The dense forest, swampy terrain, vicious insects, dangerous tropical diseases present enormous difficulties to a rapid human occupation of this territory.

2. The Northeast, which includes seven states: Maranhão, Paiuí, Ceará; Rio Grande do Norte, Paraíba, Pernambuco, and Alagoas. Although the largest part of the so-called Polygon of Drought is found in this region, it has large subareas that are fertile and well watered. The principal commercial resources, important in the export trade, are sugar cane which is locally processed, cotton and vegetable fibers, waxes, and oils.

The population of the Northeast is not excessive; its demographic density is approximately 15 inhabitants per square kilometer. This density would be much greater were it not for the great semiarid northeastern wilderness, subject to periodic droughts which force a mass exodus of the population to the coast, and from there to the South or to the Amazon region.

Included in the Northeast Region is the Atlantic island of Fernando de Noronha, of great strategic value, where by agreement with the Brazilian government the United States maintains a post for observation and control of intercontinental missiles. The Brazilian government maintains on this island, in addition to an army batallion, a meterorological observatory and an organization for oceanographic study. In the recent past the island served as a prison for the country's worse criminals.

3. The East, a large region which includes the states of Sergipe, Bahia, Minas Gerais, Espírito Santo, Rio de Janeiro, and Guanabara, the former Federal District, is a complex region which contains not only a part of the Polygon of Drought, but an interior section cut by the São Francisco. It contains large areas of pasture land, where the typical cattle of Brazil are raised—the zebu, a breed which does not produce much meat or milk, but is resistant to the difficulties of a tropical climate. The area is extraordinarily rich in iron and manganese ore, which are exported and are also being used in domestic industries. In the state of Bahia a substantial petro-

leum industry produced 100,000 barrels per day in 1961. Bahia also produces a large part of the cocoa consumed in the United States and in Europe.

The state of Minas Gerais, the traditional source of mineral wealth, is the great producer of Brazilian steel. In addition, it is a major producer of cattle, dairy products, and cereals.

The states of Espírito Santo and Rio de Janeiro are predominantly agricultural, but are being industrialized. Moreover, their agriculture is being rationalized by means of modern machinery. On the Bay of Guanabara lies the beautiful city of Rio de Janeiro, great industrial center and sea port, and until 1960 the seat of the Brazilian government.

Over practically all of the eastern region the valuable timber land of colonial times has been replaced by pasture land, farm land, and wooded areas of small economic value. The demographic density of about 18 persons per square kilometer can be very considerably increased through economic development.

4. The South is the most highly developed region, with a present demographic density of 26 inhabitants per square kilometer. This region includes the states of São Paulo, Paraná, Santa Catarina, and Rio Grande do Sul. The city of São Paulo, which is also the capital of the state, is a great industrial metropolis, containing some 5 million people within its metropolitan area, which is 47 per cent of the population of the entire state, and almost a fifth of the population of the entire southern region.

The states of São Paulo and Paraná are the coffee raising regions of Brazil, and they contribute about 50 per cent of the value of the export trade of the entire country.

Santa Catarina and Rio Grande do Sul have been favorite immigration centers for German people, and all four states have received substantial immigration from all of the European countries and from the Near East. Agriculture is highly developed through great cooperatives and through small and medium-sized individual holdings. The area is being rapidly industrialized. Railroads and highways traverse the entire region. Still there are areas of the west of Santa Catarina and Paraná with fertile land and productive forests which have not yet been adequately explored.

5. The Central West is the new land of promise, the locus of occupation and economic exploitation in the second half

FIGURE 4

STATES AND TERRITORIES

of the twentieth century by native Brazilians and immigrants from Europe. In this region lies the new capital of the country, Brasília, inaugurated in 1960. The region consists of two states, Goiás and Mato Grosso, with a demographic density of only 2.4 persons per square kilometer. The land is fertile and rich in forest products and pastoral wealth. Highways are being constructed rapidly to provide for the transportation of the produce of the region. The Central West is thought to have extraordinary mineral wealth which, allied with its hydro-electric potential, allows a vision of future industrial greatness.

Educational Consequences of the Physiography

As the rivers were the web of communication which permitted the conquest of the immense Brazilian interior, it was along their margins that the occupation of the territory took place. Sailboats, steamboats, rowboats, and canoes were the vehicles of civilization in Brazil. Primitive highways appeared slowly after the middle of the nineteenth century, but the railways and modern highways which now give access to the interior and link the regions have been built since 1930. Scarcity of highways has particular importance in education, because of the problem of school transportation for the population distributed over the vast interior. Distance is one reason for the low scholastic efficiency in the interior of Brazil. Perhaps 20 per cent of the population is so widely dispersed that if schools were built for them, none would be attended by more than thirty pupils. Distance also makes teacher recruitment for interior schools difficult, because a young teacher with a secondary education hesitates to subject himself to the isolated and lonely life of a school lost in the interior.

The only solution is the creation of a school transportation system and the location of the schools in population centers to which the pupils could be brought and where the teachers could live comfortably. In regions such as the Amazon basin and the valley of the São Francisco, this transportation system could operate with motor boats which would collect children on the shores of the river. Even so, the success of this solution would be endangered because in Brazil the occupation of the river shores is not continuous. In the Amazon region, one can journey for hours before seeing two or three isolated homes of backwoodsmen who live by fishing and by the gathering of forest products. Moreover, the rivers, although they permit the occupation of the territory, do not always favor the rapid introduction of civilization. Because they permit men to go farther in search of a better place for a home and a livelihood, they tend to make the population distribute itself sparsely and irregularly—an extraordinary difficulty for the development of educational institutions.

In the South and a part of the eastern region, where the development of railways and highways is more advanced, the education of the population of the interior has proceeded much more rapidly. The major educational problem of Brazil exists in the Northeast, where the rivers are not navigable and where the system of communication and land transportation is still precarious. There the population is fairly dense, but the school system is deficient in quantity and quality. The situation in the Northeast results primarily from economic backwardness caused partly by the climatic situation already described and partly by the process of colonization and agricultural exploitation in colonial and imperial times which will be described later.

The great tropical forests and the mountain chains of Brazil made occupation of the inland territory difficult; on the other hand, although the river system facilitated the conquest of the immense interior area, this particular form of conquest led to a distribution of the population so sparse and intermittent that the work of education was made extremely difficult. Consequently, even today the Brazilian educational system from higher education to the primary school is mainly urban.

Demographic Aspects and Problems

Brazil is outstanding among the Latin American countries of South and Central America for the numerical size of its population. At present it is the largest Latin country in the world. At the beginning of this century, Brazil had a population of 17.5 million which rose by 1920 to 30.5 million. According to the 1940 census the population had increased to more than 41.2 million, in 1950 to approximately 52 million, and in 1960 to almost 71 million. (Basic facts about the population are given in Table 3.)

None of the populous nations of the world maintains today an expansion of population as rapid as that of Brazil or as regularly maintained during the current century. Jacques Lambert, a professor in the University of Lyon, France, who has studied the demography and the social institutions of Brazil, says that, "It is not the present number of inhabitants, large as this number is,

TABLE 3

The Population of Brazil
(in thousands)

Year	Total population	Age distribution, 1950	
1819	4,396	0- 4	8,371
1851	7,344	5- 9	7,016
1857	8,044	10-14	6,309
1872	10,112	15-19	5,502
1878	11,311	20-24	4,991
1882	12,202	25-64	18,235
1890	14,199	65+	1,406
1900	17,984		
1910	22,216	*Literacy, population aged 15+, 1950*	
1920	27,404	Literate	14,917
1930	33,568	Illiterate	15,273
1940	41,114		
1950	51,976		
1955	60,183	*Urban-Rural, 1950*	*1960*
1958	65,740	Urban	12,958	
1960	70,967	Suburban	5,825	} 32,185
		Rural	33,162	38,654

Source: *Anudrio Estatístico do Brasil,* 1960. For the year 1819, the number is an estimate made by Veloso de Oliveira. The first census was taken in 1872.

which gives a measure of the demographic pressure of Brazil; this force results from an exceptionally great fecundity which creates grave social and economic problems and gives the Brazilian population a rapid rate of increase, which is seldom equaled. . . ." [1] Lambert estimates that if the rate of population increase which was maintained between 1900 and 1950 is continued for the next forty years, at the end of the century Brazil will have a population of about 170 million.

There appears to be no reason to expect a substantial reduction of the birth rate in the foreseeable future, in spite of the increase of the middle class, which tends to control its birth rate. On the contrary, the progressive reduction of infant mortality and the governmental policy of encouraging immigration suggests that the population will increase at a rapid rate during the next thirty or forty years.

The rate of infant mortality fell between 1930 and 1950 from 500 per thousand to 200 per thousand, and in the South it is now less than 100 per thousand. Average life expectancy in 1939 was 40 years, and had increased to 56 years in 1955. There is no essentially uninhabitable area in Brazil, in the light of modern technology. Even the area of the Polygon of Drought can be

FIGURE 5

POPULATION: 1851-1960

1,000,000 inhabitants

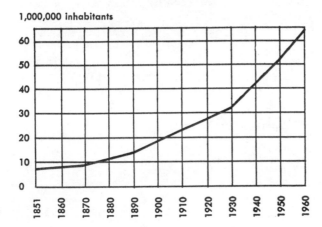

States with more than one million inhabitants

(1,000,000 inhabitants)

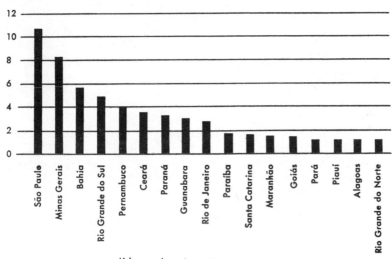

Urban and rural population in 1950

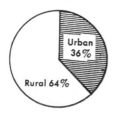

irrigated by means of reservoirs, irrigation canals, and wells. The country has the capacity to support a population of 500 million, which would be 60 inhabitants per square kilometer. However, this would require a rate of economic development at least as great as the rate of demographic increase, and here rises the major social problem of contemporary Brazil.

A nation which possesses a human potential of this order for the creation of a new generation loads the adult generation excessively with the task of providing food, clothing, and housing for the coming generation. In 1958 Brazil, with about 33 million people less than 21 years of age, had about 28 million between the ages of 21 and 59. Thus Brazil is not only a young nation historically (137 years of political independence, 70 years of republican government, and 30 years of modern industrialization), it is also a nation biologically young. If it is assumed that the period of educational preparation should be continued to about 15 years of age for the mass of its youth, Brazil had 25.2 million or about 40 per cent of its population under this age. Adding to this the 2.8 million people 60 years of age and over, the dependent and economically inactive population in Brazil in 1959 was approximately 28 million. The economically active population from 15 to 59 years of age was approximately 35 million, which meant that each five active persons had to support four persons who were completely unproductive economically. In the more developed countries, such as the United States and England, every five active workers must support approximately three dependents.

Economists and demographers generally conclude that an annual increase in the population of 1 per cent requires an investment of 4 per cent of the national income for the maintenance and the education of the additional child population, over and above what would be required if the population was merely reproducing its numbers without growth. The annual increase of the population of Brazil is at present approximately 2.3 per cent. This suggests the need for an investment of approximately 9 per cent of the national income in the maintenance of children who are increasing the population, but are not yet productive.

The national income of Brazil has increased considerably during the last ten years. Economists and financial experts estimate that the increase in real income has been about 60 per cent in the decade 1950–60 and that the per capita income has increased about 30 per cent. Thus there is at least the possibility of finding the necessary increase in income to guarantee the maintenance and education of the new and ever larger Brazilian generations.

However, the new capital which is generated in the country is needed for productive enterprises, and the amount available for investment in consumer goods, such as houses, education, welfare, and public health, is always relatively small. Nor can the government force an investment in these social enterprises by means of substantial taxation to pay for increased public services, as might be done in the United States, because this would reduce the productive short-term private investments which are necessary for economic development and which are required for the continual generation of new capital.

A consequence of this combination of demographic and economic problems is that the rate of rise of the standard of living is very slow. Millions of Brazilians are able to find only a subsistence level of living. Millions labor to cultivate the land by the most primitive process. In spite of the increase of government investment in public education, which has been considerable in the last decade, even in 1960, 50 per cent of the children spent less than four years in school. Between 40 and 50 per cent of the Brazilians aged ten and over are illiterate.

It appears that the process of development is intimately bound up with urbanization, which in a large part will provide its own solution. In 1920 the urban population of Brazil was less than 7 million, while in 1960 it was approximately 32 million. In 1920 some 25 per cent of Brazilians lived in urban and suburban areas, whereas today 45 per cent live in such areas. In 1920, 70 per cent of Brazilians over 15 were illiterate, whereas today this proportion has fallen to about 46 per cent. In 1920 Brazilian schools of all types served 45 students per 1,000 inhabitants. In 1960 for each 1,000 inhabitants primary and secondary schools and higher institutions of Brazil served 105 students.

Nevertheless, considering the number of children of school age, the educational needs for economic development, and the large percentage of illiterates, Brazil should have some 225 students for each 1,000 inhabitants, i.e., some 15 to 16 million in educational institutions. The country does not have sufficient resources to achieve this goal rapidly, at least in its present economic situation.

Composition of the Brazilian Population

Originally the Brazilian population consisted principally of three ethnic groups: the Portuguese, the Indian, and the African Negro. However, in studies made of the ethnic strains that form the contemporary Brazilian people, Oliveira Viana claims that none of these elementary groups was ethnically homogeneous during the first two centuries of Portuguese occupation. He says: "Within each of these original races, their representatives failed to show either a morphological or a mental unity; on the contrary, they varied more or less observably in the one or the other sense, the black and the red races presenting types of such accentuated somatic and psychological diversity, that one might say the members of each group came from races entirely distinct and dissimilar." [2]

The same writer indicates that the Portuguese race was a complex formed of Iberians, Arabs, Celts, Romans, Goths, and Suevi, because all of these peoples occupied substantial parts of the territory that came to constitute the Kingdom of Portugal at the close of the Middle Ages. Viana contends that Portuguese have always been far from a racially homogeneous group. It is possible to distinguish several well-defined types among them with two major contrasting groups: "One, blond, tall, long-headed, with nomadic and warlike customs; the other, brunette, short, long-headed or broad-headed, with sedentary and pacific customs." [3] The first group predominated in the aristocracy, the second formed the base of the middle and lower classes. From the former group came the conquerors who tamed the wilderness of Brazil; from the latter came the populators and the cultivators.

Viana's generalizations have the flavor of traditional racist theories appropriate to the early twentieth century in which he wrote. They are reported here only to show the possibility of wide ethnic variety in the makeup of contemporary Brazil. With respect to the contribution of the aborigines (Indians) of Brazil, it is clear that they consisted of well-differentiated ethnic groups. At the time of the discovery and first colonizations, the various Indian groups differed in skin color and stature, and they presented clearcut differences of culture and social organization, although in general they had not yet passed out of the polished stone age. Some were essentially warriors and nomads, while others were more or less sedentary and practiced a rudimentary subsistence type of agriculture.

In social organization they ranged from patriarchal to matriarchal forms. Their material culture included the use of the bow and arrow and rudimentary agricultural tools. They used fire for cooking food and for the preparation of certain tools and vehicles, such as canoes hollowed out of tree trunks with the aid of live coals. They wove fibers and flexible vegetable materials, such as bamboo, into cloth, hammocks, and baskets. Practically all groups had a developed art of using feathers. They did not cast metals.

When the Portuguese came into contact with the Indians, they appropriated much of their material culture, especially the weaving of vegetable fibers and other native materials. And from the very beginning the Portuguese began a process of unrestricted racial miscegenation. Thus, the mamelukes—sons of whites and Indians—became the pioneer race, the *bandeirantes*, nomadic and adventurous, who conquered the Central West of Brazil in the name of Portugal. This miscegenation of Portuguese and Indians with such great racial differences produced at the very beginning of the colonization what Oliveira Viana has called, "Ethnic chaos, confused and rebellious." [4]

When the Portuguese failed in their attempts to enslave the Indians, and to make them work the land, they had recourse in the seventeenth century to the importation of Africans for the heavy agricultural work. Then the African contingent began to contribute progressively and in an extraordinary way to the ethnic differentiation of the Brazilian people. It is difficult to say how and to what extent this fusion of the three races contributed to the formation of the present-day Brazilian, and which of the ethnic characteristics have been most important. Azevedo summarizes the problem:

If, as one sees, the origins of the Brazilian people are clearly tied up with the mixture of the three races or with the progressive assimilation, in the early centuries, of red and black races by the European whites in a great blood transfusion, there still remain to be entirely clarified questions relative to the various ethnic types, Portuguese and Negro, which flowed toward Brazil, to their respective anthropological characteristics, to the geographic distribution of the Negroes and the Indians, and to the proportions in which the crossings with the white colonists went on. It seems to us that one can now conclude . . . that the white sources from which the mestizos were derived were very varied; and . . . the variety of "nations" and of culture areas from which the Negro slaves were transported, ranging from the most savage tribes of the Kaffirs to the Sudanese Negroes of advanced culture who predominated in the development of Bahia. . . . The light which historic documents throw on this question . . . is not sufficient to clear up, except perhaps in a general way and in some of its essential aspects, the origin of the Brazilian people.

Not fewer, or less deep, are the shadows which surround on all sides the questions as to the various American Indian people of the "Amazon Basin," of the plateau, and of the southern coast of Brazil.[5]

It is a fact that Brazil from the beginning of its colonization has been a constant melting pot of three diverse races. Students of the subject agree that the most extensive miscegenation took place between whites and Negroes and that the mixtures of these two groups—the mulattoes—showed a great variety of types, both in their sociocultural traits and in their physical characteristics.

The mixture between Indians and Negroes was indirect, because the Indian always showed an active repulsion toward the Negro. It was only through the mamelukes, the mixture of Indian and white, that the aboriginal blood was infused in a major way into the Negro group, producing the *cafusos, caborés,* or *carijós*—mixtures of white, Negro, and Indian.

Thus it is difficult to consider the Brazilians, from the point of view of anthropology and of ethnology, as a single national type. It is even difficult at the present time to establish with any exactitude the size of the white contingent, the mulatto, the Negro, the mameluke, and the *cafuso.* The one known fact is that the Indian, as a distinguishable race in the Brazilian population, has practically disappeared, with only small contingents remaining in Goiás, Mato Grosso, and Amazonas, secluded in little-explored regions and contributing nothing to Brazilian culture. Probably their numbers do not exceed 80,000.* Considering that between pure white and pure Negro there is today in Brazil a continuous variation of skin color, type of hair, and other physical characteristics, the distinction between white, Indian, Negro, and mestizo is not clear. One individual apparently white can be mestizo with blood of the three fundamental races, just as another mestizo is apparently Negro.

There is no doubt that continuous miscegenation in Brazil has resulted in a process of "whitening" or lightening of the population. This process is generally a source of self-congratulation for the Brazilians, which demonstrates a degree of racial prejudice. This prejudice does not give rise to a deliberate segregation of such form as to create difficulties to the free movement of colored people; nor are their rights aggressively attacked.

* Darcy Ribeiro, after studying all of the existing facts, estimates that the total number of Indians now in Brazil cannot be less than 68,100 nor more than 99,700. "Culturas e Línguas Indígenas no Brasil," *Educação e Ciências Sociais,* II, No. 6 (Nov. 1957), 38.

Nevertheless, it is significant that the greatest proportion of Negroes and mulattoes (80 per cent) is found in the lower classes of Brazilian society, while Negroes are almost never encountered in the upper-middle and the upper classes, even in the state of Bahia, which has the largest proportion of colored people. In the primary and the secondary schools the major incidence of failures, which is concentrated among those who come from the lower social classes, affects particularly mestizos and Negroes.

It appears that the so-called racial democracy of the Brazilians exists mainly among the common people, and there, especially, the process of "lightening" takes place and is a condition for upward social mobility. In those social levels the general rule is to seek a person of lighter skin color for marriage. The consequence of this practice is the progressive augmentation of the proportion of white and mestizo in the population, with the compensatory reduction of the Negroes.

With this basis for understanding of the words "white," "mestizo," and "Negro" in the official statistics, Table 4 shows some

TABLE 4

Racial Distribution of the Population
(in thousands)

Date of Census	Whites	%	Negroes	%	Mulattoes	%	Asiatics	%
1872	3,787.3	38	1,954.5	20	4,185.7	42		
1890	6,302.2	44	2,097.4	15	5,954.3	41		
1940	26,171.8	63	6,035.9	15	8,744.4	21	242.3	1
1950	32,027.7	62	5,692.7	11	13,786.7	27	329.1	1

data which demonstrate the process of "lightening" of the population; but we should keep in mind that the distinction between whites, mestizos, and Negroes is highly precarious, and based only on external appearance.

It is possible to divide Brazil into areas of predominantly white or predominantly mestizo or predominantly Negro population. The northern region is predominantly mestizo, with 64 per cent of its population having a skin color somewhere between white and black and 5 per cent Negro; the Northeast is semi-mestizo, with 45 per cent of mixed color, 11 per cent pure Negro, and 44 per cent whites; and the East has the largest proportion of Negroes, with 16 per cent Negroes, 32 per cent mixed color, and 52 per cent whites, which makes it a region more dark than light in color; the South is the lightest region in the country—the proportion of Negroes and mixed does not exceed 10 per cent; and the Central West is similar to the Northeast.

Summing up, one can say that the South is an area of white dominance; the East is an area of dark dominance; and the remainder of the country shows an equilibrium between whites and mestizos. In none of the regions is there a dominance of pure Negro. The one state which has the largest proportion of mestizos and Negroes is Bahia, with 23 per cent Negroes, 51 per cent mestizos, and 26 per cent whites. The state which has the largest proportion of whites is that of Santa Catarina, in the South, with 94 per cent.

In spite of the fact that the prejudices which exist are sufficiently strong to create a desire to be white, and act to bring about the process of whitening of the population, the Brazilians are proud of their racial democracy, and this sentiment has sufficient social and political force to prevent deliberate segregation. There is no school in Brazil which refuses a pupil explicitly because he is Negro or mulatto; if one or another private institution attempts to do this, it hides the real reason alleging a lack of space or some other reason. Thus, the Brazilian schools, both public and private are attended by all—white, Negro, and mestizo. Naturally, however, the private schools matriculate Negroes and mestizos in a smaller proportion, because, since they charge fees, they exclude the poorest classes of the population in which the percentages of Negroes and mulattoes are the greatest.

The principal problem which the Brazilian school has, with respect to the racial situation in the country, is that of internal organization. Following the European standards, which go back to the Napoleonic era, each school attempts to be selective. Commencing in the primary school, the educational system is always selective, and passes on to the higher levels those intellectually most capable.

Until recently in Brazil, to fail large numbers in the scholastic examinations was thought to be synonymous with rigor and scholastic efficiency, i.e., with scholastic democracy because it signified the choice of the most apt and energetic without favoritism. But this selective process gives a natural advantage to the middle and upper classes of society, which by their standard of living, their habits, and their customs are better adjusted to the impartial intellectual competition in the schools. This fact explains the high percentage of failures, even in the primary schools, and the phenomenon of dropping out of school by those who fail, and are judged—or judge themselves—to be incapable of the intellectual life.

Since the overlapping between those who fail in school and members of the lower social classes is 90 per cent or more, and since Negroes and mulattoes make up the major proportion of these classes, it is clear that the school has serious limitations as an instrument for promoting upward social mobility of Negroes and mulattoes.*

Proposals to achieve a real democratization of the primary school were initiated in 1930. Changing its internal organization, the school was to be transformed from a selective institution to an instrument for the cultural development of the entire population. The principal leader of this movement, the Horace Mann of Brazil, was Anísio Teixeira, who is now Director of the National Institute of Pedagogical Studies. In the last ten years the economic and social development of Brazil has facilitated this task. The idea of giving the primary school the basic function of providing a minimum level of culture, common to all of the people, has gained ground and concrete measures toward this goal have been taken both by the federal government and by the several states.

Immigration from Europe and Asia

When the Brazilians speak of immigration, they have in mind the coming of non-Portuguese foreigners to take up their lives in the new country. In addition, the Portuguese immigration to Brazil has been continuous since the period of initial colonization in the sixteenth century, with the result that the 1950 census indicated the presence in the country of 300,000 persons born in Portugal.

The non-Portuguese immigration to Brazil commenced in the middle of the nineteenth century, although already in 1819 a group of 2,000 Swiss had founded the city of Nova Friburgo in the mountains of the state of Rio de Janeiro. Furthermore, at about the same time small groups of Germans established themselves in the southern part of the country. The major migratory

---

* The problem of promotion and failure in the primary schools has been studied intensively by Roger Seguin and his colleagues of the Center for Educational Research in Rio de Janeiro; cf. Chapter VIII.

movements from abroad to Brazil built up momentum in the period 1850–1860 with the first significant colonies of Germans in the states of São Paulo, Paraná, Santa Catarina, and Rio Grande do Sul.

This process of immigration was not stopped until World War II, and there were periods of special intensity of immigration: 1875–1900, 1906–1912, 1920–1928, 1935–1939, and a postwar period beginning in 1950 and still continuing. The first of the periods was the most important; it contributed approximately 40 per cent of all of the immigrants who entered the country since 1850—close to 2,000,000, including Portuguese. In the short period from 1887 to 1892, when Negro slavery was abolished in Brazil, about 600,000 immigrants entered Brazil, or some 12 per cent of the total immigration from 1850 to 1960.[6]

The total number of immigrants who have entered Brazil since 1875 is about 5 million, including Portuguese, or an annual average of more than 60,000. For a country which had a population of 12 million in 1880 and about 70 million in 1960, this total is not of great consequence; but when we remember that this immigration was concentrated principally in the four southern states, the population of which was about 25 million in 1960, it can be seen that the contingent of foreigners made a fairly heavy contribution.

Leo Waibel estimated for 1934 that there were at least 1,643,000 descendants of European immigrants in the state of Paraná, Santa Catarina, and Rio Grande do Sul.[7] This estimate excluded Portuguese and amounted to about 29 per cent of the population in these three states. This explains why the process of "lightening" of the population is especially intensive in the South.

Japanese immigration commenced about 1910 and was localized primarily in the state of São Paulo and in the neighboring states of Rio de Janeiro, Minas Gerais, and Paraná. There has been a substantial immigration from the Near East, mainly from Syria and Lebanon, which however has not averaged more than 3,000 per year in the last thirty years. In order of numerical importance, the various immigrant nationalities since 1850 would be ranked as follows: (1) Portuguese, (2) Italians, (3) Germans, (4) Spaniards, (5) Japanese, (6) Russians and Polish, (7) Syrians and Lebanese, (8) Spanish-Americans, (9) Romanians, (10) Austrians, (11) Yugoslavs.

In 1950 the foreign populations of most consequence were Portuguese, 300,000; Italian, 200,000; Japanese, 120,000; Spanish,

115,000; Russian and Polish, 100,000; and Germans, 65,000. A large proportion of the foreigners living in the country at this time were postwar immigrants. Table 5 shows that the percentage of foreign-born has never been high in modern times.

TABLE 5

The Foreign-Born in Brazil

Date of Census	Native Brazilians	%	Naturalized Brazilians	%	Foreigners	%
1872	9,547,149	96.09	1,288	0.01	382,041	3.90
1890	13,982,603	97.50	*	—	351,312	2.50
1900	16,159,371	93.40	*	—	1,074,511	6.40
1920	29,045,227	95.00	52,326	0.17	1,513,635	4.83
1940	39,822,487	96.00	122,735	0.30	1,283,883	3.50
1950	50,727,113	97.40	128,897	0.20	1,085,287	2.40

*Not reported.

Between 1954 and 1959 the average annual number of immigrants was 58,000, with the Portuguese the most important group (40 per cent). The Italians represented 19 per cent, the Spanish 17 per cent, the Japanese 5 per cent, the Germans 2.5 per cent, and the North Americans 2 per cent. The Latin group, composed of Portuguese, Italians, and Spanish, is thus the largest group, with some 76 per cent of the total. This fact explains why the process of assimilation of immigrants in Brazil has not created major problems. However, during the period from 1933 to 1945, there was some German national socialist propaganda in Rio Grande do Sul and Santa Catarina, which created some conflict with Brazilian government authorities during world War II. This was quickly forgotten after the close of the war.

At present the Brazilian government encourages the immigration of certain types of people, with an eye to the needs of the market and the labor force. However, there are no severe restrictions on voluntary immigration, even though fixed quotas for the different nationalities were established a little before the last world war, in proportion to the numbers already entered from the various countries. The quotas were liberal, and none has been exceeded up to the present time.*

* Immigrants with technical skills in industry and agriculture have been specially needed. As a result of the recent surge of economic development, the scarcity of labor supply with special skills in industry and agriculture has created an atmosphere favorable to technological training and has led the Brazilians themselves to give up slowly their old preference for academic studies in favor of study and training in science and technology.

Through its selective immigration recruitment policy, the Brazilian government has attempted to avoid augmentation of the number of unproductive people, particularly adults who are illiterate or are suffering from disease. However, immigrants have been admitted without much restriction. In some of the states, laborers coming from Eastern Europe and the Near East have not shown the capacity in rural labor to better the level of agricultural production per worker, which is already extremely low. Thus in 1956 some 9,000 illiterates entered the country by means of immigration outside of the official recruiting service. The immigrants who entered Brazil on their own initiative in the three years from 1955 to 1958 were four times as numerous as those who entered on the basis of recruitment and labor contract.

Immigration might have contributed to the formation of permanent ethnic minorities in Brazil, and indeed at the times of maximum immigration a number of ethnic communities consisting of Germans, Italians, Japanese, or Poles were formed in the South. Nevertheless, none of these communities has maintained itself intact and isolated from the Portuguese-Brazilian community. They have assimilated customs and traditions of Brazil and at the same time have transmitted a considerable part of their own trades and techniques, with the result that in the South there has been a rich experiment in reciprocal assimilation.

Immigration has contributed a great deal to the complexity of the ethnic mixture of the country, and even more so through a major internal migration from the North to the South, because of the rapid development in the southern part of the country. The people in the Northeast, who are biologically vigorous and fecund, are attracted by the economic development in the South, and undertake a series of transmigrations, at first seeking the less specialized kinds of work in the southern agricultural community and then moving on in search of more specialized employment in the urban and suburban areas of the industrial cities. On the other hand, there is a demand in the Northeast for some of the highly specialized labor force from the South. These people are needed by the industry, commercial concerns, public work projects, and projects for the mechanization of agriculture in the Northeast; they serve as business managers, engineers, technicians, agronomists, artisans, and workers with special skills. This leads to a spreading of the descendants of immigrants into Brazilian regions which are not sought out by voluntary first generation immigrants. Some numerical data will explain this process. In

São Paulo in 1950 there were 1,100,000 persons who were born in other states, but these other states contained 500,000 Paulistas born in the state of São Paulo. In Paraná there were 700,000 persons born in other states, but some 71,000 natives of Paraná lived outside of the state. In Santa Catarina the numbers were 152,000 and 119,000 respectively; in Rio Grande do Sul, 45,000 and 206,000.

This mixing of southern and northern Brazilians added more complexity to the already complex European "race" who first colonized Brazil. In Europe, from the time of the Roman Empire up to the epoch of the great maritime discoveries, there was an immense crossing and recrossing of peoples, including Greeks, Britons, Latins, Slavs, Germans, Gauls, Iberians, the Mongols of Attila, Arabs, Semites, and others. Perhaps it is more exact to say that Brazil, from colonial times until the present, has been experiencing a major racial assimilation of the Negro to the previously mixed stock of the European. The new contingents of European immigrants integrate themselves into this process of assimilation; they are attracted by the capacity of the lighter mulattoes to adapt themselves to the social system in Brazil, to overcome barriers, and to rise economically and socially. Besides, as is witnessed by the popular Brazilian music, the *morenos* appear to have a special physical attractiveness for European men and women. Slavery in Brazil created the mulatto, product of sexual intercourse of the white lords and administrators and their slaves, and the mulatto has been the great intermediary in the process of racial "whitening"; he is the favorite object of amorous conquest of both whites and Negroes. He succeeds in breaking down all barriers and rising to the highest political and administrative positions. To cite a typical example, for more than twenty years a mulatto was the political chief in Joinville, a city founded by Germans and populated predominantly by descendants of Germans. Today his name graces one of the avenues of that city of the state of Santa Catarina.

Presidents of the Republic, ministers of the Union, governors of the states, have been mulattoes. The major Brazilian author, Machado de Assis, founder of the Brazilian Academy of Letters, was a mulatto. But the Brazilians say, "When a mulatto overcomes the barriers and obtains a high position he ceases to be a mulatto." He loses the social characteristics of the mestizo and becomes "white" because he has the social characteristics of the white. This possibility of surmounting the social barriers and losing the stigma of a slave heredity tends to stimulate the mestizo and make him vigorous, striving, and capable. These characteristics, added to the erotic romanticism which folklore attributes to the physical type, make him the object of amorous desire by white and black.

The white sees in the mulatto, when he has a good position, an equal with specially desirable qualities, and the Negro sees in him, even when he is in the lower social strata, a means of becoming more white, or of making himself more nearly equivalent to the white. This explains why the European immigrants, as they acclimatize themselves socially in Brazil, follow the same process of racial assimilation, contributing to the "whitening" of the Brazilian people. In Rio Grande do Sul, Santa Catarina, Paraná, São Paulo, Minas Gerais, Rio, and other Brazilian states many people with German, Italian, Slav, and even English family names show some physical characteristics of the ancient Negro race. If this is not a true form of racial democracy, it contributes to helping the country avoid the acute racial conflicts between white and black people so common in other parts of the world.

These facts explain why foreign immigration has never constituted an educational problem in Brazil. As Fernando de Azevedo said, the Portuguese group "through its reproductive activity, its mobility, and its adaptability to the tropical climate became the very center of the national formation. . . ." [8] And this center of national structure is so powerful that the five million European immigrants moving into Brazil over the last seventy years have never, except sporadically, created problems of assimilation and of acculturation. Some German colonists during World War I and afterwards during the Nazi ascendancy in Europe, worked for pan-Germanism and caused some concern for the Brazilians. And in order to discourage separatist movements, the Brazilian constitution adopted in 1946 states that primary education, whether public or private, must be given in the national language, i.e., Portuguese.

The German colonists have cooperated through their honorable and peaceful work in industry, business, and agriculture. Possessing an effective and modern technological culture, they have been a factor in the development of the techniques of production in the South, contributing both by their education and by their work to all of the population with whom they come in contact. Valuing the school so highly, they have made it a social necessity for everybody, so that today southern Brazil can claim the best and most complete system of public schools in the whole country and perhaps in all of South America.

Bilingualism became the general rule for the first generation, but today in Joinville and other cities founded by the Germans there is little German spoken. The Germans have come to participate in the political life of the country and some of their descendants, such as Viktor Konder, Lauro Mueller, and others, have attained high administrative positions in the country.

Something similar has happened with the Japanese and their descendants. At one time they too caused apprehension, but are now integrating themselves progressively into the national life. In the National Chamber of Deputies some Japanese family names are beginning to appear.

Thus, Brazil attracts more and more immigrants, without questions concerning their ethnic and national origins, certain of its power to assimilate them to its Portuguese base, which is always being renewed by the thousands of Portuguese who enter the country annually. Not only is a continuous crossing of the races and national groups occurring in Brazil; more important, there is a continual renovating process of acculturation and enculturation which brings the immigrant into the national body and at the same time gives the nation some of the qualities of the immigrant. This being so, Brazil deserves the name of an anthropocultural democracy *sui generis,* perhaps alone in the contemporary world.

NOTES

1. Jacques Lambert, *Os Dois Brasis* (Rio de Janeiro: Centro Brasileiro de Pesquisas Educacionais, Ministério de Educação e Cultura, 1959) , p. 35.

2. Oliveira Viana, *Evolução do Povo Brasileiro,* 4th ed. (Rio de Janeiro, 1956) , pp. 123-24.

3. Ibid., p. 125.

4. Ibid., p. 137.

5. Fernando de Azevedo, *Brazilian Culture,* trans. William Rex Crawford (New York, 1950) , p. 33.

6. F. Bastos de Avila, S. J., *L'Immigration au Bresil* (Rio de Janeiro, 1956) , p. 63.

7. Leo Waibel, "European Colonization in Southern Brazil," *Geographical Review,* XL (Oct. 1950) , 531ff.

8. Azevedo, p. 37.

2

Colonial Brazil: Society, Politics, Economy, and Education

The Birth of Brazil

CONTEMPORARY Brazil appears to an observer to possess one of the most complex social landscapes in the world. In order to understand these social contrasts, it is necessary to know the origins and historical conditions of Brazilian society.

When, in April 1500, Pedro Alvares Cabral landed his Portuguese fleet in the present state of Bahia, he not only took possession of the newly discovered land in the name of the king of Portugal, but he sent back a detailed report about this land which he christened Terra de Santa Cruz (Land of the Holy Cross) : "We cannot know," said the report, "whether the land has gold, silver, minerals, or iron. We have not seen these things, but the land has such good air, and so much water, and is in general so pleasant, that if one wishes to cultivate it, it can produce almost anything, because of the abundance of water. However, the best harvest to be obtained in our opinion, is that of bringing to its inhabitants, the Indians, the salvation of their souls." [1]

During the first thirty years Portugal had little interest in the newly discovered land. Only when the English and the French commenced to exploit the trade with the Indians in brazilwood, which brought lucrative prices in Europe, did the Portuguese king decide to take effective possession of the Brazilian territory. But the financial resources of Portugal had been drained by its colonial policies in Africa and the Far East, and there were no means to meet the expenses of exploitation, settlement, and improvement of the new land. The king had recourse to private initiative.

He adopted a custom which had been practiced during the Medieval centuries and had proved effective after the reconquest of Portugal from the Moors: the granting of vast areas of land to military leaders and noblemen as proprietors, under the condition that they would cultivate these lands with the local labor force. Thus in sixteenth-century Brazil a feudal experiment was reinstituted. The shoreline of Brazil was divided into fourteen sections, each of which constituted a "Hereditary Captaincy." The western boundaries were unlimited, so each proprietor could annex as much land as he wished in that direction. The proprietors had the power to administer justice personally; to distribute the land and collect payments for their own use; and they promised to found cities and towns, colonize them, and to work the land by means of Indian slaves.

But the experiment failed. There was insufficient money to pay for conquest and colonization, and without military support the proprietors were harassed by the constant attacks of pirates and the fierce resistance of the Indians. The proprietors bombarded the king with complaints. In 1548 one wrote: "If your Majesty does not come quickly to the aid of the Captaincies of the Coast, we will not only lose our lives, but your Majesty will lose the whole country." [2] The king replied in 1549, when the Regime of the Captaincies was practically extinct, sending a governor general to Brazil, Tomé de Souza, with the mission of founding the capital of a new colony in Bahia. He was to govern Brazil in the name of the king and to distribute land to all who wished to engage in a colonial adventure, planting mandioca, maize, tobacco, and principally sugar cane, which was transplanted from the Azores, and flourished in the humid climate and moist land near the coast of the Northeast.

The Adventure of the First Colonization

Tomé de Souza brought with him, soldiers, administrators, artisans, and six Jesuit priests. "From this time forth a double conquest was to go on, that of the land by the soldiers, and of the souls by the Jesuits." [3] The interests of the conquest of land could not always be reconciled with those of the conquest of souls, and during this first century of colonization Jesuit fathers and military captains often came into conflict.

The Jesuit reductions—rural settlements of Indians who had become docile and had learned agricultural skills and certain crafts—were frequently pillaged by the Portuguese and their de-

scendants, who were quick to learn that Indians already domesti-
cated by the priests would more readily submit to slavery. Several
times the governor general of the colony and even the king had
to intervene to resolve conflicts between colonizers and Jesuits.

In this period school and scholastic education made little sense
in Brazil. Portuguese who sought to occupy the Brazilian coast
had no other aim than to seek wealth, which would permit them
to live a better life in Portugal. Survival in a tropical land and
the difficulties of the Atantic Coast of South America gave them
enough trouble to fill their time and their minds. The common
people who were not slaves and who made up the later population
of small cities and towns sought only the necessities of life. They
practiced simple crafts for which reading and writing were not
necessary; or they fished, hunted, entered military service, or
engaged in similar activities which did not require intellectual
instruction. But in spite of all these unfavorable circumstances,
some scholastic instruction was given during this initial period of
colonization in Brazil.

The Jesuit priests who arrived in Brazil with Governor General
Tomé de Souza, aimed their first educational projects at the
Indians. At this time the Society of Jesus, created in Europe as a
means of combating the protestant reformation, had not yet
defined its educational aims. Its primary goal was the expansion
of the Catholic faith. The first educational experimentations of
the Jesuits in Brazil were a kind of trial and error, as is shown
in the writings of Father Nóbrega, one of the first Jesuits of
Brazil. Nóbrega formulated a general educational scheme which
would range from instruction in reading and writing to the teaching of philosophical and theological studies. He had in mind an
adaptation of the plan of studies of the fourteenth century, including apprenticeship for the skills of an artisan.

Many writers suppose that the principal objective of the Jesuits
was the organization of one or more theocratic states in South
America, based on the religious teaching and development of the
Indian populations. As proof, they point to the early reductions
and Jesuit missions on the shores of the Uruguay and the Paraguay rivers in the interior of South America, where the social
and administrative organization had an aspect of theocracy. It
is a historical fact, however, that the initial concern of the Jesuits
was limited to the religious teaching of the natives.

In this work, José de Anchieta stood out above the others. He
wrote the first grammar of the Tupi-guarani dialect, and at-

tempted to establish good relations between the forest-dwelling Indians and the Portuguese. He was the teacher of Latin and the humanities in the first school in the area of the present-day city of São Paulo, organized to prepare priests and catechists.

The first schools of reading and writing in Brazil were organized as a means of religious instruction of Indian children. Later they came to serve the children of whites and mestizos as well.

England, Portugal, and Spain in the Colonization of America

There are fundamental differences between the Portuguese colonization of Brazil and the British colonization of the United States. Their only initial similarity was that both commenced on the sea coast. Both, according to Roger Bastide, at first limited themselves to the areas along the shores, because they feared to lose contact with the European cities and their traditions, but the one kind of colonization was based on adventure and luck, while the other was based on labor and rational organization.[4]

The Anglo-Saxon colonies of the north, which have given rise to the richest and most powerful democracy of the world, grew out of groups of people dissatisfied and unhappy in Europe, but highly capable because their maladjustment resulted from their religious independence and their capitalist individualism. The Pilgrims came to America with the determination to construct a new state, a new fatherland, which they planned and carried out by means of an organization in which the religious and intellectual leaders predominated. They opposed the English monarchy with dignity and vigor. As early as the seventeenth century representatives of diverse religious sects came together to formulate and approve a rule of religious tolerance, which as well as being necessary and practical was also an act of liberty. A deliberate individualism, disciplined with a conception of rights and civil duties, developed in economic, social, and political relations. The success of these colonies is reflected in the fact that even in their first century of existence they secured some investment of European capital, provided by the rising capitalism which was carrying Europe toward nineteenth-century industrialization.

While all this was characteristic of the thirteen North American colonies, the Portuguese in Brazil and the Spanish colonists of America never came with any other intention or desire than for adventure and riches; they represented only the interests of the mother countries, Portugal and Spain, which were in bad financial condition. They were impoverished noblemen and military leaders without resources, without any interest in liberty, and with no capitalist concern over the social organization and the construction of a liberal economic basis for society.

At the time of the colonization, both Portugal and Spain were countries in which capitalism had not taken an important role in the direction and organization of the economy. In place of large private organizations for colonization and colonial trade, the king and his court had to provide the means of conquest and later of making the new possessions profitable. Profits were secured by means of heavy taxes, which forced a kind of irrational short-term exploitation that devastated the natural resources of the colonies. These contrasts in motivation and method provide an explanation for the extraordinary difference in rates of development between the British colonies in the North and the Iberian colonies of the South.

The educational systems of the North American and the South American colonies reflected these differences. In the British colonies the colonists carried on the traditions and the newly developing educational practices of England. They sought to continue the cultural activities of the homeland, just as they continued the market economy of the old country. But the Portuguese and Spanish colonists either lived like aristocrats, if they could acquire land, slaves, or peons; or they retrogressed to a subsistence economy that did not require education. This difference should not be overstressed however, since some North American colonists became aristocrats and slaveholders, while others took to the mountains and subsistence economy.

There were also some differences between the Spanish and the Portuguese colonizations; both were Iberian and Latin, fundamentally, but different in their methods of colonial behavior. One result of these differences can be seen in the political consequences at the time of the movements for independence in South America. Although Portuguese America maintained its unity and formed one country, Spanish America divided itself into numerous independent republics. Geographical factors, particularly the Cordillera of the Andes, partially explain this division of South America, but they do not account for the divisions within Central America. Certain of the geographic factors which applied in Spanish America might also have contributed to the division of Brazil.

The Spaniards sought to organize centers of colonization and exploration, each one directly subordinate to the king of Castile, and independent of the others. On the other hand, the Portuguese, having a governor general in Bahia since 1549, even though they did not effect a true centralization of power, established at least a single channel of political and administrative relations with the Lisbon court. Furthermore, the general government at Bahia was the coordinating center for the defense of the colony. In the war against the French, who attempted to establish themselves at Rio de Janeiro in the sixteenth century; in the war against the Dutch, who established themselves in the Northeast in the sixteenth and seventeenth centuries; and later in the war against the Spanish for possession of the land to the south of São Paulo (Santa Catarina and Rio Grande do Sul), the entire colony mobilized forces through a general, though not very rigid, central command.

On the other hand, although the Portuguese administration was coordinated during the first two centuries by a governor general of the colony, it was not a rigid intermediary between the Court at Lisbon and the diverse colonial nuclei. The general government in Bahia maintained relations but exerted no centralized influence, and left the leadership largely to the plantation owners. Thus, when Portugal attempted to make peace with Holland in the seventeenth century, by ceding her the Brazilian Northeast, it was the plantation owners, with the assistance of the government in Bahia, who took on themselves the responsibility of expelling the foreigners, and having won the war, offered to the king their obedience and the rule of the reconquered land.

To establish their policy of colonization and exploitation, the Spaniards took the city as the basic unit of government. Roger Bastide writes:

The Conquistador sought out a plateau in the mountains, where the air was good, and laid out there a quadrangular plaza—the Plaza Mayor—with the church and the Governor's Palace, and around the plaza, in a regular quadrilateral, laid out streets which cut each other at right angles. This rigid rectilinear planning was superimposed both on the city and on the administration.

It was not the Spaniard who would submit to the customs of the Indians when such customs were better adapted to the climate. It was the Indian, suppressing his beliefs in the silence of his heart, who had to borrow from the conqueror his saints, his feast days, the customs of Europe and the mores of Castile.[5]

The cities founded by the Portuguese, with a few exceptions resulting from the early city planning of the Jesuits (as in the case of São Paulo), were not laid out according to any administrative plan. They were built along the shores of the rivers or along the highways in the shade of banana, palm, and coconut trees. They had no rational urban structure; they were constructed to fit the situation, in keeping with the taste and the powers of those who built them, following the natural caprices of hills and valleys, lakes, ponds, and twisting roads, whether on hillsides or on level places, in a tasteful confusion of dead-end streets and criss-crossing alleys, with mansions, two-story houses, one-story houses, huts and barracks, all painted in variegated colors—white, blue, red, yellow.

These small cities contained town councils which might be thought to be Portuguese replicas of the *cabildos* of the Spanish cities. But there was one notable difference: the Portuguese-Brazilian councils consisted of rural proprietors, owners of plantation and sugar mills, who were not concerned with the urban interests of nobles, military leaders, business men, government officials, and artisans. This rural aristocracy gave leadership to the Brazilian society for centuries and finally lost control of the nation in 1930.

The Brazilian cities only commenced to develop toward the end of the nineteenth century, at the beginning of the Republic. The heavy concentration of population in the Spanish-American cities, such as Mexico City, Lima, Buenos Aires, and Montevideo, stood in marked opposition as late as 1900 to the wide dispersion of the Brazilian population, where the urban nuclei necessary for commerce and administration had somewhat the same pattern of distribution as the country homes of the great plantation owners, always separated by considerable distances and often by rivers and forests. The practice of marriage between first cousins and in general the relations of consanguinity of the great landowning families took the place in Brazil of neighborhood relations, so that the widespread family relationship of the rural aristocracy constituted the major form of social solidarity, and was also the major factor in colonial unity and later of national unity. Brazilian literature of the nineteenth century is full of stories of male cousins who came from afar to get acquainted with their female cousins with whom they were to marry. Marriages were arranged by means of letters carried by messengers on horseback from one rural principality to another, at times requiring four or five weeks for the trip. The Brazilian custom of using a number of family names was the common way of indicating the diverse family trees which a given individual represented. Very long names such as, for example, Joaquim Soares Veloso de Andrade e Silva, were very common in Brazil. Furthermore, as a result of wide intermarriage over considerable distances, certain family names such as Silva, Machado, Oliveira, Moreira, Soares, and Veloso are found in all of the contemporary Brazilian cities with about equal frequency.

This essentially rural structure of Brazil impeded urban development and urban cultural resources for four centuries. While the Spanish-American cities saw growth in the number of officials and professional workers as well as in the development of urban business and of industry based on the work of local artisans, the Brazil of the great rural properties developed almost no internal commerce and had no significant development in the professions. Therefore, it was easy for Portugal to take a course antagonistic to the cultural development of the colony: prohibiting the press, not encouraging higher institutions and universities, creating commercial monopoly, and so forth. Only primary schools were tolerated on the plantations, and the Jesuit college, which was a kind of secondary school, was founded in provincial capitals. A Brazilian youth who wished to follow higher studies had to go either to Coimbra in Portugal or to Montpellier, in France.

The immensity of the territory and the endless possibilities for adventure made the native Brazilian a being independent in his own land, little limited by the laws and regulations of the mother country—indeed he loved to break them and to rebel against them—and without nostalgia or any great love for distant Europe. He lived in a "society of Patriarchs without bondsmen, without true servants, with a clientele of mestizos and Indians, served by the slave labor of the Negroes, in whose midst, however, he lived, knowing intimately each one of the Africans, caring for them, and esteeming them as though they were members of his family." [6] Thus the Brazilian patriarchal society possessed a democratic aspect, although with no similarity to the democracy of the English and the North American colonies. It was an emotional democracy characterized by the paternalism of the landlords and the fraternalism of the races. The first was generous and kindly, and the second was without aggressive and rude discriminations.

Work and Social Organization in Colonial Brazil

But all of these factors in Brazilian society which were so positive from the Christian—philanthropic point of view were in some ways negative, when seen from a pragmatic—social point of view. A conscious and directed social organization never was a strong element of Brazilian life, whose grand features always gave the impression of spontaneity and an almost complete absence of controls.

Portugal was preoccupied with a financial policy of tax collection which depended more on customs officials than on legal and cultural institutions. For their part, few of the first settlers had opposing objectives. When they arrived on the coast of South America, they had only the desire to solve their financial problems —to get rich—without thinking of organizing any society. It is true that the majority did not have success in this venture. The few who became rich never returned to Portugal except on tourist excursions to "quiet their yearnings," to use a Portuguese expression. They came eventually to have no other objective than to conserve the power which they enjoyed in the colony. Consequently, the rich, the average, and the poor did little, and could do little, for the progressive development of colonial society, which expanded without getting any better. With an undeveloped technology in the motherland, the Portuguese could not bring to Brazil the technical and material means necessary to carry on rationally the work of population and exploitation of the land. They had to improvise almost everything that they needed.

It was difficult, and sometimes impossible, for such people, few in number, with no other qualifications than military experience and noble antecedents, to cultivate the land and extract from the forest the richness which lay there. Initially, there was a system of trade with the Indians, during the period of exploitation of brazilwood, the reserves of which were depleted in sixty years. Then as agriculture began to expand, the colonizers initiated and developed a system of exploitation of native slave labor. It is easy to understand how the Indians reacted against this system, since they had always lived according to their primitive standards of culture and social organization free of regular and organized work. There followed a century of warfare, which hindered the development of the colony.

As sugar production developed, the Negro slave trade flourished, and the settlers solved their labor problem but created other obstacles to development. Not only did the Negro satisfy the needs for labor in the sugar cane industry, but he was also a factor of major importance in the development of Brazilian culture. Living in *senzalas*, a kind of low barracks, joined to the great house of the plantation, the Negro was not segregated from the life of the landlord and the other whites and mestizos who lived on the plantation. Through their "Mammies" and their "Uncle Toms" the Negroes developed intimate relations with the white families. They were submissive, but they had a certain power. They influenced the everyday vocabulary, the style of cooking and interior decoration, and they even introduced some African religious practices. To some extent, this explains the difference between popular Catholicism of Brazil and that of the other Catholic nations of America and Europe. The church and the priest were limited to a somewhat complementary function in religious practice, because the Catholic saints, humanized and hybridized with African deities, were worshiped outside of the church in the family chapels and altars and in the courtyards, with their own semi-African rituals. A set of superstitions and beliefs developed within this cult, entirely outside Roman Catholic ritual, for the purpose of securing good fortune in marriage, travels, and the cure of illness.

But Negro slavery was a limiting factor in the efficiency of work production, since they were a primitive people lacking a culture necessary for the rational development of technology. They worked patiently enough under the improvising direction of their masters, who operated by a system of trial and error, without any concern for experimentation leading toward more intensive production. Semifeudal lords endowed with an immense unexploited territory did not need to be concerned with the rational treatment of the land. It was enough to get immediate results. Who cared about the future? One could always take over more land and buy more slaves. If money was needed to finance new planting and sugar mills, to buy more slaves and more hatchets, it was always possible to borrow from the private money-lenders who had established themselves in the principal semi-urban areas. What did it matter that their interest rates were above 8 per cent per month? The white colonizer of Brazil did not possess practical foresight, partly because he was not capable of working efficiently in the tropical areas and partly because he lacked habits and traditions for systematic business management.

None of the common Portuguese agricultural products such as grapes and olives could be acclimated in tropical Brazil, and thus the settler turned to improvisation, the defects of which were increased by his lack of a technical, experimental nature. Indeed, the Portuguese were not interested in agriculture; they devoted themselves almost entirely to the sea and to navigation. For example, on the coast of Santa Catarina, where there was no large-scale monoculture to make use of Negro slaves, the settlers coming from the Azores and the Island of Madeira engaged in fishing in preference to agriculture. The Portuguese were not able to transmit efficient productive techniques to the Negro slaves. If it were not for this perhaps the socioeconomic condition of the great mass of the people of Brazil would not be as low as it is today.

The Economic Cycles of Colonial Brazil: Brazilwood, Sugarcane, and Gold

Exploitation of brazilwood was the first economic activity of the Portuguese in Brazil. To extract and sell the dye-making material known as brazilwood, it was necessary to have a special concession from the Portuguese king. (This was the system used by Portugal in all of its foreign commercial activities: spices from India; gold, ivory, and slaves from Africa; brazilwood from America.) The reserves of brazilwood in the coastal forests were used up in a few decades and the first phase of exploitation declined very quickly. Little or nothing of the income obtained in this business remained in Brazil, because the royal monopoly was granted to favorites of the Court in Lisbon and not to colonists in Brazil.

Between 1560 and 1700 the production of sugar was the unique base of the Brazilian economy, and the labor problem was solved by the African Negro. When the enslavement of the Indian did not work out well, the Portuguese had no hesitation about utilizing the African as a slave; African slavery had already been tried on a small scale in the mother country and in the Atlantic islands. So advantageous was this commerce in human beings that the traffic was made an official royal monopoly.

The slaves were sold by the Negro chiefs of the African tribes in exchange for knives, mirrors, and other trifles, but in spite of the low original cost a slave arrived at Brazil at a high cost. Transportation was expensive, the mortality of slaves was high during the journey. Badly fed, confined in poorly ventilated ship holds, without any sort of sanitation, the slaves died in great numbers. Some 50 per cent of each human cargo was thrown dead into the sea. At such high prices only the richest regions and the large farmers and sugar planters could acquire slaves. Thus only the large estate, the *latifúndio,* could be successful during the colonial period.

Exploitation on a large scale, both of land and of slaves, was the only possible way of organizing labor and production. The principal feature of the *latifúndio* was the *engenho,* a kind of mill run by oxen or waterpower, which served in the manufacture of sugar. In time *engenho* came to stand for the whole property, with its lands and equipment.

Sometimes, when the land possessed by a proprietor was so extensive that he did not have enough slaves to work it, he would rent out a part of it to small-farm workers, who planted sugarcane and were obliged to process it in the mill of the landowner. These lands were rented out at varying rates in terms of a percentage of the product, the percentage never being less than 55 and sometimes going as high as 70. No doubt this was a form of severe exploitation of the landless workers. But even then some of them succeeded in acquiring a few slaves, which permitted them to take on more land and to increase their own income. Thus was established a sequence of extortion and exploitation: the king through his monopoly of the slave trade and through taxes on the sugarcane produced exploited the sugar producers. The money lenders or private bankers collected high interest rates, and the great landowners in turn passed on the major part of the burden to the workers to whom they rented land.

Thus the first system of economic production in Brazil never had the function essential for a continuous economic development—that of generating local capital which would be available for productive reinvestment. The colony produced capital for Portugal, where, rather than being used for production, it was squandered to build monuments and to support a life of luxury. The little which remained in Brazil was wasted on local imitations of the sumptuousness and ostentation of Lisbon. Caio Prado, Jr., writes: "The colonial population, with the sole exception of the wealthiest classes, lived always in a state of chronic undernutrition. On the one hand abundant prosperity and great economic activity and on the other hand hunger and lack of the most elementary necessities of life for the great mass of the population." [7]

In spite of all these deficiencies and problems, Brazil was the major world producer of sugar in the seventeenth Century. Only in the latter half of this century did the colonies of Central America and the Antilles begin to compete with Brazilian sugar. Considering all the factors adverse to development in colonial Brazil, the sugar economy provided a basis for the development of Brazilian colonization which simple extractive exploitation, such as that of brazilwood, could not provide.

From Rio Grande do Norte to São Vicente (in the South, on the coast of São Paulo) sugar plantations and sugar mills extended along a coastal strip a few kilometers deep and served as the base for the conquest of the interior. Until the eighteenth century, the center of Brazilian economic life remained in the Northeast, in the States of Pernambuco and Bahia. Although the sugar mill owners took care to maintain a small subsistence agriculture, in addition to the cultivation of cane, this was never sufficient to satisfy Brazilian needs. The subsistence agriculture had an indigenous origin and was not transplanted from Europe. Mandioca was the basic food product of the colony followed by maize and black beans. Of lesser importance were the tropical fruits. The consumption of green vegetables in Brazil only commenced to be significant in the twentieth century.

Since the land suitable for sugar was held by large proprietors, those who did not have land, namely, mestizos of white and Indian blood, migrated to the semiarid lands of the Northeast (the Polygon of Drought) where they developed a cattle raising industry with a type of animal not very valuable but capable of withstanding the climate and having a great fecundity. These people were able to supply the areas of sugar production with the dried meat, even now appreciated in Recife and other cities of the Northeast and known as "sun-dried meat"; a semi-liquid butter known today as "bottled butter"; and with an indigenous cheese, strong and ripe, still very popular.

The second great phase of colonial economy extending from the seventeenth century through the first seventy years of the eighteenth century included the occupation of the Central South, the development of mineral industry there, the development of cattle raising in the Northeast, and the occupation of the Amazon Valley.

The new Portuguese advance which enlarged the frontiers of the colony was retarded perhaps by sixty years because Portugal was reunited with Spain. In the late sixteenth century, the young king of Portugal, Dom Sebastian, was killed in battle in a crusade in North Africa. He died without leaving heirs and his nearest relative was the king of Spain. Although Portugal retained a degree of autonomy, its viceroy was subordinate to the Spanish king and its internal and foreign interests tended to be confused with those of Spain during this period. As one consequence, Brazil was the subject of attack by the English and the Dutch, with whom Spain had an intermittent war. Portugal lost practically all of its African and Asiatic colonies at this time. Also the richest part of Brazil, the Northeast, was occupied by the Dutch from 1630 to 1654. During the period of Spanish dominion, 1580–1640, Portugal saw its merchant marine destroyed and its empire cut to pieces.

When the Spanish dominion was terminated, Portugal had no choice except to make peace with the enemy countries to Spain and to confirm the loss of its colonies to them. It did not lose the Brazilian Northeast because the Dutch policy of extreme mercantilistic exploitation provoked a rebellion on the part of the Brazilians who were able with their own resources to expel the invaders and to reunite with the Portuguese community. The Brazilians today are proud of this feat of their ancestors, and partly because the Brazilians of various racial sources—white, Negro, and Indian—united in a common cause for the first time.

After 1640 emigration from Portugal to Brazil intensified to the point that the Portuguese king was obliged to take measures to prevent a depopulation of whole areas of the mother country. The territory expansion in Brazil as a result of this emigration began about 1650. When it ended the Portuguese and their Brazilian descendants had possession of all the territory which today constitutes the largest Latin nation of the world. When, about 1750, treaties were drawn up to define the boundaries between the Portuguese and Spanish possessions in South America, Spain had to recognize Portuguese sovereignty over half of the continent.

Having lost her other possessions, Brazil became Portugal's sole basis for economic reconstruction, and consequently Portuguese policy toward its South American colony was completely modified. Portugal reenforced its centralized control and administration of the colony with a view to a more effective collection of tax monies, and perfected its system of commercial monopolies. Every effort was made to channel the income of Brazil's productive activities to the mother kingdom. As a consequence, separatist sentiments manifested themselves; men born in Brazil felt discontentment and hostility against the so-called Royalists, and at times bloody warfare broke out.

The grand epoch of mineral exploitation began in the second half of the seventeenth century, and Portugal intensified its policy of economic restriction and administrative oppression. Gold was a great discovery but also a great factor in retarding Brazilian development. Portugal concentrated its attention on gold mining for three-fourths of the eighteenth century, and the center of Brazilian production was transferred from the Northeast toward the Southwest; all other economic activities declined and the original zones of occupation became almost depopulated. Minas Gerais grew at their expense, and was, until 1920, the most populous state in Brazil, being at present in second place with ten million inhabitants.

As soon as the Paulistas discovered gold, Portugal established a complete fiscal and production control, called "Intendencias de Minas," directly subordinate to the crown. The fifth part of all production was immediate tribute, and all the gold produced could only be sold in Portugal, at the price fixed by the king. If the collection of taxes of the fifth part did not reach the sum of 100 arrobas annually, the miners had to contribute the difference. The king required a minimum annual contribution of 1500 kilograms of gold (nearly 3,307 pounds in weight).

After 1770 the gold production of Brazil almost ceased, for two principal reasons: exhaustion of mineral veins and deficient methods of exploitation. The most common explanation of the exhaustion of the mineral veins is that the gold of Minas Gerais was alluvial, being found in the beds of rivers and streams and in their nearest banks. This accounts for the small concentration of gold and the rapid exhaustion of even the most important deposits. Almost all the Brazilian rivers contain this type of gold in small quantity, economically not exploitable. A gold ore which is economically more exploitable is found in the mountains or in rocky lands, but, even there, the gold content is low, not surpassing 10 grams per ton (1,000 kilograms) of ore.

Gold production came back into minor importance in the nineteenth century, when English mine operators were allowed to extract gold with a Brazilian labor force. They applied a better technology and have mined gold up to the present, with a production of about 3,500 kilograms annually.

The British success indicates that the Portuguese did not know how to extract the gold efficiently. "As to the technical deficiencies" says Caio Prado, Jr., "one has to put the principal blame on the public administration which kept the colony in complete isolation, not having organized here [Brazil] any efficient educational system (rudimentary as it may have been), and rendering technical knowledge relative to their activities inaccessible to the colonists. . . ." [8] The ignorance of the Portuguese colonists always constituted a very serious obstacle to the development of their economic activities, in mining as well as in other areas.

In 1770 the gold cycle ended, and the inhabitants of the colony found themselves poorer than they had been during the sugar cycle. Mining had almost liquidated the agriculture which had been implanted in the previous century. And yet mining had positive results for Brazil: it caused the transfer of the economic and administrative center more towards the south and it opened perspectives for the exploitation of new areas. The capital of the colony was transferred in 1763 from Bahia to Rio de Janeiro. The center of Portuguese colonization moved to the very center of the South American continent. The territories of the present states of Minas Gerais, Rio de Janeiro, and São Paulo, began a domination of the social and economic life of Brazil that continues to the present day. From them the colonization was to expand through Paraná, Santa Catarina, and Rio Grande do Sul which, with São Paulo, now constitute the richest region of the country.

Parallel with the development of the gold cycle, two important events took place as a result of the administrative and fiscal politics of the Portuguese crown: the occupation of the interior northeastern states and the development of cattle raising which had started in the previous century. The occupation of the Amazon valley and the beginning of exploitation of forest products were additional developments in this period.

Cattle-raisers established their ranches on the shores of the São Francisco river, the inland highway from the Northeast to the mines of Minas Gerais. But commerce between the cattle-raisers and the miners was discouraged by various devices adopted by the king's administrators, because it was a way of smuggling out gold and avoiding the payment of the government tax of one-fifth of the gold produced. The only legal commercial outlet from Minas Gerais was Rio de Janeiro.

The illegal cattle trade continued, but was forced away from the southern stretches of the São Francisco further into the interior. Cattle-raisers moved in search of pasture and water to the plateau of Maranhão, almost in the Amazon basin. If this form of settlement of a new territory does not constitute an epic page in the history of Brazil, it is certainly proof of the tenacity and capacity for resistance to the most adverse natural conditions, both on the part of the Brazilian and of his cattle. The population managed to increase in areas where the running water and ponds were more permanent, not disappearing totally with the prolonged droughts.

The Northeasterners also turned to the occupation of Amazonia in their unrelenting search for less arduous ways of making a living. In 1616 the Portuguese had founded the fort of Belém (Bethlehem) at the mouth of the Amazon, beside which a town and some sugar mills were established. In the eighteenth century the colonists began to exploit a variety of indigenous animal and vegetable products which served as a base for commerce and livelihood almost independent of agriculture and cattle raising. Cloves, cinnamon, chestnuts, sarsaparilla, cacao, river fish and other animals, hardwood, and medicinal woods—all came to constitute the economic base for migration from the Northeast through the great tropical basin.

The Indians cooperated with the colonists, since they were asked only to do things they had always done—hunt, fish, and gather forest products. Transportation of merchandise to Belém was by means of canoes, the usual Indian method. The whole technology of exploitation and occupation was an adaptation of indigenous culture by the colonists.

Results of the colonization of the Amazon were poor. Caio Prado, Jr., writes that "the operation was more a speculative adventure than the solid building of a stable and organized society, due to the instability and uncertainty of the types of economic activity available, and to the complex problem of assimilating the large numbers of natives. In the exploitation of the tropics the general characteristics of Brazilian colonization revealed themselves in all their cruelty and brutality. These were not diminished, as in other parts of the colony, by a parallel development of more fruitful elements leading to higher and more organic social forms. The Brazilian evolution from a simple tropical colony to a nation, so difficult and painful, and still uncompleted today, was especially retarded in that region. Amazonia has remained the most backward of the occupied and colonized regions of Brazil." [9]

When the cycle of gold came to an end, the Northeast and the South Central regions had to return to agriculture. Production of sugar was revived, and new products were cultivated, such as cotton which became a source of income for the crown as it was exported by way of Portugal to England and other European markets. Cattle raising followed the valley of the Sao Francisco into Minas Gerais. Rice was grown successfully in practically the entire coastal area, although it never achieved the importance of sugar or cotton.

At that time a system of economic exploitation that persists today took form in relation to the population distribution. Agricultural production designed for export was concentrated along the coast in the humid lowlands and close to the ports. Cattle raising, which demanded less labor and less transport, remained in the interior: Minas Gerais, the hinterland of the Northeast, and the Central Plateau. Both forms of economy remained extensive rather than intensive; that is, they remained technologically primitive up to the twentieth century. There was no attempt to improve the breed of cattle or to conserve the soil. This led to ups and downs of production, in response to the cycle of exhaustion of soil and pasture and the occupation of virgin productive areas.

The most important event of the late colonial period (1770–1808) was the occupation of southern Brazil. After 1640, Portugal and Spain disputed the territories south of São Paulo. In 1680 a military expedition left Rio de Janeiro to plant the Portuguese flag and to establish a strong military garrison on the northern shore of the Rio de la Plata, facing Buenos Aires.

It was called the Colonia de Sacramento, today the Uruguaian city of Colonia, which till the nineteenth century was to be cause for dispute between the Portuguese and the Spanish, and after independence between Argentinians and Brazilians; a problem which only resolved itself in principle with the independence of Uruguay (1828) and, definitively, in the middle of the nineteenth century when Argentina, Brazil, and Uruguay established peace treaties and neighborly relations.

Following the military occupation, the eighteenth-century Paulistas established themselves in Santa Catarina and in Rio Grande do Sul, as well as in part of Paraná. Furthermore, Portugal, interested in maintaining these lands under its power, started a new system of colonization by recruiting families from the Azores and from Madeira, which had excess population, and by locating these families on the coast of Paraná, Santa Catarina, and Rio Grande do Sul.

Since tropical products did not grow there, Portugal financed the purchase of small farms and furnished agricultural tools free or at low cost. Thus was developed a new type of social organization, based on small parcels of land each worked by one family. This growth prevented the establishment of the great patriarchal structure of the Northeast that was based on slave labor, and it led to the formation of a homogeneous free population which had an important function in the occupation and development of the southern interior.

Paulistas and Azoreans became the human base for the occupation of the South. Paulistas developed a cattle culture on the prairies of Rio Grande and on the plateaus of Lages and São Joaquim in Santa Catarina. On the coast the Azoreans developed a subsistence culture of various cereals. These patterns led to the establishment of large ranch properties in the interior, and small mixed farming and fishing on the coast.

At first the cattle were driven to market in herds across the open lands of Santa Catarina and Paraná. Later, after the perfecting of a process for making jerked beef (by drying and salting), the product was shipped from the ports of the southern states, Pôrto Alegre, Rio Grande, Pelotas, and Laguna. At the same time the South developed the breeding of horses and mules which were used for transportation of people and freight from the interior to the coast. In 1800 Rio Grande provided horses and mules for the whole of Brazil—horses for transporting humans, mules as cargo carriers.

This form of economy created in southern Brazil a strong individualism which, beginning in the second half of the nineteenth century, served as a base for Brazilian liberalism. Added to the aristocratic liberalism developed in the Northeast at the time of independence, this brought about the progressive extinction of Negro slavery (1850–80) and the institution of the Republic (1889). It is still in that liberal individualism that the economic revolution and the social changes of the twentieth century have their basis.

Education and Culture

In a society which developed at the mercy of economic cycles, the product of an almost blind search for means of survival and maintenance, without orientation or planning, it was difficult to achieve a cultural consciousness that would bring about the development of satisfactory educational institutions. Had it not been for the catechistic activities of the Jesuits, probably the first educational institution would have appeared only at the time of independence from Portugal.

At the end of the sixteenth century, in 1586, the Company of Jesus resolved to define its educational goals, hoping by means of secondary and higher education to educate the lay leaders of Catholicism as well as the priests. In 1599 the plans were described in the *Ratio Studiorum*. With the new educational orientation of the *Ratio Studiorum,* the Jesuits transformed their schools originally founded for the Indians into colleges for instruction in liberal arts. They already had institutions which were to prepare clergymen for the religious service of the colony; now these institutions were enlarged and were opened to the layman.

The rich families, owners of sugar plantations and sugar mills, were immediately interested in the Jesuit colleges. They were seeking to imitate the Lisbon court life, and humanistic learning was a cultural accomplishment which all rich young Portuguese should possess if they aspired to a prominent position in politics, administration, and literature. Henceforth, humanistic culture in Brazil was to become a class distinction for the owners of large sugar plantations and landed estates. This social stratum was to constitute a rural aristocracy until the end of the Empire.

The Jesuit colleges were almost the only centers of intellectual culture in Brazil during its three centuries of colonial life. They also provided the basic education of the Brazilian leaders in the first few decades of the Empire. Even after they disappeared they served as the models for the organization of the first secondary schools of the Empire.

Moreover, due to the general desire of aristocratic families to have at least one son as a man of letters and one as a priest, there developed within the *casas grandes* a kind of primary school for teaching the white and mestizo children and at times also the Negro children—a literate slave could be rented out by his master to perform services for illiterate whites. The priests who were born in the *casa grandes* returned to them in the role of chaplain joined to that of schoolmaster. Thus, after the passing of the phase of conversion of the Indians, the Jesuit colleges had an indirect result in the small scale diffusion of primary schooling, by means of chaplains and teaching priests who dwelt on the larger agricultural estates.

In the middle of the eighteenth century the Jesuits had in Brazil seventeen colleges and seminaries. Of these the most important, at Rio de Janeiro and Bahia, had complete courses in the humanities, philosophy, theology, and religious sciences. The famous Padre Antonio Vieira was educated at Bahia; his works constitute one of the landmarks of the evolution of Portuguese literature, and his political activity was distinguished both in the colony and in the Lisbon court, where he was an effective advocate of Brazilian rights and interests.

The Jesuit education, always in accordance with the *Ratio Studiorum* elaborated in Rome, was neither popular nor vocational, for it only had in view the humanistic and Catholic formation of the ruling classes. As Fernando de Azevedo says: "Here as everywhere, today as in the colonial period, their colleges are established preferably in the first cities of Brazil and in the shadow of the 'Casas Grandes,' on the landed estates of the coast, where their disciples are recruited; and the stability of the patriarchal family offers them a secure and necessary base for the construction of their system of instruction." [10]

But the instructional program that these colleges offered could only be brought to completion by a theological training. Portugal was opposed to the development of institutions of higher learning for laymen in the colony. The Jesuit college commenced at the secondary level with instruction in literature, followed by philosophy and science. For laymen the Jesuit education stopped there. Those who aimed for an ecclesiastical career could go into the seminary at the level of higher education and study theology and sacred science.

The sons of the more well-to-do, if they wished to be graduated in the juridical sciences, had to go to the University of Coimbra (Portugal) which was also equipped to give them a doctorate in the sacred sciences or in theology. Those who preferred the medical and natural sciences would go to the University of Montpellier (France) on the shore of the Mediterranean.

Eventually the Jesuit colleges came in for serious difficulties. The eighteenth century in Europe was the "age of enlightenment," the reign of enlightened despots. The kings and their ministers thought that reason would be able to solve all the social and economic problems of their time. They peopled the European courts with artists, philosophers, and scientists, and they placed the systems of education under the direction of the state rather than the church.

Portugal as well as Spain had its "enlightened" rulers during this period. Almost all of the sovereigns in Catholic countries engaged in disputes with the Roman Catholic Church and especially with the Company of Jesus, to which they attributed political designs as well as responsibility for the excesses of the Inquisition. With respect to education, they were charged with attempting to inculcate intellectual uniformity; their course of study, dogmatic and abstract, was said to be inflexible; their methods authoritarian and encouraging to rote-learning. Classical literature and rhetoric were their principal subjects, and they neglected the sciences and contemporary languages.

In the second half of the eighteenth century the European Catholic countries began to expel the Jesuits in their respective territories and to destroy their educational institutions. In 1759 the Marques de Pombal, prime minister of Portugal, decided to expel the Jesuits from the kingdom and from its colonies. France did the same in 1763, as did other Catholic monarchies, until Pope Clement XIV in 1773 had no alternative but to close the order to avoid any more harm to Catholicism. The Society of Jesus was not reorganized until the nineteenth century after the period of instability brought about in Europe by the French Revolution and Napoleon Bonaparte.

It is said that the expulsion of the Jesuits by the Marquis de Pombal was a disaster for the colonial educational system. However, considering that the colleges maintained by them were not dedicated to the general public, we may conclude that the expulsion only affected the formal and literary education of the rural Brazilian aristocracy. In fact, the aristocracy had to resort in greater volume to the Portuguese schools and to the University of Coimbra, a result which from a political-social point of view was useful. At Coimbra the Brazilian boys, originating from various regions of the colony and under the influence of liberal ideas from the end of the eighteenth century, were able to dream of independence and to think of political ideals. Thus were educated the Brazilian leaders who brought about the events of 1808–22 out of which emerged the independent empire.

With the Jesuits expelled, the Marques de Pombal tried

for the first time to organize in Portugal and in the colony an educational system designed to reach a more substantial part of the population, at least with instruction at the elementary level. He created a tax to finance a program of education including primary instruction, or, as they called it at the time, schools for reading and writing, which used itinerant teachers; and secondary education offering lessons in the humanities and the sciences.

To accomplish his plan, Pombal initially thought of secular teachers. The poet Silva Alvarenga directed a class of rhetoric and poetry in São João Del Rei (Minas Gerais). A few teachers, educated in Coimbra, came from Portugal to teach Latin, Greek, Hebrew, French, and philosophy. Pombal's program of secular education was supplemented after 1774 by the teaching of Franciscan monks who established a number of schools in Brazil. They organized graded courses which fitted in a general way the ideas of Pombal.

The prime minister did no more than the Jesuits toward achieving education for all. His so-called "regal courses" were only attended by the social class who had previously gone to the Jesuit colleges. Then, and for a long time after, schooling had no great meaning for the people.

The failure of Pombal's plan was caused less by the fact that he extinguished the Jesuit school system than by his failure to foresee the cultural, economic, and political forces which opposed his endeavor to give a new and wider meaning to education. His intentions are made clear in his decree of 1759, treating the reform of education, the accomplishment of which would necessitate "not only repairing the study of humanities so as to prevent their falling into total ruin, but restoring to them their former brilliance which made the Portuguese renowned in the republic of letters before the Jesuits interfered in their instruction with sinister intentions and unfortunate success." [11]

Finally, just before the close of the eighteenth century (1798–1800), the Seminário de Olinda was created by Bishop Azaredo Coutinho. Educated in Portugal, where he was influenced by Pombalian ideas, Bishop Azaredo was interested in training both priests and laymen. His seminary, located on a hill just to the north of the city of Recife, taught Greek, French, history, geometry, physics, natural history, and drawing—all in addition to the traditional curriculum of grammar, Latin, rhetoric, poetry, philosophy, and theology.

Olinda was the last educational project in colonial Brazil, a decade before the country became the seat of a European monarchy. Already the United States was a sovereign nation and through all of Spanish America the people and their leaders were agitating for political emancipation. All the Spanish colonies of America had their universities and their school systems. Brazil, with the Seminary of Olinda, was barely taking the first steps of cultural independence.

NOTES

1. Quoted in Roger Bastide, *Brésil, terre des contrastes* (Paris, 1957), p. 20.

2. Ibid., p. 21.

3. Ibid., p. 23.

4. Ibid., pp. 23-24.

5. Ibid., p. 25.

6. Gilberto Freyre, *The Masters and the Slaves,* trans. Samuel Putnam, 2d ed. (New York, 1956) .

7. Caio Prado, Jr., *História Econômica do Brazil,* 4th ed. (São Paulo, 1956) , pp. 43-44.

8. Ibid., p. 62.

9. Ibid., p. 77.

10. Azevedo, *Brazilian Culture,* p. 351.

11. Quoted in Azevedo, p. 357.

3

Brazil
Becomes an
Empire

The United Kingdom of Portugal and Brazil

ALTHOUGH Brazil did not attain complete independence until 1822, the seat of the Portuguese Empire was established there in 1808, when the government of Portugal under João (John) VI was forced to flee because Napoleon ordered an invasion of Portugal. The population of Brazil was small at this time, but it was already greater than that of Portugal. Although more than 8½ million square kilometers were included within the political boundaries, only a small portion of the territory was effectively organized. Two centuries of trade and colonization over scattered areas had left behind a pattern—vast in exploration and sparse in occupation—that provided no effective system of communication. The only connections between the coast (the outside world) and the interior were trails which only packmules and horsemen could traverse. The most practicable of these trails were between Rio de Janeiro and São Paulo and between Rio de Janeiro and Vila Rica (now Ouro Preto, in the state of Minas Gerais).

João VI escaped from Portugal under the protection of a squadron from the English fleet provided as part of an alliance between Portugal and England. This alliance effectively abolished Portuguese control over Brazil. One of the first acts of King João, when he transformed Rio de Janeiro into the provisional capital of the United Kingdom of Portugal, Brazil, and Algarves, was to declare the ports of Brazil open to international trade. This was to the advantage of the English, who, with their trading facilities, their unique industrial establishment, and their unsurpassed merchant marine, were able to control the foreign trade of Brazil. At the end of the Napoleonic wars the volume of English trade surpassed the total of all European countries. As a result of this arrangement, Brazil was able to derive tremendous benefits, substituting it for the impoverished trade with Portugal which was burdened by monopolistic privileges.

On his return to Portugal, in 1821, the King tried to reestablish the dependent status of Brazil, but neither Brazilian nor British interests would permit it. Brazilian patriots led by José Bonifácio de Andrade e Silva persuaded Dom Pedro, Prince Regent of Brazil, to disobey orders from Lisbon to sail for Portugal. Shortly thereafter, on September 22, 1822, Brazil proclaimed her independence as an empire, and the Prince was crowned emperor, with the title of Dom Pedro I. In Europe, British diplomacy secured immediate diplomatic recognition for the new empire from the great powers. Similar diplomacy was also successful in Portugal. In exchange for recognition of Brazilian independence the Brazilian government assumed certain debts which were owed by Portugal to the banks and the treasury of England.

Portugal was unable to offer any resistance to the independence movement in 1822. The small forces that she had in Brazil were quickly overcome. A Brazilian naval squadron, organized under Lord Cochrane, a British admiral, made the power of the new Empire respected in all the provinces.

Education at the Beginning of the Empire

King João, during his brief reign in Brazil, established a number of cultural institutions which were necessary in a capital of an European-American nation. He founded the royal press in 1808 and commenced publication of the *Gazeta do Rio de Janeiro*. The first public library was established in 1810 with a collection of 60,000 volumes. The naval academy was created in 1808 and the Royal Military Academy in 1810.

Although another century would pass before the creation of Brazil's first university, the reign of João VI saw the establishment of several higher educational institutions which formed the building blocks out of which universities could later be fashioned. Courses in surgery, anatomy, and medicine were established in Rio and in Bahia between 1809 and 1813, thus beginning the training of doctors on Brazilian soil. A chair for the teaching of economics was founded in Bahia in 1808, a course in agriculture in 1812, in chemistry in 1817, and in technical designing in 1818. The Royal School of Sciences, Arts, and Professions was founded on August 12, 1816; it functioned under that title until 1820, when the name was changed to the Royal Academy of Painting, Sculpture, and Architecture.

For the first time Brazilians were beginning to develop an educational system designed to meet the social and economic needs of a society emerging from colonial status and agricultural simplicity. Higher institutions were designed to meet these needs, and at the same time there was the beginning of a system of free popular education aimed to make the common people literate and to improve their efficiency as workers and citizens.

At this time no more than 10 per cent of the free adults were literate, and even fewer of the slaves. Progress toward a system of universal education was to be very slow, much slower than in North America and in the countries of northern Europe, because of the socioeconomic structure of Brazilian society. With an aristocratic social structure and an agricultural society based on slave labor, the principal social functions of education were to give literacy and a few professional skills to the small group of individuals who would become merchants, bankers, lawyers, doctors, priests, and government officials; and to give the education befitting a "gentleman" to the children of upper-class families, as a mark of their social status. It would be a century before the social functions of education in an industrial democracy became important enough to allow Brazilian education to make an important contribution to the development of an industrial and urban society.

Preparation for Liberalism: 1822-50

Although the arrival of João VI in 1808 and the declaration of independence in 1822 freed Brazil from the exploitation of a Portuguese trade monopoly, its position as a simple exporter of tropical products and an importer of manufactured goods continued for more than a hundred years. Brazil's inheritance of colonial inefficiency stressed quantity rather than quality and neglected a developmental technology. The backwardness of the country forced the importation of everything that bore the least trace of manufacture, including primitive agricultural implements. In 1812 total exports were £1,233,000 (gold sterling), and the imports were £770,000; but in 1816 exports (£2,330,000) were exceeded by imports (£2,500,000). In the year of independence, 1822, merchandise valued at £4,030,000 was exported against imports worth £ 4,590,000. Up to the year 1860 this imbalance appeared to be irremediable, entailing continuous foreign loans which constituted a heavy lien on future generations.

Moreover, in view of the pressure first exerted by England and, subsequently, by other European countries, the import duties from 1812 to 1844 could not legally exceed 15 per cent ad valorem—a rate that did not afford adequate protection for the development of domestic industries. Also foreign capital for investment in Brazilian enterprises was difficult to obtain, since the products resulting from such enterprises would be in direct competition with goods produced by the countries furnishing the capital.

Because of all the foregoing reasons it was impossible to establish a sound monetary system. In 1808 the old Brazilian milreis (now replaced by the cruzeiro) was worth 70 English pence. In 1822 the milreis was worth 49 pence, and by 1850 it had dropped to 28 pence. In 1960 the cruzeiro was worth less than an English half-penny, or 0.6 of a United States cent, and in 1963 the cruzeiro fell to 0.1 of a cent. In reality, as we shall observe later, today the appreciation of foreign currencies in relation to the cruzeiro constitutes in part a Brazilian policy of protecting the native industries.

These meagre economic data suffice to demonstrate that the socioeconomic situation of the Brazilian people did not change greatly after independence. Throughout the nineteenth century the economy was characterized by a slow and halting kind of transition, with occasional periods of growth followed by plateaus. This development continued until the beginning of the true industrial revolution in Brazil.

If the coming of the royal family to Brazil in 1808 paved the way for independence, it is equally true that the Empire constituted a long preparatory stage for the Republic and for economic liberalism; the latter, in turn, was to create a favorable climate for the industrialization and economic planning which took place after 1930. In our times these factors have culminated in a democracy which is progressively becoming more efficient.

At the time when Brazilian independence was achieved, Europe was directing its attention to great industrial ventures and was offering tremendous opportunities for the investment of capital. But Brazil was virtually devoid of experienced men who were capable of long-range planning; and its population, shut off from active contact with the outside world for over three centuries, felt no urge for development. The Brazilians were content to remain in the obscurantism in which the country languished. In many of its basic economic and administrative aspects the Empire was simply a semicolonial organization, and not a truly democratic nation.

To be sure, Brazil did possess elective legislative bodies in the provinces (now states) as well as in the capital. A small elite of lawyers, barons, and counts held seats in these legislatures and formulated codes and statutes which were very learned at times, but were always difficult to enforce, since they were largely incomprehensible to the masses. Erudite oratorial controversies were common in those assemblies, while political maneuverings existed behind the scenes. All the legislaters were chosen by a small minority of enfranchised citizens who were controlled by local political bosses from the rural aristocracy. This was the political result of the trinity of slavery, latifúndia, and single-crop agriculture that was to persist until the end of the nineteenth century.

In the meantime the vanguard of an intellectual elite and of a commercial middle class in the cities had launched a slow but persistent fight against the status quo. Their struggle at times assumed the aspect of political agitation, at times that of a more active warfare. Behind this unrest was the development in the urban centers of a stratum of unemployed. These were for the most part artisans who, by virtue of freedom of import trade and the resultant competition offered by goods manufactured abroad, had been deprived of a market for their handmade products and had affiliated with the city middle class, itself a victim of that competition.

Possessed of greater resourcefulness, the European-bred foreigners enjoyed marked advantages in competing with the natives of a new country that until recently had been an isolated and backward colony. The English came to dominate big business and the financial transactions of the Empire, while the French concentrated largely on luxury trade, especially fashionable clothing. The city bourgeoisie, both Brazilian and Portuguese in its makeup, had largely to content itself with dealing in basic commodities—a less lucrative activity—and in doing business with the broad masses, the unemployed, a small middle class of persons engaged in commerce, and the public officials, who for the most part were poorly paid.

These factors led to two partially contradictory movements. On the one hand the urban classes arrayed themselves against slavery, regarding that institution as degrading to labor and as contributing to poverty in the cities. This sentiment became so powerful that José Bonifácio de Andrade e Silva, father of independence and prime minister of the Empire, wrote: "It is high time to do away gradually with the last vestiges of slavery among us, so that in a few generations we may come to constitute a homogeneous nation; for otherwise, we shall never be truly free, respected and happy." [1] In 1826, 1827, and 1830 Brazil undertook measures against the importation of slaves, a trade then carried on by Portuguese slave traders and their intermediaries.

On the other hand, the same social and ideological factors that sustained the movement against slavery were exploited by the rural aristocracy in an effort to protect the slave traffic. Just as they were concerned about freedom to work, the urban classes resented foreign competition, especially English domination of Brazilian commerce and finance. The loss of Great Britain's American colonies had obliged her to undertake the development of her colonies in Africa and in Asia, where an ample unskilled labor force was needed. Buttressed by this necessity, English liberalism forced the replacement of the slave traffic with a system of contract labor for agricultural work in the colonies. Numerous slave ships in transit to Brazil were captured by British warships, and their occupants were removed to the English colonies as wage workers. (Brazilian writers often expressed doubts whether these "rescued" slaves enjoyed more favorable living conditions in Africa than they would have on the plantations and in the sugar mills of Brazil.)

The hostility of the urban classes against English competition in Brazilian trade and finance was readily transferred to the British antislavery position. Brazilian slaveholders made much of the British attacks on slave ships sailing along the Brazilian coasts. The nationalist outcry against these violations of Brazilian sovereignty smothered the antislavery movement until about 1850.

Between 1845 and 1850 the English intensified their attacks on the slave traffic—even assaulting ships that were anchored in Brazilian ports. The local slave trade fell entirely into the hands of the Portuguese, who took advantage of the difficulties of transportation and charged the rural aristocracy exorbitant prices for the Negroes they sold.

The Imperial government resolved to put an end to the slave traffic at this point, and was able to get some support from the rural aristocracy who were being exploited by slave-traders. At the same time the government reduced the dangerous tension that existed between Brazil and England. In the three years after 1850 the slave trade was completely ended.

Political Liberalism and the Change in Conditions of Employment

The Imperial government reestablished friendly relations with England, but tried to stimulate the inflow of French and German capital, thus mitigating English predominance. The France of Napoleon III, as well as Prussia and Austria of that period, cheerfully acquiesced in that policy. Furthermore, trade between Brazil and the United States was assuming considerable scope, since the latter was lacking in the tropical agricultural and extractive products that the former could supply. The vigorous competition that arose between various European nations and the United States on the Brazilian market, both with regard to exports as well as imports, provided another factor making for economic emancipation.

In 1851 immigration from Germany to Brazil began to assume considerable proportions, thanks to the influence of the Imperial family which was intimately related, through maternal lineage, with the Austrian and German nobility. Dom Pedro II manifested particular interest in this immigration, for it meant the introduction of a new agricultural and artisan technology into Brazil. The present industrial cities in the states of Santa Catarina and Rio Grande do Sul had their origin in German settlements founded after 1850, such as Joinville, Blumenau, Brusque, Nova Hamburgo, São Leopoldo, Jaragua, and São Bento. In 1870 the immigration of Italians into São Paulo and the other states in the South became intensified, and the economic development of these areas in turn served to attract additional waves of immigrants from Europe.

By the mid-eighteenth century it was becoming possible for the urban middle class, reinforced by portions of the rural aristocracy that moved to the cities, to organize and dominate the internal trade of the country and penetrate foreign trade. The way was paved for the accumulation of Brazilian capital, and these resources were, for the most part, invested in the states of the South, in Rio de Janeiro, and in Minas Gerais.

Southern Brazil showed the most rapid economic growth after the middle of the nineteenth century. Immigrants with European technology utilized the soil of the southern states more efficiently than had the Brazilians. The small craftsmen of city and countryside fared better as domestic trade developed Meanwhile the Northeast and East slowly outgrew slavery and a colonial economic system.

The War With Paraguay and the Movement towards the Republic

In the second half of the nineteenth century some foreign capital became available, especially for public utilities. This led to the establishment of an extensive banking network and systems of communication (the first telegraph lines were built in 1852 and the first railway was inaugurated in 1854). Parallel with this development, a political crisis developed that was to have profound repercussions upon Brazilian life, contributing mightily to a transformation of the system of employment and of production, as well as of the social and political institutions of the country:

Although it was a small country, the Paraguay of that era was possibly the best organized and most firmly disciplined nation in South America. Organized on a theocratic base by the Jesuits who dominated the country until 1767, Paraguay was noted for its resistance to the fiscal and administrative demands made upon it by Spain, a resistance facilitated by the comparative isolation of the country. Under the dictatorships of Francia (1814–40), of Carlos Lopez (1840–62), and of Francisco Solano Lopez (1862–70), Paraguay became sufficiently strong from 1845 to 1852 to defy the claims of the Argentine to dominate it. Moreover, it never acquiesced in the intervention by the Brazilian armed forces in the political conflicts between Uruguay and the Argentine, because such intervention would pose a threat to its own security.

Organized militarily, well disciplined, and armed by England—which looked askance at Brazilian claims to hegemony in the La Plata basin—Paraguay was in a position to challenge the Empire. And it did so with determination and courage, achieving several military victories. Brazil was obliged to improvise armies, produce armaments, organize a supply system, and mobilize its manpower and productive facilities.

For a period of five years public opinion in Brazil was entirely absorbed by events in the southwest of the country. In the ranks of the combatants a new phenomenon appeared: free men and slaves fought side by side. The officer corps in general was provided by the urban middle class, whereas the senior commanders of the army corps came from the rural aristocracy. All members of the fighting forces—soldiers, officers, and commanders—were obliged to fraternize in the course of the savage and merciless battles. And a great many soldiers, free men and slaves, distinguished themselves by their heroism and by their capacity for making decisions and thus rose to the rank of lower-grade officers. A new feeling of equality was born, along with a better realization of the needs of Brazil. At the end of the war in 1870, in the wake of demobilization, a wave of liberalism swept Brazil. Henceforth, the officer corps of the army would be a potent factor in the democratization of the country. All this tended to strengthen the new socioeconomic conditions that were being created, thus further accelerating the democratization of Brazil.

While the war with Paraguay led to social and political benefits for Brazil, its consequences were disastrous for Paraguay. The last three years of the war were waged on Paraguaian territory, and its ruler, Francisco Solano Lopez, would never agree to capitulate. He died, sword in hand, in the last desperate battle. Prudently avoiding the creation of a feeling of mistrust among the other South American countries, Brazil refrained from taking reprisals against Paraguay and renounced any claims to war indemnity or to any portions of enemy territory. Thus the war against Paraguay was also the last armed conflict in which Brazil was involved with any of its neighbors. All disputes which henceforth arose were resolved through peaceful arbitration.

After 1870 the industrial production that the war had forced upon the country—especially in the areas of metallurgy, textiles, footwear, and construction of vehicles and ships—began to be channeled into peaceful paths. Although the government initiated a policy of tariff protection by increasing import duties, some of the industries were unable to meet foreign competition. Soon, however, Brazilian exports began to exceed imports, and the ensuing favorable balance of trade made possible a series of measures essential to the development of the country: the organization of transportation companies, expansion of railway facilities, improvement of harbors, construction of better highways, development of a telegraph system and a merchant marine, an extension of mining and forest production, and an increase in agricultural exports. Parallel to these were the enlarging of public services in health and education and progressive steps in the administrative services of the provinces.

Urban life was now beginning to assume greater importance, giving rise to an expanding middle class of public officials, teachers, business office employees, bank clerks, physicians, lawyers, and journalists. At the same time the urban public services, the textile industry, and the transportation services were beginning to create a class of free workers. Even in the agricultural and extractive industries, the European immigrants, chiefly Italians and Portuguese, were a new and potent element of competition with slave labor. The free labor was found to be more highly competitive, more technologically progressive, and more productive. Only slave owners clung to the old mode of production.

These socioeconomic factors, combined with an active liberal ideology, conditioned in 1871 the first decisive blow against slave labor. In September of that year the congress voted the so-called "Law of the Free Womb," according freedom to every individual born on the soil of Brazil.

In the meantime, the idea of a republic was being openly advocated in the congress and in the press. The political and administrative institutions of the Empire had not succeeded in adapting themselves adequately to the new economic, social, and cultural conditions of the period. The Emperor himself, Dom Pedro II, appeared excessively conservative. He regarded the abolition of slavery as a reform to be achieved gradually, so as to avert the bankruptcy of a large part of the rural aristocracy which was still heavily dependent on that institution.

The most decisive of the political blunders committed by the Empire was its failure to perceive the significance of the change that had taken place in the army ranks. Recruited in large part from the newly constituted, urban middle classes, influenced by the social and political impact of the war with Paraguay, alert to the crucial problems facing their country, the army men refused to remain silent or to confine themselves to the routine life of the barracks. Many entered the political arena while officers who could not easily enter civilian pursuits sought to elevate military service into a professional career.

The Imperial government, counting on the traditionally passive discipline of the armed forces in times of peace, was unable to grasp the realities of the new situation, with the result that the republicans gained their most powerful allies. Rejecting the police task of recapturing fugitive slaves, the army precipitated the abolition of slavery in 1888. Refusing to acquiesce in the discharge and replacement of the liberals among its higher cadres, the army, under the influence of the foremost republican leaders, deposed the Emperor and proclaimed the Republic in 1889. When the new regime was consolidated, power was turned over to a president, who was elected in accordance with the new constitution. At no time has any general or other military chief in Brazil been permitted to become dictator in his country. One general was the provisional president, the proclaimer of the Republic (Marshal Deodoro da Fonseca) ; another was vice president and constitutional president, the consolidator of the Republic (Marshal Floriano Peixoto) ; two were presidents elected by democratic processes (Marshal Hermes da Fonseca and Marshal Eurico Dutra). Of the twenty-three presidents who held office between 1888 and 1963 nineteen were civilians.

Economic Situation at the End of the Empire

Let us now examine the economic situation in Brazil in the years 1870–89. During that period coffee assumed first place among Brazilian exports, becoming the primary means for obtaining foreign exchange for provisioning the country with the necessary industrial equipment. From 1870 to 1880 an average of 3,250,000 bags, 60 kilograms each, were exported each year, and in the period of 1881–90, the annual average rose to 5,163,000 bags. Whereas in the decade of 1821–30 the total foreign trade of Brazil fell short of 10 million gold pounds per year, in the ten-year period from 1880 to 1890 that total exceeded 50 million gold pounds sterling per annum. Over one hundred textile factories were already in existence in the country in 1889, located in Rio de Janeiro, Minas Gerais, Bahia, Pernambuco, and Maranhão. São Paulo had not as yet been transformed into an industrial center.

In 1889 the railroads already had a total mileage of some 9,000 kilometers, and an additional 1,500 under construction. River and coastal maritime navigation had undergone a broad development. The regular riverboat traffic extended over nearly 50,000 kilometers. The telegraph lines, connecting all the capitals and important cities in the country, totaled more than 11,000 kilometers in extent.

The population of Brazil, in 1822 short of 4 million, totaled nearly 14 million toward the end of the Empire; of these some

2.5 million might be regarded as urbanized, 1.5 million were able to read and write, and less than 300,000 attended schools of any kind. Thus the demographic picture still reveals a country which is predominantly rural and culturally backward.

Education During the Imperial Era

After independence was proclaimed on September 7, 1822, both the Imperial government of Pedro I, as well as the Regency * and the government of Pedro II sought to organize a free popular system of education that was capable of stimulating the cultural development of the nation. The effort was not altogether successful. The good intentions of all the governments were defeated by the relative impoverishment of the country, the shortage of qualified teaching personnel, the lack of means for training teachers on the one hand, and the lack of interest in the professions on the part of potential students. These causes were aggravated by the public's lack of enthusiasm for public education. Furthermore, there was almost a total absence of educational specialists to plan and to put into effect an educational system adequate to meet the cultural needs of Brazil.

In many of the basic aspects of its economy and administration, the Empire was little more than a semicolonial organization rather than the democratic nation desired by Pedro II. Contrary to technological progress and accelerated cultural advancement, Negro slavery, which brought wealth only to the rural aristocratic minority, continued as a base for national production. Beyond any doubt the Imperial court at the Quinta da Boa Bista in Rio was brilliant and sophisticated, and the parliament or the Imperial congress enjoyed a large measure of freedom in their legislative proceedings. Still, the representatives of the people were elected by a small minority or elite. As a rule these were brilliant men of high intellectual attainment, educated in Europe or in the few advanced academies extant in the country, and because of that very fact they were more or less alienated from the everyday problems of popular education. During the entire Imperial period, the illiteracy rate among the Brazilian population was never less than 85 per cent, if we consider the free population only, and higher if we compute the Negro slaves.

* "Regency" is the name given to the period of eight years following the abdication of Pedro I in favor of his son, who was a mere child. Brazil therefore had a Regency government, in the name of the child-emperor (Pedro II), until 1840.

In spite of all these adverse circumstances, the cultural elite of the country, entranced by the liberal ideas implanted in Europe by the French Revolution, endeavored to create an educational system. There was no dearth of laws, plans, and projects during the life of the Empire. Beginning in 1823, the year after the formation of the Empire, there was an attempt to solve the problem of mass education. Experiments were made with the monitorial system of Lancaster, then quite popular in England. By this system, a single master teacher taught hundreds of children in a single classroom, assisted by advanced students who acted as monitors. But the agricultural and rural economy of Brazil provided poor motivation for such a program.

There was also no lack of legislative encouragement of education. The law of October 20, 1823, proclaimed the principle of freedom of instruction without restriction; this was tantamount to an invitation to the exercise of free initiative in the hope that it would bridge the immense gaps in schooling existing in the country. The results were meagre, since private undertakings are always predicated on the possibility of making a profit, and social and economic conditions made this virtually impossible in the realm of instruction.

Clause No. 23 of Article 179 of the constitution promulgated by the Emperor on December 11, 1823, guaranteed free primary school education for all citizens. To a certain degree, this was in contradiction to the previous law on education—only two months old at the time—since free education was incompatible with freedom of private initiative in establishing schools.

The law of October 15, 1827, provided for the establishment of primary schools in all cities, towns, and villages, as well as schools for girls in the cities and more populous towns; it did not, however, provide the technical facilities and necessary funds, and the consequences were sterile.

The law of August 11, 1827, established two courses in law: one at the Convent of São Francisco in São Paulo, launched March 1, 1828, and the other at the Monastery of São Bento in Olinda, inaugurated on May 15 of the same year. These schools were of the utmost importance in training the political elite and in shaping the juridical mentality of the Empire, and in addition they became centers for new philosophical ideas, literary movements, and the cultural debates and discussions that appealed to the intellectuals of that era.

Clause No. 2 of Article 10 of the amendment to the constitution, promulgated in 1834, decentralized the organization and administration of elementary and secondary instruction, turning it over to the competence of the provinces (later to become states), so that only higher education, and schools in the "Neutral Municipality" (Rio de Janeiro) remained within the jurisdiction of the national government. In the provincial domain there then ensued a duplication of what had already happened on the national level: a multiplication of laws, administrative measures, offices, recommendations, and governmental pronouncements—all aimed at creating regional systems of elementary instruction and making popular education available to all. However, the melancholy reports of school administrators revealed the failure of all legislation, and for obvious reasons: shortage of teachers, weaknesses in teaching, low registration, resistance to high scholastic standards, and lack of school supplies.

To gain a better idea of the status of public schools during the golden years of the Empire and of the conditions which explain the constant but futile reforms introduced by the provinces, let us examine an account written in 1872 by Diego de Mendonça, director of education for the province of São Paulo:

In the province of São Paulo, rich in talented and illustrious people, seat of a Faculty of Law, from where, as from a brilliant source, the light radiates out over all parts of the Empire, the state of public instruction is far from being satisfactory. The number of schools has increased in recent years, and with this the cost of maintaining them, but without a corresponding profit. And so it must be, because schools are worthless without teachers; and teachers are worthless without training. There has been one normal school in the province, but it was abandoned by Law 16 of 1867. . . . The program of compulsory education meets great difficulty. Difficulties of travel and transport hinder this development in the rural areas, but perhaps something can be accomplished in the towns and cities. In a population of some 700,000 souls the school enrollment has not gone above 11,160 in the last five years, and the actual attendance has not exceeded 8,688. . . . It is also necessary to point out the shortage of school buildings. It is not within the power of the province to meet this need in all of the places where school classes exist.[2]

The historical publication from which this quotation is taken is a veritable anthology of similar reports. The educational officials responsible for public education in the days of the Empire were tormented by problems that defied solution. They produced an abundance of laws and administrative measures that had little relationship to the reality which consisted of a few rudimentary a-b-c schools with meager registration and poor attendance.

Several types of secondary schools were established, some with public and others with private support. As was the case in Europe, the secondary schools were quite separate from primary schools. A pupil might prepare for a secondary school either by attending a primary school or by studying with tutors. There were several different names applied to secondary schools, the most common being *colégio,* after the European practice. A bachelor's degree was given at the conclusion of the course, when students were in their late teens.

One of the most interesting accomplishments of the Empire was the founding in 1837 of the Colégio Pedro II in Rio de Janeiro. Maintained by the national government, this school was eventually to become an official model or standard for secondary schools throughout the country. Here the students, after seven years of study, received the degree and diploma of bachelor of letters. Parallel with the founding of this *colégio* was the establishment of several others through private initiative; these duplicated the old-time Jesuit colleges in spirit and in curriculum. In 1820 the Lazarist fathers founded the Colégio Caraca, whose fame endures to our days, being affectionately remembered for its rigorous discipline and high scholastic standards. In 1845 the Jesuits, who had returned to Brazil three years previously, founded the short-lived Colégio de Nossa Senhora do Destêrro (now Florianopolis) . In 1867 they organized the Colégio São Luis in Itú (São Paulo) . Also worthy of mention are the College and Seminary of Pernambuco, founded by the Jesuits; the Liceu Paraibano (1842) and the Colégio Brandão in Cajazeiras (1866) , both in Paraíba; the Ginásio Baiano of Abílio Cesar Borges, founder of secondary schools in Rio de Janeiro and later in Barbacena; and the Colégio Meneses Vieira in Rio de Janeiro.

Nearly every province had at least one *colégio,* maintained by a religious order or by a group of lay teachers. This form of school bestowed upon the youth of the upper classes the intellectual bouquet fitting their social position. To a lesser degree it provided for the growing middle class and for mestizos the opportunity for advancement by means of the liberal professions or by a political career. The *colégio* led easily into a law school, medical school, or other higher institution.

Some provinces also sought to organize secondary schools with public resources. These were the *liceus,* most of which failed due to inadequate numbers of both teachers and students.

In addition to the founding of secondary schools and *colégios* for instruction in the arts and letters—all professing a narrow humanistic intellectualism—some attempts were made to develop instruction in technology, agriculture, commerce, and industry. These were notably unsuccessful. By 1864 not more than 150 students were enrolled in the few existing technical and commercial schools in Rio de Janeiro, Pernambuco, and Pará, while the registrations in the *colégios* rose to about 8,000, and the two law schools in Recife and São Paulo had a total enrollment of almost 800.

During the Empire the first efforts on the secondary level were undertaken to train teachers for the primary grades. The first Brazilian normal school was founded in Niterói by the provincial government (1835) and other schools opened in Bahia (1836), in Ceará (1845), and in São Paulo (1846). Registrations were at first meagre, but they gained as the schools became known as *colégios* for girls, rather than as centers for teacher training.

An earnest and resolute effort was made to provide an educational system for Imperial Brazil, but it was not possible to create an educational system without first resolving basic problems of work, social organization, economy, transportation, and communication. Following the war with Paraguay, some Brazilian congressmen began to understand the causes for Brazil's cultural backwardness. Apparently the first attempt to plan education without ignoring the fact that educational institutions bear an intimate relation to the development of society was made in 1882. Rodolfo Dantas, cabinet minister, proposed a national program involving "cooperation among the influential elements in the complex and immense task of education, for which purpose the provincial resources are and for a long time will remain insufficient." Rui Barbosa, speaker for the commission from the Chamber of Deputies that was to pass on the project, made a detailed study of the educational issues, drawing upon the thought of educators from the United States, France, and Germany. His two reports, one justifying the project and another concerning primary education, undoubtedly exerted a profound influence on the educational outlook of the Republican period.

Just before the monarchy went out of existence, at the final session of the Imperial parliament, on May 3, 1889, the "speech from the throne" emphasized educational problems. The Emperor advocated the founding of technical schools adapted to local conditions and facilities; two universities, one in the South, another in the North; and faculties of sciences and letters in the various provinces. He realized that these institutions must be based on the expansion and improvement of secondary and primary education throughout the country. He also called for a Ministry of Instruction to superivse the new program. What the Emperor proposed was an adequate and well-coordinated national system of public instruction. This took place on the eve of the proclamation of the Republic.

In 1869 there were 3,561 public schools with a total of 115,735 students (about 1.2 per cent of the population). For each classroom there were, among the free population of the country, 541 children of school age. Five years later, in 1876, there were already a total of 6,000 public schools attended by 200,000 pupils; or, if one takes into account only the free children of school age, there was a classroom for each group of 314.

In 1889 the number of public and private schools throughout the Empire was 7,500, and the number of students was almost 300,000 (about 2.1 per cent of the population).[3] There were 292 secondary schools with 10,427 students; two higher schools of law, with 1,329 students; two schools of medicine with 800 students; and one polytechnic school (engineering), with 161 students. Higher education was an exclusive professional specialty, there being no schools for the promotion of the pure sciences or of literature.

The Brazilian population in 1889 being estimated at 14 million, it follows that for each group of 10,000 inhabitants there were 214 pupils in the primary schools, 7 in the secondary schools, and 1.6 in the advanced schools. Less than 3 per cent of the population was attending existing schools at all levels. This was, without doubt, a very modest school contingent for an independent, sovereign country. At the time of the proclamation of the Republic in 1889, Brazil was still an extremely backward and underdeveloped country.

NOTES

1. Quoted in Prado, *História Econômica do Brasil*, p. 147.

2. Primitivo Moacyr, *A Instrução e as Provincias*, in *Subsídios para a História da Edução no Brasil*, I (São Paulo, 1939), 53.

3. M. F. J. Santa-Anna Nery, *Le Brésil en 1889* (Paris, 1889).

4

Republican
Brazil:
Preparation for Socioeconomic
and Cultural Development

JUST as independence was achieved through the intelligence and resourcefulness of a young Brazilian elite that took advantage of the international juncture of affairs and impelled Prince Dom Pedro to break with Portugal—thus averting a long and possibly divisive armed struggle—so, in an analogous fashion, the Republic was the product of a group of able men who were in positions of leadership. The Republic was not a triumph of the people. The politically liberal elite who furthered it were as remote from the common people as was the rural aristocracy that had been the mainstay of the Empire. The awakening of the Brazilian people to political responsibility is a relatively recent phenomenon, assuming decisive importance only since 1945. But there can be no doubt that the Republic, by virtue of its educational system and its cultural institutions, began the political and social maturing process of the masses.

One of the founders of the Republic asserted that the people were a mute and stupefied witness to the proclamation. Similarly, the common people took little part in consolidating the power of the central government during the next decade. Fewer than 5 per cent of the adults could meet the literacy and other requirements to become voters. Political power was concentrated in the hands of the large rural landowners and of the merchant class of São Paulo and Minas Gerais. In fact, the entire period from 1900 to 1930 may be characterized as an oligarchic Republic.

Some notion of how far the Republic has been able to enlist the support and understanding of the people in the processes of socioeconomic and cultural development may be gained from

77

a comparison of the situation in the Northeast in 1890 with that in the 1950's. In the Northeast of Brazil there was unrest and turmoil after the Republic was proclaimed. The sugar raising area, which had depended on slave labor, had to adjust to free labor, and the freed slaves had to adjust themselves to a new condition. In the Polygon of Drought the people were still as isolated as they had been for three centuries of life-or-death struggle against the environment. To them the new government had little meaning.

In the village of Canudos, located in the hill country within the Polygon of Drought in the state of Bahia, a strangely assorted group of people collected around Antônio Conselheiro (Anthony the Counsellor), a messianic leader with a quasi-religious, quasi-political message. Cattle-drovers of the dry *Sertão*, the backland, refugees from the cities who had run afoul of the law, and a large number of religious people of the *Sertão* were moved by the preaching of Antonio to give their worldly goods to his cause and to live with him in his backcountry principality of Canudos, which by 1896 had grown to contain 5,000 houses.

Antonio Conselheiro preached against the new government, and was openly defiant of some of its laws. His fame drew lawbreakers to Canudos as a place where they might find immunity. The more lawless people began to raid surrounding communities for supplies, and Canudos became known as a kind of pirate center.

Eventually the government sent a small military troop to assert its authority in Canudos. This troop fought a battle and killed a number of the Canudos defenders, but eventually retreated when supplies gave out; they learned, to their sorrow, that the defenders of Canudos would fight with guerilla tactics and would not surrender. Soon a larger column of 500 government soldiers was sent to take the town, and they, too, met a humiliating defeat. By this time the situation had become a national scandal. Could a ragged band of outlaws successfully defy the new government? If so, the government could hardly hope to assert its authority over this vast country. Then the national government sent a third force, this time 1,300 men, who attacked the town and actually took a part of it, but were again driven away, with 200 dead.

Finally, in June 1897, a force of 5,000 men marched on the town and managed to capture one corner of it at a cost of 900 men. Just as this army was about to retreat because its supplies had run out, a relief expedition arrived and lost another thousand men while taking another piece of the town. Then followed two months of constant hand-to-hand warfare during which the rebels gradually weakened. Government troops were reinforced in September with 2,500 men and they finally killed the last defenders on October 5. There was no surrender, and only a few prisoners were taken—women, children and old men. Antônio Conselheiro died on August 22. The outlaw leaders continued to lead their bands of desperate fighters, and were only gradually killed, one by one.

Life has continued to be hard in the Polygon of Drought in the intervening decades, and the sugar-producing Northeast has been an area of economic distress. But the years since the fall of Canudos have allowed the people to experience the advantages of a strong central government and to feel themselves a part of the United States of Brazil. For instance, the government after World War II contructed a hydroelectric plant to harness the power of the São Francisco river. One of the great water power resources of the world, it now gives light and power to the resident of Pernambuco and neighboring states. Since the war the government has assisted in providing the Polygon of Drought with 4,000 wells, over 600 reservoirs for storage of 6.4 billion cubic meters of irrigation water, and 700 kilometers of irrigation canals.

It would not be true to say that the Republic has completed the task of integrating Brazil and making it a happy, productive land. The country is still one of contrasts, with wealth and poverty often existing side by side. The poverty-stricken and isolated rural communities that were characteristic of nineteenth century Brazil still exist in dark contrast to the more productive industrial and urban areas.

In an essay on technological aspects of productivity, a leading Brazilian educator and scientist, Dr. Ernesto Luís de Oliveira, Jr., defines six conditions that are necessary for a technological revolution:

1. A long and continuous technological experience
2. Demographic pressure, due to growth of population
3. Wealth combined with change in the economy; i.e., the economy must be wealthy enough to serve as a base for systematic research and planning, but at the same time must be open to technological change

4. Social mobility in a social structure that is fluid enough to permit upward mobility

5. A technical ideology; i.e., an interest in invention and in getting work done in a labor-saving manner

6. Acceptance of the idea that the state should use its power for the social welfare [1]

None of these six conditions was present in Brazil at the beginning of the Republic. But fifty-six years later, in 1945, all but two had been sufficiently realized to serve as a base for rapid and stable economic development. In this chapter and the next we shall see how the Republic of Brazil prepared the country to enter this technological era, and what still remained to be done after World War II.

The Beginning of an Industrial Economy: 1890–1914

The export trade of Brazil increased substantially and exceeded imports during the first three decades of the Republican government. In the period from 1901 to 1910, exports averaged 50 million pounds sterling annually, while imports were 32 million. The following decade, 1911–20, saw exports climb to 70 million on the average, and imports to 55 million.

Departing from the conservative patterns of the Empire, the Republican government promoted production through its financial policies, at the cost of continuing inflation of the currency, a process very familiar to Brazilians and known by the term *ensilhamento* (putting a saddle on another saddle); but the process stimulated the agricultural and extractive industries and raised the export rate so as to provide foreign money for the purchase of railroads and other equipment necessary for further economic development. The railroad network, essential for transport of export goods and for internal commerce, reached 29,000 kilometers in 1920, not far from its 1960 size of 37,000 kilometers.

The first industries produced goods for which there was a large domestic demand, such as textiles, furniture, brick and tile, and food products. Machinery for these industries was bought from Europe with the money obtained from exports of agricultural commodities. At the same time, imported machinery was replacing manual labor in the coffee plantations and sugar mills.

A high level of industrial productivity was not to be expected from a labor force that as late as 1920 was 80 per cent illiterate, and the Brazilian productivity per worker was low in comparison with productivity of workers in more industrialized countries.

This meant that only by means of low wages could Brazilian industry compete against foreign industry in the production of manufactured goods.

Education did not contribute much to economic development of Brazil during the early Republican period. The colonial and imperial systems of education, as well as the system of slave labor which lasted almost to the beginning of the Republic, deeply affected the attitudes of people toward manual work. The educational system was concerned mainly with providing an education in literature and in the liberal arts. The school-taught man was known by his elegant appearance, delicate hands, preference for office work, and for management of public and private enterprises. Factory work, which might involve developing callouses on one's hands, was regarded as appropriate only for slaves or for the benighted masses. This made it impossible to establish an educational system stressing technological and industrial training. The meager attempts made in this direction during the Empire, as well as by the first schools devoted to the arts and crafts, founded shortly after 1910, showed a very modest registration from the people at large. Those who did attend school had no desire to learn to work; rather they aspired to become holders of a bachelor's degree and to lead the good life of the *doutores*. Hence the popular saying in Brazil that the first Republic was an "aristocracy of doctors"—that is, of university graduates. To build a class of skilled workers under such conditions was indeed a difficult task. And this very same problem continues to weigh heavily upon Brazil, as we shall see in subsequent chapters.

Education for middle- and upper-class youth had the function of helping them to maintain their social status by getting a "gentleman's education." Thus it had symbolic value, but was not actually necessary for earning a living. Only a small minority of youth from poor homes used education as a means of climbing the social ladder, and they generally aspired to be lawyers or doctors, i.e., to avoid manual work. Only engineers and military officers, of which there were a few, underwent a training close to technology.

The immigrants from Europe furnished most of the workers who could handle machines and machine tools, and many of them became foremen or superivsors in factories and railroads. Two million four hundred thousand persons came as immigrants between 1891 and 1914. The heavy inflow from Italy and Germany of men with a primary school education and training in handicrafts helped Brazil to begin the process of industrialization. It was commonly remarked in the South that the "gringos" (a generic nickname applied to immigrants) taught the Brazilians to work with their hands.

Economic Expansion: World War I to the World Depression, 1914-37

World War I gave an enormous push to the Brazilian economy. By reducing the exports of the European manufacturing nations it gave Brazilian manufacturing a stimulus; and by continuing and even increasing the demand for most Brazilian raw materials it provided Brazil with the capital necessary for industrial expansion. Furthermore, the São Paulo coffee production encountered market difficulties because of the loss of European markets and because coffee was not essential to the war effort. Consequently, the Paulistas were forced to diversify their agriculture and to invest some of their available capital in new industry.

Between 1900 and 1912 Brazilian rubber had almost a monopoly of the world market. The city of Manaus, in the center of the Amazon basin where rubber trees grew naturally, sent rubber by ship to industrial nations all over the world. Manaus grew rich enough to build a great opera house and to import opera troupes from Europe on the same ships that carried away the rubber. But an Englishman carefully collected 70,000 seeds from Brazilian trees and took them to Kew Gardens in England where they were planted. The young trees were cultivated in hot houses until they could be shipped to the East Indies to start rubber tree plantations there. After 1912 the East Indian production replaced Brazilian rubber on the world market. Later the Germans discovered a process for making synthetic rubber which has now, even in Brazil, been found cheaper and more satisfactory for some purposes than natural rubber. This is one of the few instances of decreased production in Brazil during the first half of the twentieth century. The rule was that both agriculture and industry were expanding.

In 1907 Brazil claimed a total of 3,258 industrial establishments employing 150,841 persons. In 1920 there were 13,336 factories with 275,521 workers. Thus the average number of workers per factory dropped from 46 to 21. Many small factories were started during the war, by artisans with a little capital, often immigrants. They manufactured candles and soap, knitted goods, tin cans, footwear, iron utensils, beer, wine, and canned foods. Especially in the South there developed a number of small industrial cities, such as Blumenau, Joinville, and São Leopoldo. Textile industries accounted for 50 per cent of total production in 1907, but by 1920 food industries amounted to 40 per cent and textiles had decreased.

When the war was over, there were 1.5 million urban dwellers dependent upon industry for a livelihood. To protect them from foreign competition the government set up a system of protective tariffs. Although industry did not grow between 1920 and 1930, it held its own.

While 75 per cent of Brazilian people still lived in rural areas in 1920, the urbanized 25 per cent were creating cities and city problems. The exodus of the rural population to the cities began, and it continues to this day. Expectations of high pay and better living standards were often illusory, and many became marginal city dwellers, living in *favelas* or *cortiços* under conditions that shocked the more privileged citizens.

Most of the migrants from country to city had lived on a mere subsistence level before they migrated. If they worked for a large landholder, they got barely enough money to pay for their clothing and the additional food they needed to supplement the produce of the land allotted to them by the landlord. If they had their own land, they followed the primitive practices of colonial days. The better methods of agriculture used by the immigrants in the South made it even more difficult for the *caboclo* and the *sertanejo* to farm at a profit, and hastened their exodus to the cities.

Development of an Educational System

As the cities grew during the first thirty years of the Republic there came into being an urban educational system that was good by the standards of those days. The Republican constitution of 1891 gave major responsibility for primary education to the states, as well as power to establish secondary schools and higher educational institutions. It also gave the federal government power to establish a system of secondary and higher education. The constitution defined the secular nature of public education and guaranteed the free exercise of any "moral, intellectual and industrial profession."

The first head of the federal administration for education was Benjamin Constant, one of the fathers of the Republic and, like most of the others, much influenced by the philosophy of positivism which emanated from France. His ideas led in the direction of education for science and technology, in contrast to the tradition of literary humanism, and he succeeded in enlarging the curriculum of the secondary schools by adding the scientific subjects.

The federal government maintained in Rio the Ginásio Nacional, the former Colégio Pedro II, which later resumed this name. Its curriculum became the official curriculum for the country, and other secondary schools were expected to duplicate it. The more progressive states established their own *ginásios* in the state capitals, many of them being reincarnations of the old-time *liceus* of colonial days. Teachers in the *ginásios* were frequently obtained from the outstanding members of the liberal professions of law, medicine, and theology. Throughout this period secondary education was treated either as preparation for entrance to a university or as the conclusion of a liberal education appropriate for youth of middle-class families. There was very little interest in using secondary education for vocational training. Secondary schools did not multiply rapidly during this period, partly because educators and the government were mainly concerned with expanding primary education. The number of primary school pupils per thousand inhabitants gives a rough measure of the extent of primary school education. In 1889 there were 19 primary school pupils per thousand population; by 1907 this number had reached 30, and it increased to 44 in 1920 and to 62 in 1930. Still, in 1920 only about 43 per cent of school-age children were in school, when by "school age" is meant the five-year period from 7 through 11 (see Table 6.). However, the advance was not a balanced one, for while the cities and the wealthier states expanded their systems of primary education, the rural areas and the poorer states lagged behind.

São Paulo was the first state to deal seriously and systematically with the problem of public primary education and the preparation of teachers. Following a law passed by the state legislature in 1892, the state was divided into school districts under the supervision of inspectors. In the capital and the county seats the primary school was organized in two stages: the primary school of four years and a supplementary school of three years. The smaller communities and the isolated rural schools offered only the four-year course.

In addition, the state turned to the task of reorganizing the training of teachers. The Normal School of the city of São Paulo was reorganized by Antonio Caetano de Campos, assisted by Maria Guilhermina Louveiro de Andrade, who had made a study

TABLE 6

*Primary School Enrollment, in Relation to Total Population
and to Population of School Age*

Year	Enrollment in primary schools Public	Private	Number enrolled per 1,000 total population	Number enrolled per 1,000 aged 7-11
1857	70,500	12,500	10	68
1869	89,600	16,400	11	77
1878	154,600	21,100	16	112
1889	259,000		19	136
1907	638,000		30	202
1920	1,251,000		44	291
1930	2,085,000		62	430
1940	2,092,000	463,000	62*	460
1950	3,245,000	465,000	71	554
1958	5,079,000	723,000	90	720
1960	6,300,000		90	735

*From 1940, the enrollment figures are for "effective enrollment," whereas before 1940, they are for "general enrollment." The "general" figures are 10 to 20 per cent higher than the "effective" figures. For comparison, the figures before 1940 should be reduced perhaps 10 per cent. "Effective enrollment," the enrollment in the last month of the school year, is about 15 per cent greater than "average attendance."

Sources: *Sinopse Retrospectiva do Ensino no Brasil, 1871-1954* (Rio de Janeiro: Serviço de Estatística da Educação e Cultura, Ministério de Educação e Cultura, 1956); *Anuário Estatístico do Brasil*, 1960; Ruy Barbosa, "A Lição dos Numeros Sôbre a Reforma do Ensino," *Revista Brasileira da Estatística*, II (1941), 927-1024.

of the educational system in the United States, and by Marcia Browne, a school principal from Boston. They added experimental primary school classes for practice teaching by student teachers, organized the curriculum on a four-year basis, and required that the student complete a three-year supplementary primary course before entering the normal school.

São Paulo was influential as a model in Brazilian education. Teachers were sent there to observe the school system or São Paulo loaned educators to other cities to reorganize their educational systems. Santa Catarina, Paraná, Ceará, Mato Grosso, and other states followed the lead of São Paulo, while Minas Gerais, Bahia, Pernambuco, and the Federal District went in another direction. The São Paulo program followed the theory of Herbart, which was then in vogue in the United States; the opposing program followed the French version of European pedagogy, with the educational theories of Froebel and Pestalozzi as a basis, and reinforced later by Binet, Decroly, and Montessori.

There remained a major problem of getting primary education into the rural areas, where as late as 1950 two-thirds of the children were living. The isolated rural school was not an inviting place for a young woman to teach, and the great majority of primary school teachers were women. The school was generally maintained physically by a large landowner, because it served his employees. In all except the southern states the land was generally held by *fazendeiros* with as many as fifty or a hundred families living on the fazenda and working it. Sometimes the teacher was the wife or daughter of the owner or manager of the fazenda. Otherwise, she would be a girl who had to live near the school, unless the distance was short and there was a road good enough for her to ride a bicycle out from the county seat or another town. Writing about the teacher of rural schools in the middle 1930's, Professor A. Almeida, Jr., said:

There are *fazendeiros* and farm managers who consider the teacher to be an employee of the fazenda under the orders of the master and subject to the general discipline of the laborers. . . . Frequently the girl must find shelter in the house of the *caipira*, where the mistress of the house, although an excellent person, cooks the beans badly with no fat. Cleanliness is unknown. . . . The teacher is given a room, with the walls full of holes, which is also used for keeping saddles and harness. . . . [2]

The task of teaching in an isolated rural school was not always pleasant for a city-bred girl, but these crude schools did much to cut down the illiteracy of the rural population. However, Brazilian educators differed about the value of the one-room rural school. Professor Sud Menucci led the group that favored the maintenance and expansion of this type of school, while Professors Almeida, Jr., Fernando de Azevedo, and others regarded the isolated rural school as a weak and ineffective institution. At any rate, the number of rural schools continued to grow, from 26,600 with 27,600 teachers in 1936, to 67,000 with 79,000 teachers in 1959.

Thus primary education increased, if gradually, and because of more urban and rural schools the percentage of illiteracy among adults dropped from 75 in 1920 to 50 in 1950.

Political Unrest and Social Change: 1922-37

The rule of Brazil by a conservative rural oligarchy centered in the states of São Paulo and Minas Gerais was sharply challenged after 1920. By then, Rio de Janeiro, São Paulo, Recife, Salvador, Belo Horizonte, and Pôrto Alegre were industrial cities with a new social structure and a new economic leadership. An urban middle class and an urban industrial working class were growing. The social structure was more fluid: able and ambitious children of the working class moved up into middle-class positions in business and the professions; members of old aristocratic families were obliged to accept minor positions in business and government; and some middle-class people sank into the working class.

In the cities, as far back as 1920, members of the same family (Oliveira, Campos, Sobral, Moreira, Santos, Souza, etc.) could be found in three different social classes. The popular literature of that era reflects the new social mobility in accounts of rich cousins and poor cousins, of sons who acquire great wealth and help their impoverished parents, or of the wicked rich who are reduced to penury.

After World War I the government adopted an economic policy that was intended to protect local industry, but which also raised prices and caused discontent. At the same time a welter of new ideas and ideologies swept in from Europe and were picked up by the intelligentsia and by the urban leaders who were concerned with the mass poverty of their country. From 1922 to 1930 the agitation and debate that focused on the cities was instigated by the fundamental contradiction between the semipatriarchal, backward Brazil of the interior and the modern Brazil of the industrial cities. The time was coming when there must be political changes. The urban intelligentsia and the emerging leaders of the working class vacillated between the political right and the left from 1930 to 1945, when eventually they settled upon a centrist position. Meanwhile the greater part of the nation languished in boundless ignorance. "Brazil is a sleeping giant, eternally reposing in a splendid cradle," was a common saying, ironically enlarging on a verse of the national anthem.

Pre-revolutionary Movements

Accompanying and to some extent reflecting the political unrest was a new aesthetic movement. Beginning with a gathering of new writers in São Paulo in 1922, the movement revealed two principal objectives: emancipation from the old European patterns that still held sway in Brazil and the discovery of indigenous artistic themes. The new literature concerned itself with daily life, with the realities and problems confronting the Brazilian people, and was written in a style that gave full recognition to the spoken language. Frequently it featured themes of social protest. Monteiro Lobato portrayed Jeca Tatu, the typical man of the interior: sickly, afflicted with verminosis, and incapable of sustained labor. Graça Aranha described the suffering of immigrants, and Gilberto Freyre, in two books entitled *Casa Grande e Senzala* (*The Masters and the Slaves*) and *Sobrados e Mucambos* (*The Mansions and the Shanties*) which combined in masterly fashion belles lettres and a social study, recounted both the greatness and the decadence of the Northeast area. Mário de Andrade, Manoel Bandeira, and Carlos Drumond de Andrade transmuted into free verse the melancholy and the tragic apathy of the life of the common man and of the middle class of São Paulo, of the Northeast, and of Minas Gerais.

The impact of this literature upon the middle class as well as the elite of the cities was virtually revolutionary. Novels, romantic tales, and poems were avidly read and discussed by all social classes, and Brazilians found themselves wanting to learn more about their country. It is not at all surprising that during this period (1922–45) the social sciences gained prominence under the leadership of such Brazilian scholars as Fernando de Azevedo, Gilberto Freyre, and Emílio Willems, and of such foreign professors as Donald Pierson and Roger Bastide.

REVOLUTION OF 1930. Parallel with the development of this new intellectual life was the growth of political unrest. The political movements took the form of attempts to break the system known as the São Paulo-Minas Gerais axis. The Republican oligarchy had developed a custom of alternating the presidency between the two most powerful states, Minas Gerais and São Paulo, both of which were controlled politically by rural landlords. In the elections of 1922 and 1930 there were candidates opposed to this political practice, the leader of the 1930 opposition being Getúlio Vargas, governor of the state of Rio Grande do Sul. This was a confused election, because President Washington Luís, who had been governor of São Paulo, designated another Paulista, Júlio Prestes, as his candidate, and thus antagonized the governor of Minas Gerais. Rio Grande do Sul combined with the Northeast to attack the oligarchy at this strategic time, supporting João Pessoa, governor of the northeastern state of Paraíba, for vice-presidential candidate to run with Vargas as candidate for the presidency, João Pessoa was assissinated during the election campaign, and feelings ran high. When Prestes was declared elected, Vargas charged the government party with election fraud.

After the election Getúlio Vargas raised the standard of rebellion in Rio Grande do Sul, Antonio Carlos did the same in Minas Gerais, and in the Northeast a young army officer, Juarez Távora, launched a third revolutionary movement. The army sided with the rebels, and the garrison of Rio de Janeiro deposed President Washington Luís a few days before he was to hand the office over to his successor. The army gave power to Vargas, who set up a provisional government.

Vargas assumed leadership just as Brazil was feeling the full force of the worldwide depression. All countries had been forced to curtail their imports, and the demand for Brazil's coffee, cacao, mate, rubber, and lumber was greatly reduced. The average annual export trade of Brazil dropped from 85 million pounds sterling (1925–29) to less than 40 million (1930–34). The government suspended payments in foreign currency, raised customs duties in order to force a reduction in imports, and withdrew excess coffee from the market. Brazilian industry was given some impetus at this time, since foreign goods could not be imported easily. At the same time the agriculturists were encouraged to diversify, with the production of cereals and fruits. Only the old-time aristocrats of São Paulo, the coffee-planters, opposed these trends. But an increasingly powerful set of industrialists and business men in São Paulo were for the changes.

Industrial production increased and agriculture became more diversified. Domestic trade grew. In the decade 1921–30 the value of foreign trade (exports plus imports) was £ 1,235,044,000, whereas in the following decade the total shrank to £ 677,373,000. By way of compensation, the domestic commerce in Brazil for 1931–40 tripled in value and doubled in tonnage.

Industrialization and diversification in farm crops were not uniformly distributed throughout the country, and the reduction in the exportation of raw materials and tropical products caused certain areas to become stagnant. A large part of the eastern area, the Northeast, and the North suffered in this respect. The South and the southern portion of the East and Central West benefited from the new phase of the Brazilian economy.

There was currency inflation at this time, and in order to resolve this problem the government enacted wage-price legislation designed to maintain a fair balance of wages and price. A special judiciary body was formed to settle problems in labor relations. Thenceforth, every drop in the purchasing power of the currency was compensated by a rise in wages. In lieu of waging a strike, the workers were given the right of "collective dissent" which could be brought before the "tribunals of labor justice" and resolved by them. Generally speaking, these labor courts sought a middle ground between the conflicting interests of labor and management.

These economic events were related to political movements that threatened the stability of the government. A new constitution, which introduced the secret ballot and other reforms, was drafted in 1934, and Vargas was named president by the congress. Shortly afterward, in 1935, the Communist party infiltrated several army garrisons and attempted to seize power. Although this *coup* was unsuccessful, it heightened the tension that gathered about the approaching presidential election of 1938. The Vargas supporters were for José Américo de Almeida, of Paraíba; São Paulo sponsored the candidacy of its governor, Armando Sales de Oliveira; and a new political party of a fascist nature appeared —"Integralismo." Vargas used the fears and uncertainty of the time, together with the threat of a new communist uprising, to secure army and navy support for his *coup d'etat* of 1937. He dissolved the congress, proclaimed the "Estado Nôvo" (New State), and established a new constitution by decree. In the following year the Integralistas made an attempt on the life of Vargas by launching an attack on the presidential palace, and when the attempt failed the party was outlawed.

From then until 1945 Getúlio Vargas ruled the country absolutely. For a period of eight years he and his cabinet wielded power by means of decrees that had the force of law. Brazil seemed to be entering into a political synthesis that embodied phases of fascism, the corporative Italian state, and the semi-authoritarian-bourgeois state directed by Salazar in Portugal.

Toward the end of World War II, in which Brazil participated on the side of the United States by sending an army corps to Italy, new internal and external conditions obliged Vargas to call for the election of a new congress. Various liberal political groups demanded that a presidential election also be held; they promoted the candidacy of an old-time revolutionary, Eduardo Gomes, then an officer in the Brazilian air force. Vargas countered by launching the candidacy of his Minister of War, General Eurico Dutra. The armed forces, doubting Getúlio's sincerity, purged him and called upon the president of the Supreme Court to take over the presidential post. In the elections, however, General Dutra triumphed. In 1946, with a new constitution in effect, Brazil entered into another phase of its democratic career.

Educational Reform and Reaction

The social, political, and economic changes that led up to the Revolution of 1930 had their counterpart in the field of education. During the decade of the 1920's there was a movement in Europe and the United States for educational reform that stressed two quite different and possibly contradictory aims. One was to form education around the interests of the individual, who would "learn by doing," to use a phrase common in the United States. The other was to use the school as a means of social, political, and rural reconstruction so as to realize a higher measure of democracy. This movement was known as "progressive education" in the United States and as "the new school" or "the activity school" in Europe. One of the ablest young educators, Lourenço Filho, was appointed by the state government of Ceará to organize and develop a system of elementary education and a teacher-training program. After that he went to São Paulo, where he became a professor in the State Normal School and later Director of Public Instruction. His book on the philosophy of the "new school," *Indrodução ao Estudo da Escola Nova*, was published about 1930 and has gone through several editions, the latest in 1961.

Among the leaders of the new movement were Anísio Teixeira, Carneiro Leão, Fernando de Azevedo, Luís Trindade, Coelho de Souza, Francisco Campos, and Mario Casassanta. These reformers had the opportunity to direct educational reform in several states: in Minas Gerais; in the Federal District under three virtually successive administrations—those of Carneiro Leão, Fernando de Azevedo, and Anísio Teixeira, and São Paulo, with Fernando de Azevedo and Lourenço Filho.

Anísio Teixeira is an example of the leadership of those days. At the age of twenty-four, a law school graduate, he was placed in charge of the schools of Bahia. To orient himself in the field of education, he travelled to Europe and later studied with John Dewey. In 1928 he wrote in his report to the governor of Bahia: "We are a state with a large illiterate population living under primitive social conditions, with a tiny class of educated persons whose standards and way of life were directly copied from the more mature educated classes of Europe. . . . Within the framework of the contrast between that intellectual aristocracy and the backward inhabitants of the interior lies the explanation for many problems afflicting the country. . . . Four years of administration are as but a minute for a solution of the problem." [3] When Teixeira was summoned to direct the educational system of the Federal District, he had the opportunity to apply the principles of Dewey's philosophy.[4]

The aims of this group of reformers were to make the primary school an instrument for bettering the social life of the community and to create a system of secondary and advanced schools that would support the technological and cultural aspects of a developing democracy. They took steps to reform the rigid curriculum of the secondary schools, and they created the first universities of Brazil. However, the efforts of these reformers were paralyzed by the political regression that began with the 1937 dictatorship. They lost their power, and most of them left the government for university positions, where they could be relatively free. A period followed in which education was "simplified" and made more formal, partly under the public pressure for additional schools to reduce illiteracy. The result was the impoverishment of the educational system that had been built up with such labor in the years before 1930. The three-year supplementary course to the four-year primary school was virtually abandoned. The four-year primary course of the cities was reduced to three years in the rural areas, and the schools were limited to the teaching of reading, writing, and arithmetic. In 1937, out of 29,406 primary schools, 90 per cent were one-room rural schools, indicating that the states were stressing the task of fighting illiteracy in the rural areas. At the same time, among the 74,000 primary school teachers, about 65 per cent lacked specific training for their job. The federal government established a normal school course for training primary school teachers in two or three years after the first four-year cycle of the secondary school, which was completed at the age of fifteen or sixteen. And training for teachers of rural schools now required only four years beyond the four years of primary school. The salary of a primary school teacher in 1937 varied from 80 cruzeiros a month to 400, with an average of 160 (worth about $8.00 U. S.).

Meanwhile, in the cities the pressure of increasing population was met not by building more new buildings as in the pre-1920 period, but by shortening the school day so that each classroom could serve two classes, one in the morning and one in the afternoon.

Thus, from 1937 until about 1950 there was a decline in the quality of the primary school system as it was forced to expand rapidly and accommodate a rapidly increasing enrollment. Only after 1950 were attempts to improve the quality of primary education resumed.

Dictatorship and Industrialization: 1937–46

Subsequent to 1937 the government held in its hands an extraordinary degree of power which enabled it to resort to unprecedented intervention in the realm of commerce. It created such a complex bureaucratic apparatus for regulating domestic activities that the civil service came to be the largest profession in the country. However, the steps in the direction of a "directed economy" were taken without any consistency or coherent plan, each measure aimed at solving an emergency situation that was sometimes more private than national. This was an era of corruption and of economic favoritism, but at the same time one of speculation which led to continually advancing production.

As World War II approached, Brazilian exports of raw materials began to recover from the depression. The value of exports in 1940 was double that of 1935. After 1940 the exports of raw materials doubled again in five years, and Brazil began to export cotton textiles and to increase exports of meat. Since there was little that could be imported from the belligerent countries during the war, domestic industry was again stimulated to produce goods that had formerly been imported. The increase of industrial production during the war was approximately 50 per cent.

The growth of industry was costly. Brazil had no industry capable of creating and maintaining a transport system, and there was a staggering amount of wear and tear on roads, railroads, trucks, and airplanes. Stocks of gasoline and oil were exhausted. There was also a chronic shortage of electric power.

In the meantime, with an abundance of money available, the government began a great program of public works. This was the golden era of Brazilian architecture. The government erected in Rio de Janeiro the large and beautiful modern buildings of the Treasury and the Ministries of Education, Labor, and War, as well as the Central Railway Station. Skyscrapers were constructed by private enterprise in São Paulo, Rio, Pôrto Alegre, Recife, Belo Horizonte, and Curitiba.

Although the period of the Vargas dictatorship lacked systematic economic development and saw a recession of political democracy and of education, some progress was made. Two of the six conditions formulated by Oliveira for the making of a technological society were achieved. The need for a fluid social structure was met by the Revolution of 1930, which broke down the aristocratic structure of the society and laid a basis for the rise of enterprising people through the industrialization that came between 1930 and 1946.

The people also accepted the idea that the state should use its power for social welfare. This too was met by the Revolution of 1930, which introduced government wage and price control mechanisms, and was followed by a variety of governmental economic activities. One of the most important was the construction of the government-planned steel plant at Volta Redonda, and of the hydroelectric plant at the falls of Paulo Afonso on the São Francisco river. These were basic steps in the development of a modern industrial economy.

At the end of the war, the prevailing mood called for a rational approach to the problems of the country. A substantially increased number of technically trained people were available to assist in technological development. Since the dictatorship had discouraged young men from entering politics or public life, enrollments in the law schools decreased while the number of university students in the schools of engineering, economics, and philosophy and letters increased sharply. The engineers were needed for the development of industry, the economists for the development of industry and business, and the graduates of the philosophy faculties were needed to teach in the rapidly growing secondary school system. Thus the close of World War II saw the return of democratic constitutional government in a situation that was favorable to economic development.

NOTES

1. Ernesto Luiz de Oliveira, Jr., *Ensino Técnico e Desenvolvimento* (Rio de Janeiro: Instituto Superior de Estudos Brasileiros, Ministério de Educação e Cultura, 1959), p. 16.

2. A. Almeida, Jr., "Os Sete Pecados Capitais da Escola Rural," *Revista Brasileira de Estatística*, II, No. 8 (1941), 1215ff., quoted in T. Lynn Smith, *Brazil: People and Institutions*, rev. ed. (Baton Rouge, 1954), pp. 565-66.

3. Anísio S. Teixeira, *Relatório da Diretoria de Instrução Pública ao Govêrno do Estado* (Salvador, Bahia, 1928).

4. See his *Educação Progressiva* (São Paulo, 1932).

5

Social Structure, Education, and Social Mobility

DURING its first three centuries, Brazil remained a simple society with only a rudimentary social structure. The great landowners and the slaves formed the two poles of the society, with a shapeless mass of free workers in between. A more definite structure of working classes and middle classes would have existed if it had not been for the variation of economic cycles which caused a kind of tidal movement of population from one part of the country to another and tended to prevent social stratification. Only in the last half of the nineteenth century did a more complex social structure begin to take definite shape. This process was stimulated by European immigration into the South and the consequent development of a larger middle class and a free working class. In this chapter we shall look at the social structure of the country during the epochs of 1870, 1930, and 1960.

Social Structure in 1870[1]

An estimate of the numerical size of the various socioeconomic groups in 1870 indicates that the number of slaves was about 1.5 million, while the free population totaled 8.6 million. The number of students in school was about 138,000, and one may infer that these were almost entirely children of upper-class and upper-middle class families. The average family had five to six persons according to the censuses between 1900 and 1950, and the families with children in school had an average of 1.5 children attending school. Assuming that 20 per cent of the families of this level did not have school-age children, we may estimate that there were about 620,000 persons of all ages in the upper and upper-middle classes, or about 5 per cent of the total population.

This group included 6,800 landowners with an annual income of 15 contos or higher and 1,200 large property owners in the cities, including bankers and merchants of substance. Fifteen contos was equivalent to about $8,000.00 (U. S.) at the time, and would have been worth substantially more than that sum is worth today.

There was a second group of lesser rural property owners with annual incomes between eight and fifteen contos; this group numbered no more than four thousand. In addition, about 70,000 graduates of secondary schools (some of them university graduates) —physicians, engineers, lawyers, higher officers in the army, professors in institutions of higher education, merchants, and bankers—constituted an analogous social group in the urban areas. These made up what might be called an upper-middle class.

Approximately 120,000 business employees and government officials, city artisans, and small rural proprietors might be said to constitute the lower-middle class. One and a half million slaves and about 800,000 sharecroppers or landless peasants with their families made up the lower-lower class, while the remaining urban workers and a few small farmers were at the upper-lower level.

On the basis of these crude figures we can estimate the socio-economic distribution of the population as shown.

The socioeconomic status of the slaves differed from that of the free laborers, but their material standard of living was no worse, and often better, than that of the lower working class. After 1851, when it became illegal to import slaves, and with the enactment of "the free womb" and the "sexagenarians" * laws, the prices of slaves increased, making it more economical, by 1871, to employ free laborers for agricultural work. Thus the decline in the economic importance of slave labor and its abolition in 1888 added to the existing oversupply of unskilled labor. According to Nelson Werneck Sodré, "The transition from a system of slave labor, with no compensation, to one of wages which had to be figured in the cost of production, tended to preserve the colonial system of production. The social class which provided labor for Brazil simply grew larger without gaining social or political power, and the resultant increase of labor force merely aggravated the moral degradation of labor with a corresponding economic degradation."[2]

---

* Laws were passed which provided that all children of slaves were to be born free and that every person who passed the age of sixty became free.

At the higher level there was very little social distinction between upper and upper-middle classes, though some differentiation was made in Rio de Janeiro. The Imperial court was under the influence of bankers, barons of the Empire, the higher echelon of government officials, and the members of the liberal professions (the "sheepskin aristocracy"). But the Emperor in his daily life at the Quinta da Boa Vista led a rather simple social life, not unlike that of the bourgeois rural aristocracy of that period, with conventional attitudes and habits and a tranquil family life. Thus the upper-middle and upper classes lived under such similar material and cultural conditions that their differences were small compared with those between them and the lower class.

Social mobility in such a society was possible only along two paths: movement through family connections or through acquisition of an education. Social ascent through marriage alone was more feasible for girls than for boys. A girl of the working class might marry a man of the lower-middle class, and a girl of the lower-middle class might marry a man of slightly higher social status. But a young man could rarely marry a girl of higher social status unless he also had a superior education.

Another form of social mobility through family connections was based on the godparent relationship. Upper-class men frequently accepted the honor (and the responsibility) of becoming godfather to a number of children of employees or of people who were lower in social status and recognized the upper-class man as a patron. The godfather would often provide encouragement and the small financial means necessary for a primary school education, and upon the boy's completion of primary school the godfather would help him obtain a government job or a clerical job in business. Occasionally the godfather would assist a talented boy to get a secondary or higher education. In the popular literature of the era this process of social ascent is frequently used as a romantic theme.*

The idea that school should be a prerequisite for a middle-class job was gaining general acceptance at the close of the Empire. In 1882 Ruy Barbosa's plan for educational reform proposed that anyone who completed an eight-year program of primary school should have preference for government positions

---

* For example, in the novels of urban life by José de Alencar and M. Mode Macedo.

as well as special priority in competitive examinations for administrative positions.

Social Structure in 1920

As late as 1900 the structure of Brazilian society was hardly distinguishable from that of 1870. Only the gap between the base and the apex of the socioeconomic pyramid may have widened: whereas in 1872 the national income was 30.5 billion cruzeiros (1958 value) with a per capita income of 3,050 cruzeiros, in the year 1900 the national income was 53.4 billion with a per capita income of 3,085 cruzeiros. By this time there was more wealth in a few hands, and this concentration was the first phase of the capital formation that would facilitate the twentieth-century economic growth.

By the beginning of the twentieth century there were signs of the emergence of the modern, industrialized, and productive country that was to develop alongside the archaic Brazil. Most representative of the new trends were São Paulo and Rio de Janeiro, as well as the other regions of the South that were receiving large European immigration. The immigrants brought with them more efficient productive techniques as well as a will to build for themselves and their posterity a better pattern of life. They introduced new crops and a diversified agriculture. Among the crops successfully introduced in the South were grapes, barley, rye, and garden vegetables. They grew corn and beans as well as barley, oats, and rye; they maintained orchards with fruit trees and grape vines, and kitchen gardens with cabbage, carrots, onions, and lettuce, in addition to flower gardens with rose bushes, carnations and violets; and without fail they kept a few milk cows, chickens, and pigs.

In their small towns and cities they developed workshops that later grew into the factories of today. Thus were founded, among others, the great Renner establishments (textiles and garment manufacturers) ; the Walig and Bertha metallurgical works of Rio Grande do Sul; the factories of Rennaux, Collin, Wetzel, Garcia, Hoepcke, and others in Santa Catarina; and the large and powerful Matarazzo Enterprises in São Paulo.

The entire South became a rich and more prosperous variant of Brazilian core culture. The higher standards of living created a domestic market for the developing industries and the new agriculture. With the construction of the São Paulo-Rio Grande and the Sorocaba and São Paulo Railways, the movement of goods in the state of São Paulo was intensified, and the occupation of traveling salesman became lucrative. In the south of Minas and reaching to the plains of Rio Grande do Sul, the salesman became a familiar figure—even to the point of providing a character for literature.

During this period the middle classes were increasing in relative numbers, and an upper stratum of workers was emerging to demand education for their children. The school enrollment statistics reflect the socioeconomic changes, with the number of children in primary school increasing from 14 per thousand inhabitants in 1872 to 22 per thousand in 1900 and 62 per thousand population in 1930.

The South was leading Brazil toward a social structure with a larger middle class and an upper working class that was growing at the expense of the lower working class. And led by their southern representatives, the middle and upper working classes were clamoring for more primary schools and for a system of free public secondary schools. Analysis of the 1920 census data on occupations and property ownership gives the socioeconomic

TABLE 7

Social Class Distribution in Brazil at Various Dates

Class	1870-72	1920	1950	1955
Upper	1.0	1.5	2	2
Upper-Middle	5.0	2.0	3	4
Lower-Middle	6.0	9.5	12	16
Upper-Lower	} 73	10	33	36
Lower-Lower		70	50	42
Slaves	15			
	100	100	100	100

Sources:
1870-72
  Caio Prado, Jr., *História Econômica do Brasil*.
  Afonso Arinos de Melo Franco, *Desenvolvimento da Civilização Material do Brasil* (Rio de Janeiro, 1944).
1920 The 1920 Census of Occupations. Data analyzed by J. Roberto Moreira in a way similar to the analysis of the 1950 data, cited below.
1950 The 1950 Census of Occupations. Pompeu Accioly Borges, "Estratificação e Mobilidade Social no Brasil," *Desenvolvimento e Conjuntura* II, No. 10, (Oct. 1958), 93-104; Robert J. Havighurst, "Educação, Mobilidade Social, e Mudança Social em Quatro Sociedades," *Educação e Ciências Sociais* II, No. 6 (Nov. 1957).
1955 Statistical data published by the Ministry of Labor, Institute of Workers' Pensions and Retirement, Institute of Business Employees' Pensions and Retirement, Income Tax Division of the Ministry of Finance, and the Ministries of Agriculture and of Commerce.

distribution shown in Table 7. Still, in 1920 industrial production was scarcely 15 per cent of the gross national product, and the industrial workers constituted only 2.7 per cent of the gainfully employed population. (In the South the industrial workers made up 5.7 per cent of the labor force.)

Social Structure in 1960

After 1920 the pace of social change quickened, as industrialization and urbanization increased. The number of factory workers increased, and with it the numbers of foremen, factory managers, engineers, and research scientists. At the same time more people were employed in business offices and banks. The government expanded its school system as well as its health and social services, with a resulting demand for teachers, nurses, doctors, and social workers. These new positions in the economy were generally in the upper-middle, lower-middle, or upper working class. As they increased, the relative numbers of farm workers and unskilled urban workers decreased. Table 7 shows how the social class distribution of 1950 compared with that of earlier times.

The modernization that paralleled the changes in social structure has not affected all of Brazil equally, as we have already noted. The states of the South led the rest of the country, and

TABLE 8

Socioeconomic Structure of the South of Brazil Compared with Brazil in General, 1920
(percentage distribution)

	The South (São Paulo, Paraná, Santa Catarina, and Rio Grande do Sul)	Brazil in general
Upper Class: Large landowners and the urban upper class	1.3	1.5
Upper-Middle Class: Medium-sized rural landowners and upper level professional and business men	4.7	2.0
Lower-Middle Class: Smaller rural property owners, public employees, small merchants and manufacturers, lower level professional men	10.5	9.5
Upper Working Class: Workers employed in factories, railways, public service, transportation and communication	27.5	17.0
Lower Working Class: farm laborers and unskilled urban workers	56.0	70.0

TABLE 9

Socioeconomic Distribution in Various Regions of Brazil, 1950

	Percentage of employed persons					
Socioeconomic Class	North	North-east	East	South	Central West	Brazil
Upper	1.5	1.5	2.0	2.5	1.5	2
Upper-Middle	5.0	2.0	3.0	5.0	2.5	3
Lower-Middle	11.0	11.0	12.0	13.5	11.5	12
Upper Working	16.5	15.5	33.0	37.0	15.5	33
Lower Working	66.0	70.0	50.0	42.0	69.0	50

Note: Analysis made by J. Roberto Moreira, based on occupational data in the 1950 census.

large areas were almost unchanged. Tables 8 and 9 show that the percentages of middle-class positions varied from 13 to 18.5, while the percentages of lower working-class positions varied in the opposite direction, from 70 to 42.

But even the regional distinctions in these tables do not reflect the complexity of present-day Brazilian social structure. If we analyze the South in more detail, we find a coastal strip running from Porto Alegre to south of São Paulo with a social structure resembling in some ways that of the Northeast. Similarly, if we study the western parts of the states of Paraná and Santa Catarina, we find a frontier with a society still in the making, somewhat similar to the Central West. On the other hand, in the Northeast, in Pernambuco, in Paraíba, in Sergipe, and in Rio Grande do Norte, we encounter areas in the process of industrialization or of economic diversification, and consequently in the throes of intense social change. Recife, for example, is a metropolitan area probably as important today as Rio de Janeiro was in 1920.

The industrial and urban areas, wherever they are, have become targets for internal migration, as have the frontier areas in process of settlement—the Central West, Southwest, and the North. In the year 1950 there were a million and a half persons living in the South, Central West, and North who had been born in the Northeast and East, people in search of better opportunities for earning a living. In this process of internal migration there are elements of vertical social mobility similar to those which figured in the European emigration to the South of Brazil. Bernard J. Siegel found that the migrants from the Northeast settling in a semirural community near the city of São Paulo were able to achieve an income as high as that of the upper half of the local society. Some 50 per cent of these migrants from the underdeveloped Northeast attained an income equal to that of the upper half of the old-time residents, who were descendants of German, Italian, Portuguese, and Spanish immigrants. Whereas the local *caipira* averaged 11,000 cruzeiros in annual income, the Northeastern *caipira* earned 70,000 to 90,000 cruzeiros in the same period. Siegel writes: "In no case did the migrants from the North begin with more resources than did resident *caipiro* In fact the latter did in several cases own property. Nevertheless, within the space of a few years more than half of the northern immigrants had saved enough money to purchase a small shop or a little land, or both." [3]

Meanwhile, accompanying industrialization were economic growth and increase of per capita income. In the period of 1870, per capita income was about $45.00 (U. S., 1958 value). By 1920 the figure had risen to $90.00, to $180.00 in 1940, and to $285.00 in 1956. This increase means there was a substantial degree of upward group mobility, especially for the urban factory workers. These people improved their standard of living in comparison with that of their parents, even though they remained in a working-class status.

Education and Social Mobility

From Table 7 it appears that the proportions of upper-middle and lower-middle class positions in the Brazilian working force must have approximately doubled between 1920 and 1960, while the proportions of upper-working class positions more than doubled. This development took place in a population that more than doubled in absolute numbers during this period, and it thus accounts for a great deal of upward social mobility. Many people who were born into families of the lower-lower class must have risen at least one step in the scale, and others who were born into upper-working class families must have moved up into middle-class positions. Even if every middle-class family produced as many as four children who reached adulthood and if their four children had maintained their middle-class status, there would have been room in the rapidly growing Brazilian society for upward mobility into the middle classes from below.

Some notion of the extent of upward mobility is given in Hutchinson's study of social mobility in a sample of men in the city of São Paulo.[4] Here the degree of individual social mobility was probably greater than in most parts of Brazil, since São

Paulo is the industrial and commercial center. Comparing men aged 30 and over with their fathers, Hutchinson found that 43 per cent had the same occupational social status as their fathers, 40 per cent had occupational status above that of their fathers, and 17 per cent had lower status. Thus there was a net upward mobility of 23 per cent of the São Paulo men.

With the fact established that there has been a great deal of individual upward social mobility in Brazil during the present century, we may now investigate the relationship of education to social mobility.

The data showing the increased numbers of children and young people attending primary schools, secondary schools, and universities are presented fully in other chapters. We can anticipate these data here by saying that while the numbers of primary school pupils increased between 1920 and 1960 from 29 to 74 per cent of the age group 7 through 11, the numbers of secondary school pupils grew from about 1 per cent to 10 per cent of the age group 11 through 17, and the numbers of university students increased from 0.5 per cent to 1.8 per cent of the age group 18 through 21. In other words, it has become customary during this century to attend primary school (though not to finish the fourth grade), but it is still unusual to attend secondary school and extremely rare to attend the university.

It appears, then, that most of the upward social mobility that has occurred during the past century in Brazil has been achieved with no more than a primary school education. Many sons of agricultural laborers and unskilled urban workers have secured semiskilled and skilled jobs. A few of them have become successful small business men. They have no doubt been assisted in the process of social mobility by the literacy and the general knowledge they obtained in the primary school, but it would be difficult to prove that their primary schooling was the efficient cause of their mobility. Rather, the industrialization of the country and its economic growth provided opportunities which these people grasped, assisted by native ability, education, and luck.

Mobility into the middle classes is probably more strictly associated with education. The proportion of middle class positions increased from about 11 to more than 20 per cent between 1920 and 1960. Since far less than 20 per cent of Brazilian men had a secondary school education in 1960, it is clear that secondary schooling was not essential for middle-class status. Many landowners and many small businessmen had middle-class status without any more than a primary school education. But a large part of the increase in middle-class positions between 1920 and 1960 consisted of jobs as technicians, as teachers, and as members of the free professions, all of which required at least a secondary school education. With the proportion of young people entering secondary school (about 13 per cent in 1950) substantially below the proportion of middle-and upper-class positions in the society, it would seem that two conclusions may be drawn: (1) it is possible to maintain middle-class status and perhaps to achieve it without a secondary education; (2) a secondary education is almost a sure guarantee of middle-class status.

TABLE 10

Social Class Origins of University Students in Brazil
(percentage distribution)

Class	A	Institution B	C
Upper	} 74	10	7
Upper Middle		41	29
Lower Middle	16	37	48
Upper Working	8	} 12	16
Lower Working	2		

Note: Institution A represents the first-year entrants of the University of São Paulo in 1956. See Bertram Hutchinson, "Origem Socio-Econômica dos Estudantes Universitários de São Paulo," Educação e Ciências Sociais, I, No. 3 (Dec. 1956).

Institutions B and C represent the first-year students of the Technological Institute of Aeronautics at São José dos Campos (São Paulo) and the School of Architecture of the University of Brazil, respectively, during certain years in the 1950's.

Ratings of social status are by J. Roberto Moreira and are based on occupation and income of the father.

The relation of university education to social mobility is suggested by the data in Table 10. Perhaps half of the university students of Brazil come from lower-middle-class and working-class homes, and practically all of these students will achieve upper-middle-class status. However, the proportion of university students is so small (less than 2 per cent of an age group and about 3 per cent of young men) that there are many people who maintain the upper-middle or upper-class status into which they were born without a university education, and there are others who achieve this status without a university education.

Education and Social Mobility in the Future

In the recent past the rapid economic development of Brazil has created an upward draft of social mobility that has carried many people in its sweep, some assisted by education, some by native ability, and some by luck. What of the future?

The class system will probably become more open in Brazil in the future. That is, the balance between ascribed status and achieved status will move toward more weight on status achieved by the individual in his own lifetime, as against status conferred on him by the accident of his birth. This change has occurred in every country that has gone through industrialization and urbanization. A larger proportion of the higher status positions in the society requires education and training, and the free education of a democracy opens the way for children of lower status to compete for these higher status positions. However, this type of mobility will require a major expansion of both secondary and higher education—an expansion over the next twenty years at least as rapid as that of the past twenty years.

In the absence of such educational expansion, it is likely that social mobility will be reduced during the next two decades. At present both secondary and higher education are rigorously selective in Brazil, more so than in the countries of North Europe and much more so than in the United States. Entrance examinations must be passed in order to enter the secondary school, and families with money to pay for tutors or an extra year of primary school bestow an advantage upon their children in these examinations. Further entrance examinations must be passed for the university, and as many as 50 per cent of the candidates fail to quality for the university course of their first choice. Again, families with money can assist their children to prepare for the entrance examinations. "Pobre para ser doutor, tem que queimar as pestanas"—"If a poor man is to become a doctor [Ph.D], he must feel his eyes burn with fatigue"—is a well-known adage in Brazil.

The Cultures of the Social Classes

A social class is a group of people that shares a common set of beliefs and ways of behaving, which makes them different to some degree from other groups in the same country. While they share a common Brazilian culture with their countrymen, they also have a subculture which sets them off from other Brazilians.

Following is a brief description of the social class cultures of present-day Brazil.

UPPER CLASS. The members of the upper class are generally rich, with a tradition of wealth in the family for several generations. Some few of them may not be wealthy, but being near relatives to an upper-class family with wealth, they share the status of this family. A person who has a position of great prestige in a profession or in business may be an upper-class person even though he is not extremely wealthy. There is also a group of "new rich" who lack the manners and the style of life of the upper class, and are generally counted in the upper-middle class.

The elite group belong to exclusive social clubs, and are members of the boards of directors of art museums, symphony and theater associations, and charitable societies. They ordinarily give liberally to charity and to churches and religious organizations. They belong to political parties of the right and center. Generally their support of political organizations is discreetly semi-anonymous, and they permit the official leadership to be held by upper-middle class persons. Among their interests are the history and genealogy of their families. In their homes, gardens, summer houses, automobiles, and clothing they seek a moderate kind of elegance, avoiding the flashy and the ostentatious.

Education for an upper-class person is a way of learning the art of living. Formal schooling is only a part of education. Training for a profession or other kind of work has some value, but is not essential for the upper-class person. However, the occupation for which one seeks training must be appropriate to the class. Girls of this class study French or English, art, music, and literature, without planning for a job. Boys may prepare for one of the liberal professions or for business. Boys and girls generally go to exclusive and expensive private schools.

UPPER-MIDDLE CLASS. The majority of the adults in the upper-middle class have achieved this status by their own efforts, being upward mobile from lower levels. The general notion is that members of this class are ambitious, dynamic, and energetic workers—business directors and managers, lawyers, medical doctors, etc. The upper-middle class dominates business, politics, and such professional organizations as the Rotary Club, the Brazilian Assistance Legion, and the Organization of Social Pioneers. The women, besides their domestic and social activities, are active in political and religious organizations. Those who come from poor families are likely to cultivate social refinements meticulously and to say little about their family background. Their homes are medium-sized or large, very clean and well-cared for, with a flower garden or a grassy lawn. Often there is a recreation room. If there are young children in the family, there will be a governess for them, as well as other house servants. However, the wife has certain domestic tasks and responsibilities.

Middle-class people are very careful about appearances. The salary of the family head provides for material comfort, and generally they are considered to be rich by those below them in status. They can afford the expenses of secondary schooling for their children, frequently they have an automobile, and they usually hold a modest investment in stocks and bonds.

The great majority belong to religious societies in the Roman Catholic Church, and are involved with religious activities on Sundays and holy days. A few are indifferent to the Church or agnostic; a few lean toward spiritualism as a philosophy and religion; very few belong to Protestant churches.

Education is extremely important to this group. They consider a secondary school education essential for their children, and favor a university education also. Although they can afford private schooling, they generally prefer the public primary and secondary schools.

In the medium-sized cities the children of the upper-middle and the upper classes associate together freely, since the upper class is too small to provide a separate social life for its children.

LOWER-MIDDLE CLASS. The lower-middle class is growing in the small cities, where it consists mainly of small businessmen, civil servants, and employees of banks, transportation agencies, and business firms. Income is less than that of the upper-middle class. Lower-middle-class people of the large cities tend to live in districts rather distant from the city center, generally in modest stucco houses or in apartments in the less fashionable areas. Many European immigrants belong in this class during their first generation in Brazil, after which some of them move to the upper-middle class.

In Brazil this class is a recent product of the industrial and commercial development of the country. It did not exist in large numbers in the rural society of the nineteenth century, since there were few small independent farmers who might have qualified for such a category. Even now it is less clearly definable than the classes immediately above and below it. Its members are "small people" who seek to better their position in life. They have no clear-cut political ideology. Both Protestant church membership and spiritualist affiliation are found more commonly in this than in other social classes.

UPPER-LOWER OR UPPER WORKING CLASS. When the politicians address themselves to the "workers" of Brazil, they mean the upper working class group. They are most numerous in the industrial cities, such as São Paulo, Belo Horizonte, Pôrto Alegre, Joinville, and Juiz de Fora. In the less industrialized and the rural areas they are a smaller minority, but they exercise some influence and are generally respected as productive people. Although some are skilled workers, the majority are semiskilled factory operatives. This group is much courted by the labor parties, and they are becoming more conscious of their political power. They are interested in social services and in good wages, they belong to labor unions, but they do not take a "leftist" position in politics.

Generally they live in working-class suburbs or in sections of small cities farther away from the center than the classes above them. Their houses are small, generally clean, with running water and sanitary facilities. Most of the women stay in the home to look after the children; the remainder work in factories or in small shops.

Some of the members of this class have come from rural areas in search of better living conditions. The rural immigrants with more ability and industry get steady work in factories or construction projects and establish themselves in the upper working class, while others, less skilled or less industrious, tend to remain in the lower working class.

This group spends most of its income on the necessities of life; it uses any extra money to buy furniture, a radio, television set, or refrigerator. But some of them manage to save enough to start a small business, and if this succeeds they are on the way up to the lower-middle class.

While the parents express interest in the education of their children and make strenuous efforts to get them into primary school and to keep them there, the children as a group have difficulty in school, and generally do not reach the fourth grade. Only recently have some methods been developed that seem to promise greater success for these children in school.

LOWER-LOWER OR LOWER WORKING CLASS. Most of the people who work on the farms of the interior and many of the town and city workers form the lowest of the social groups. They are without special occupational skills except the traditional, simple, and inefficient ones they learned from their fathers. Practically all of the members of this class are illiterate.

The great mass of these people are morally respectable, but this class also includes the majority of the unemployable, the irresponsible, and the criminal. The attitude toward life is one of passive fatalism, accepting their lot without making much effort to change it. They are not politically active. Their habitations are very poor—the shanties of the Rio *favelas*, the *mucambos* of Pernambuco, or the *malocas of* Rio Grande do Sul. They have no steady work. Sometimes they seek assistance from private or public charity.

Most members of this group attend mass and receive the visits of Catholic clergy respectfully; at the same time they follow Afro-Brazilian religious practices, with *macumba* and "low" spiritism. In the cities they organize *samba* societies and focus much of their energy on Carnival.

Many of this class are migrants, the men moving about in search of work or to avoid the police. The migrants from the Northeast are generally in this class, though some of them work their way up and out of it. In reality the lower working class is a heterogeneous collection of the ill-favored people of Brazil, and not a group with a single culture.

While these people say they want their children to attend school, they do not provide a home environment that stimulates a child to learn in school. Their children do not always get into the rural schools, and if they live in the cities they send their children to school later than the other social classes. The children generally do poorly in school, and their poor adjustment often leads to delinquency. In the cities these children represent a major problem group.

National Unity

While the twentieth century seems to have reduced the nationalism of some of the European countries, it has brought an intense nationalism to Latin America, as well as to other countries that are either just emerging from colonial status or are striving to become more independent economically. Some students of political development say that all the Latin American countries will go through a stage of nationalism that shows itself in political and in economic policies. In his study of the economy of Brazil, Spiegel remarks that policies of economic nationalism developed under Vargas, and suggests that these were probably a necessary aspect of the evolution of a modern nation. The formation of Petrobrás, the national company for the exploitation of petroleum, is an illustration. It would be politically unwise for a Brazilian leader to permit foreign oil companies to exploit Brazilian oil, even though it might be economically advantageous to get more oil production through cooperation with foreign companies.

Economic nationalism tends to promote domestic social solidarity. And social solidarity is needed when a weak national state is developing within a society that was formerly loosely organized in an almost feudal structure, as was Brazil until the twentieth century. Nationalism in economic policy, in relations with other nations, in literature, in religion, and in education all seem to develop as part of the evolution of a society, and to grow with the emergence of the new middle class of business men, industrialists, technologists, and salaried professionals.

Brazil has had a remarkable record of political and social integration in a situation in which several separate nations might have emerged, as happened in Spanish America. Brazil was a vast territory, with various racial groups and economies. During the nineteenth and twentieth centuries there were large groups of immigrants with alien languages (as in the case of the Germans and Japanese) and alien religions (as in the case of German Protestants and Japanese). It is true that there were some divisive movements on the part of the Germans in the South at the time of World War II, and in the case of separatist movements in São Paulo before 1940; but there never was a serious civil war, as there was in the United States, and the various immigrant groups seem to have merged into the dominant society more easily and more quickly than they have in the United States and in South Africa.

The social integration of Brazil has been facilitated by the vast country's single church and by its single language. Social unity has also been promoted by the relative ease of movement from one part of the country to another. The ocean provided an easy road between Northeast, East, and South, and there were no impassable mountains. The São Francisco river offered an inland highway between the Northeast and the South before there were roads. The highways later served the same purpose. For example, the main stream of migration for the poor people of the Northeast is by way of the highway from Bahia to Rio and

São Paulo. The importance of easy transportation is recognized in Brazil. Thus the new highway between Brasília and Belém, stretching 1,500 miles through the Amazon forest and the prairies of the Central Plateau, was inaugurated in 1960 with a motor "Caravan of National Integration," as it was called in the newspapers. Traveling in the caravan were engineers, soldiers, workers, and journalists, and their automobiles were all manufactured in Brazil, another item in the catalogue of national pride.

RACIAL INTEGRATION. With Negro slavery lasting until 1880 and with 10 per cent of the population Negro and another 25 per cent mulatto, severe racial conflict might be expected; but Brazil has less overt racial conflict than any other large mixed society. Gilberto Freyre calls the social integration of the racially-mixed Brazilian society an example of ethnic and cultural pluralism. He says that the tendency toward ethnic and cultural fusion of European whites, South American Indians, and African Negroes has always been positive, and seldom a source of social maladjustment. The critical conflicts and tensions have been between regional cultures or regional groups, with poverty-stricken regions confronting rich and technically advanced regions. Brazil, he believes, is "culturally European and sociologically Christian," in spite of having absorbed large numbers of non-Europeans and non-Christians.[5]

THE ROLE OF THE SCHOOL. A nation such as Brazil that is evolving out of a semicolonial and semifeudal condition might be expected to have a policy of using the schools to inculcate nationalistic sentiments and to stimulate internal social cohesion. This was the case with Germany in the nineteenth century and with Russia (if Russian Communism can be called a form of nationalism), Mexico, and Japan.

Yet Brazil seems to have made relatively little use of education as a means of building national unity. Nevertheless, schools do serve, and have served, in a limited way to inculcate a spirit of national unity. This was most marked during the first twenty years of the current century, when the primary school system was spreading through the towns and cities. The literature of the time reflected the intense national pride and optimism, and was much used in the schools: Alfonso Celso's popular book, *Porque me Ufano do meu Pais* ("Why I am Proud of My Country"); Olavo Bilac's poems; Alphonsus de Guimaraes' tributes to the old peaceful cities of Minas Gerais; and Machado de Assis's chronicles and short stories about Rio de Janeiro.

The words of Fernando de Azevedo are an appropriate summary of the importance of education to the unity of Brazil:

> Even though the school does not of itself make a nation, it does more than improve the material, moral, and intellectual condition of the people. In the school the various social classes can lighten their differences. The school preserves and passes on to the coming generations the music, the songs, and the moral traditions which move the spirit of a people. It maintains the continuity of a living history and engages pupils in the sweep of national evolution; and through the school the state can build solidly the national conscience, making the voice of the school into the voice of the country.[6]

Perhaps this is as far as we can go in making a case for the educational system as an instrument or agent of national unity in Brazil. Clearly, the remarkable degree of integration among people of different color and different ethnic backgrounds did not arise primarily through education. It came about for other reasons, and the school system is now an instrument for the preservation of national unity.

NOTES

1. References for the social structure of Brazil at the close of the nineteenth century are: Prado, *História Econômica do Brasil*; Nery, *Le Bresil en 1889*; Afonso Arinos de Melo Franco, *Desenvolvimento da Civilizaçao Material do Brasil* (Rio de Janeiro, 1944) ; A. Cavalcanti, *Resenha Financeira do Ex-Imperio do Brasil* (Rio de Janeiro, 1890) ; L. de Castro Carreiro, *História Financeira do Imperio do Brasil* (Rio de Janeiro, 1889) ; Louis Couty, *L'Esclavage au Bresil* (Paris, 1881) ; Freyre, *The Masters and the Slaves* and *The Mansions and the Shanties* (New York: 1956; 1963) ; M. B. Lourenço, Filho, *Tendências da Educação Brasileira* (São Paulo, 1940).

2. Nelson Werneck Sodré, *Introdução a Revolução Brasileira* (Rio de Janeiro, 1958), pp. 39-40.

3. Bernard J. Siegel, "The Role of Perception in Urban-Rural Change: A Brazilian Case Study," *Economic Development and Cultural Change*, V, No. 3 (Apr. 1957), 248.

4. Bertram Hutchinson, *Trabalho, Status, e Educação* (Rio de Janeiro: Centro Brazileiro de Pesquisas Educacionais, Ministério de Educação e Cultura, 1960), p. 219.

5. Gilberto Freyre, "Plural and Mixed Societies in the Tropics: The Case of Brazil from the Sociological Point of View," in *Ethnic and Cultural Pluralism in Intertropical Communities* (Brussels: International Institute of Differing Civilizations, 30th Meeting, 1957).

6. Fernando de Azevedo, in a speech to teachers, 1950.

6

Socioeconomic Development of Present-Day Brazil

THE fifteen years immediately following World War II can be divided into two phases: the initial phase of postwar prosperity and the following phase of economic growth and adjustment to a world economy. This second phase, commencing about 1950, will continue more or less indefinitely. This process of economic growth within an expanding and complex world economy is a mid-twentieth century phenomenon of Latin America. Not only Brazil, but also most of the other Latin American countries experience it.

Economic growth and educational development have been closely related in Latin America. One cannot be understood without the other. Consequently we shall sketch the postwar economic development of Brazil before going into details concerning educational development during that period.

Postwar Economic Development of Brazil

World War II brought temporary prosperity to Brazil, as it did to other countries that were in a position to sell agricultural products and other raw materials to the Allies. Domestic industry flourished, and employment rates were high. But this apparent prosperity was not without its problems. One major difficulty was inflation of the currency. The government gave credits to foreign buyers and issued large sums of paper money to pay Brazilian exporters. Since there were few foreign goods to be imported during the war, the money was spent on Brazilian products, and tended to raise prices. When the European governments did not permit their wartime debts to be paid in postwar European goods, the Brazilian government used these credits to acquire several Brazilian railroad lines belonging to European companies, such as the São Paulo Railway Company, the Leopoldina Railway, the São Paulo-Rio Grande, and the Great Western, all of which needed new investment in rolling stock and railroad beds.

As soon as goods were available for importation from the United States, Brazilians with money began to buy luxury goods. This was the "era of the Cadillacs," which swarmed over the streets of Rio and the state capitals. It was also the period of foreign travel by wealthy Brazilians, who in 1947, for example, spent 30 million dollars in travel abroad. By 1947 these practices had placed Brazil in arrears on commercial debts to foreign suppliers by 75 million dollars. A number of companies suspended their shipments to Brazil, and several Brazilian industries were obliged to curtail production because of a lack of equipment or of essential materials from abroad. There was danger that the supply of gasoline and fuel oil might be shut off, paralyzing the economic life of the country.

By 1948 the government began to restrict imports to economic necessities, and thus reduced the exchange deficit. By 1950, which brought high world prices for coffee and other tropical products, Brazil achieved a favorable commercial balance, and the control of imports was continued as a means of encouraging the importation of the industrial equipment and the semifinished goods necessary for industrial growth.

These measures during the early 1950's developed into a policy of using government controls over imports and exports as a means of achieving economic growth, and such practice has been continued in one form or another since that time. This policy was put to a severe test after 1953, when world prices declined for coffee, cocoa, and other Brazilian exports. Central America, other South American countries, Africa, and Asia became strong competitors of the Brazilian export trade. The world was entering a period of overproduction of basic agricultural commodities in relation to the buying power of consumers, and practically all of Latin America had difficulty in selling its national exports at prices that would permit the purchase of large quantities of goods needed for industrial development at home. Although Brazil did grow in economic production, this growth was not rapid enough to satisfy either the industrialists or the mass of the people. Serious questions of economic policy had to be answered by the government, and the answers were not altogether satisfactory. Writing about the first half of the twentieth century, the American economist Henry Spiegel significantly subtitled his book on Brazilian economy as "Sporadic Industrialization and Chronic Inflation."

One conto was worth about $1000.00 (U. S.) in 1822, when the Empire was founded. In relation to the British pound and the American dollar it lost much more than half of its value during the nineteenth century and continued to lose during the twentieth century until its value in 1950 was $50.00 (U. S.) Spiegel's remark about chronic inflation was prophetic of what happened during the 1950's, when the conto lost more ground and was worth $1.00 (U. S.) at the end of 1963. Since the dollar had itself lost purchasing power after 1940, there was no doubt about the inflation of the Brazilian currency.

Spiegel pointed out that the Brazilian economy, still very backward in 1950, was bound to develop only slowly and with difficulty into a modern industrial economy. Being tied down to the world prices of coffee, cotton, and cocoa, Brazil's economic welfare was, and is, dependent on conditions abroad, over which it has no control. Rational planning of business by private entrepreneurs is difficult, though profits are often very great. The largest industrial investments are generally made by government agencies or by foreign investors. The low per capita income stands in the way of the development of domestic industry which must be based on mass purchasing power. Nevertheless, with foreign assistance and under foreign tutelage there are good prospects for industrial development.

The decade of the 1950's was to see a plan for economic development—the first serious and systematic effort at industrialization. For the working of this plan the income from Brazil's foreign trade was essential, but it had to be shared with other interests. There were three general purposes for which foreign exchange would be used.

One purpose was to provide for the continued operation of the Brazilian economy at the existing rate of production. Replacements must be bought for worn-out or obsolete machinery. Gasoline and diesel fuel must be imported to keep motor trucks, busses, and tractors moving. Locomotives, motor trucks, airplanes, and automobiles must be imported to keep the transport system working.

A second purpose was to provide the equipment necessary for increased production by the Brazilian economy. Steel was needed for factory buildings. New machinery was needed for new factories. Equipment was needed for new hydroelectric power plants, for oil refineries to refine the native crude oil, for the new steel plants to make Brazilian steel. Machines were needed to stamp out the bodies of the Brazilian-made automobiles, tractors, trucks and to make rubber tires. If these things could be bought, Brazil might slowly become a greater industrial producer, and thus free herself from the need to purchase so many machine-made items from abroad.

A third purpose was to provide for the demands of Brazilian consumers. Those who had money wanted to live better, as well as to invest some of their savings in Brazilian industry. They wanted foreign automobiles, Scotch whisky, books, cameras, refrigerators, air-conditioners, motion pictures, radio receivers, television receivers. Young people wanted to go to the United States or to Europe to study, and every middle- and upper-class Brazilian woman wanted a trip to Paris. All of these things could be purchased only with foreign money.

Somehow the needs for these three types of expenditures had to be balanced against one another, and decisions had to be made concerning priorities. The first need, to keep the Brazilian economy going at its present rate, clearly had a priority, but the competition between purchase of consumer goods and investment in new capital goods for production was not to be settled easily. Decisions were gradually worked out during the 1950's through adjustment between industrialists, government, and the consuming public. The government acted through its control of imports to favor the importation of capital goods and to reduce the importation of consumer goods. For instance, the importation of automobiles for personal use was made almost impossible during a part of this decade. Very high exchange rates were set on such luxury items as camera film. On the other hand, lower rates were set by the government for the purchase of foreign money to pay for books, machinery, tractors, locomotives, and other items that were necessary for production or for the growth of education. For example, at one time a Brazilian had to pay eight times as much for a dollar to be used for the purchase of an automobile as he had to pay for a dollar to be used for factory machinery.

Naturally, many people were displeased at the controls laid by the government on their expenditures for foreign goods. Whether they were rich or poor by Brazilian standards they all felt poor by European-American standards, and when they had money they wanted to use it to raise their standard of living, whether this meant a São Paulo factory owner buying a Cadillac, a Rio bank clerk buying a refrigerator, or a farm laborer in Goiás seeing an American Western movie once a month.

One result of economic changes during the 1950's was a further drastic inflation of the currency. The decade was one of nearly worldwide inflation, but Brazil experienced it somewhat more than most countries. The cruzeiro lost about 85 per cent of its purchasing power between 1950 and 1960, a greater degree of inflation than occured in Mexico and the United States, but less than in Chile and Bolivia. Some economists argue that currency inflation was necessary or at least desirable as a means of maintaining economic growth. Others believe that inflation is never necessary and does more harm than good. In Brazil the argument waxed warm on both sides. President Kubitschek's slogan of "Fifty Years of Progress in Five," which he announced as the goal of his term as president, was realized at least in part, for substantial economic growth occurred in Brazil between 1956 and 1961. However, critics of his government were quick to point out that the monetary inflation which had already started before his presidency continued unabated, and was furthered by enormous government expenditures and borrowing from abroad. They misquoted Kubitschek's slogan as "Fifty Years of Spending in Five." When Jânio Quadros became President in 1961 he announced that inflation was to be controlled and reduced, but that there would have to be some immediate price increases in order to control the spending of the Brazilians. However, government spending continued at a higher rate than government income, and the government under both Quadros and his successor Goulart issued vast sums of paper money with further decrease in the value of the cruzeiro. Thus the Brazilian currency continued to lose purchasing power.

Economic Growth of Brazil

The people, as individuals, and the Brazilian industrial corporations and government bureaus, all were learning the basic lessons of economic growth in an underdeveloped country in the twentieth century. For Brazil was underdeveloped. In spite of modern factories in São Paulo, oil wells in Bahia, palatial homes on great coffee fazendas and cattle ranches; in spite of her astonishing skyscrapers and public buildings which had the architects of the world agog; in spite of the unrivalled beaches of Copacabana, Guarujá, and Salvador adorned with bathers in the latest waterside attire, the per capita income of Brazil was only $200.00 to $250.00 in the 1950's, compared with $1,875.00 for the United States and $850.00 for Great Britain. Although far richer than her neighbors, Paraguay and Bolivia, Brazil was well below Argentina, Uruguay, and Venezuela in per capita income.

A third of the population lived at a bare subsistence level in the rural parts of the country. These "20 million economic zeros" were not going to be content with mere subsistence indefinitely. Gradually they were moving out of their primitive habitations and drifting toward the cities and the industrial South. The economy had to grow in order to provide jobs at decent wages for these people. The slum dwellers in the cities also demanded better living conditions, more and larger houses, with electricity, refrigeration, and schools for their children. The economy had to grow.

But Brazil, like most other underdeveloped countries, was caught in the vise of pressure on one side for heavy investment and pressure on the other side for higher wages and salaries to be spent on more consumer goods so as to raise the standard of

TABLE 11

Economic Growth of Brazil, 1949-60
(relative to 1949)

Year	Gross national product per capita	Gross national product	Agricultural product	Value of services	Industrial product
1947	95				
1948	98				
1949	100	100	100	100	100
1950	104	107	103	106	112
1951	108	114	105	114	124
1952	111	119	113	116	132
1953	112	124	113	122	138
1954	118	132	122	130	150
1955	119	137	129	133	158
1956	122	144	127	138	178
1957	130	157	140	148	199
1958	137	169	142	157	243
1959	140	178	155		279
1960	143	186	160		337

Source: Fundacão Getúlio Vargas, "Contas Nacionais do Brasil," *Revista Brasileira de Econômica*, XIV (Mar. 1960).

TABLE 12

Aspects of Economic Growth in Brazil, 1949-60

Year	Gross national product per capita	Agricultural production prices of 1948		Industrial production prices of 1949					
		Domestic products	Export products	Capital goods	Consumer goods	Minerals	Construction	Electrical energy	General total
1947	95	100	100						
1948	98	104	106						
1949	100			100	100	100	100	100	100
1950	104			118	111	101	106	108	112
1955	119	138	135	170	155	127	152	156	158
1956	122	141	106	207	165	142	152	176	179
1957	130	154	136	260	165	168	158	193	202
1958	137	147	155	352	167	199	165	213	243
1959	140	154	179	425	178	299	168	232	279
1960	143	170	168	550	190	359	171	255	337

Source: Instituto Brasileiro de Economia de Fundação Getúlio Vargas.

living. And the population was growing rapidly—2.5 per cent a year—demanding that the economy grow at that rate merely to maintain the existing per capita income. Between 1949 and 1960 national income (the gross national product, measured in stable prices) did increase in Brazil at the rate of 6 per cent a year, leaving a net gain of 3.5 per cent per capita income per year. This was fairly good, better than the growth rate of the United States, but Brazil was starting from a lower base, and had to invest substantial sums in economic growth while gradually bettering the standard of living of her citizens.

An examination of the economic indices of Tables 11 and 12 shows that there was a striking gain in industrial production in Brazil during the 1950–60 decade, while agricultural production increased at a much lower rate. In fact, food production for the domestic market barely kept pace with the increased purchasing power of the people. Since a considerable proportion of the population is undernourished, increase of food production for the domestic market is essential. On the other hand, there was a great increase in the production of industrial capital goods—motor trucks, hydroelectric plants, and machinery—much greater than the increase in manufacture of consumer goods. This means that the economy was investing resources in future production. During the period 1951–55, 18 per cent of the national product was invested in expansion and improvement of factories and farms, and 14 per cent during 1956–59. These figures are not as large as some Brazilian economists hoped, but they show that the country was saving and investing in economic growth.

It is a favorable sign that the rate of economic growth was greater in the latter half of the 1950–60 decade than in the first half. Although President Quadros inherited inflation and an unfavorable foreign trade balance from President Kubitschek, he also inherited a growing economy and passed it on to President Goulart. The society was becoming more industrialized. Whereas 22 per cent of the national income came from industry in 1949, this figure increased to 32 per cent in 1958. And the Brazilian domestic market was growing, which was a good sign. As the purchasing power of the people increased, their buying accounted for more and more of Brazil's business, while foreign trade, always a gamble, became a smaller factor in the total economy. In 1957 the domestic business of Brazil was greater than the total foreign trade (both exports and imports) of all of Latin America, Brazil included.

Means of Economic Growth

Modern studies of economic growth identify five factors that determine the level of economic production of a society.

1. Land and natural resources
2. Quantity of labor
3. Reproducible capital; i.e., factories, power plants, railroads, highways, motor trucks
4. Human skills and knowledge
5. The arts of production (A general term for the efficiency with which labor and land and machines are used, it includes size of factories and farms and other units of production, efficiency of transportation and of communication, and the utilization of research for the development of better methods and materials.)

In order to grow economically a society may increase any or all of these factors. Certain factors are crucial at any given time in a given society, while others are relatively unimportant in causing increased productivity at that time. Hence the allocation of effort and of resources among the growth factors is a matter of extreme importance to the growth rate. Governments and private planning agencies are much concerned with the problem of allocation of resources so as to maximize economic growth.

LAND AND NATURAL RESOURCES. Vast amounts of arable land are unused in Brazil. For example, the frontier of coffee-culture is being pushed into the northwestern part of the state of Paraná, beyond the booming city of Londrina, which has grown since World War II to a population of 75,000. In the southwest of Paraná fertile lands are being cleared of valuable timber and opened up to general farming. The states of Mato Grosso and Goiás are vast reaches of rolling and well-watered country which are now sparsely populated by cattle ranchers. They may develop as the plains states developed in the United States after 1850.* However, the present need is not so much to bring more land into cultivation as to increase the productivity of land already in use.

* Such growth will require a major development of highways and railroads. In 1957 Brazil had 7.4 meters of highway per inhabitant and 0.6 meters of railways, being inferior to Argentina (2.9 meters of railway per person) and Chile (1.6 meters of railway per person) but superior in this respect to all other Latin American countries. Probably the major methods of travel and transport in Brazil will be the motor vehicle and the airplane. In 1956 Brazil was second in the world in the mileage of internal airplane flights (surpassed only by the United States) and in air freight transportation; and ranked third in aerial passenger transportation.

Mineral resources essential to an industrial country are being rapidly developed. Oil was discovered in Bahia in 1939, and in 1961 100,000 barrels a day were being produced. The government has organized a corporation, Petrobrás, to take charge of oil production and refining, and has not permitted foreign companies to come in and exploit the oil resources. Oil production has developed slowly when compared with the increasing rate of consumption, but the domestic production has stabilized imports of petroleum.

The steel industry was born in Brazil during World War I and became an important national asset during World War II, when (with the aid of money from the United States) a modern steel mill was built at Volta Redonda in the state of Rio de Janeiro. Brazil has abundant reserves of iron ore, perhaps the largest in the world, but the abundant Brazilian coal of the Santa Catarina region could not be used for cooking until the discovery of a process that improved its quality. Production of steel exceeded 1 million tons in 1955 and, with the addition of another steel mill near Belo Horizonte, was about 3 million tons in 1962. These figures compare poorly with the 100 million tons achieved per year by the United States, and Brazil's production does not meet her own needs. However, it seems likely that Brazil will eventually become self-sufficient in steel and also become a principal supplier to other Latin American countries, most of which have no iron ore of their own.

Brazil also produces a considerable amount of aluminum, and will produce more as electrical energy becomes cheaper and more readily available. Domestic production reached 2,000 tons in 1955, and about 20,000 in 1960.

Vast resources of water power put Brazil among the four leading nations in potential hydroelectric energy. Half of this potential is on the Paraná river and its tributaries, as yet hardly touched.

LABOR. Like many other countries that have benefited from modern health services before they become industrialized, Brazil has no shortage of labor. But like these other countries, a large part of the labor force works with low efficiency because it uses only simple tools. This is true especially in the rural areas, where a primitive agriculture is practiced and many farmers own only a hoe and a cutting tool. In 1950, 34 per cent of the farms had plows, and 84 per cent of these plows were in the four southern states. In 1962 there was one tractor to 600 farm dwellers, while the ratio in the United States was one to four. Tools and equipment are often inferior for urban occupations as well. For example, in preparing the foundations of buildings in the solid rock sections of Rio de Janeiro, workmen laboriously chip away the rock by hand. The per capita productivity of industry is also relatively low.

Economic growth is not likely to result because of an increase in the quantity of labor. While there are some areas of recent industrialization and of new agricultural exploitation where labor is somewhat scarce, these shortages are more than offset by the general super abundance of unskilled manpower. Any substantial gain in production that comes from the use of labor must arise out of improving the quality rather than the quantity of labor.

TABLE 13

Distribution of the Labor Force, Brazil and the United States

Percentage of the labor force occupied in:					
	Brazil 1940	Brazil 1950	USA 1850	USA 1870	USA 1950
Agriculture	68	58	65	52	12
Mining	3	2.8	1	1.5	2
Manufacturing and Construction	10	13	17	22	32
Commerce, Transport, Communication	9	10	5.5	11	33
Services: Professional, Personal, Domestic	10	16	12	13	20

The distribution of the labor force among the various sectors of production is shown in Table 13. Comparable figures are given for the United States. The Brazilian labor force distribution in 1940 and 1950 was similar to that in the United States in 1850 and 1870. As the labor force evolves, it will increase in the urban categories of industry, commerce, and services. But urban workers require more education than rural workers, and furthermore the deceasing proportion of the labor force occupied in agriculture must become more productive, which will require more education.

REPRODUCIBLE CAPITAL. Until recently all reproducible capital except the most simple tools, buildings, vehicles, and crude highways had to be imported or to be made with imported equipment. This reliance on importation set a severe limit on industrial expansion, because foreign money was so difficult to obtain. Nevertheless, Brazil did import large amounts of capital for the equipment of its productive economy during the nineteenth century and the first half of the twentieth century. The fifteen years after World War II saw major developments in this critical area.

Factories increased in number almost six-fold between 1920 and 1957, with a seven-fold increase in the amount of power used industrially and a four-fold increase in number of factory workers. In agriculture the application of machinery also increased greatly, the number of plows going from 141,200 in 1920 to one million in 1959, and the number of tractors increasing during the same period from 1,700 to 70,000.

The manufacture of motor vehicles began in Brazil shortly after 1950, through a government-owned truck factory and through assembly plant operations by such foreign automakers as Volkswagen, General Motors, Ford, and Willys. Gradually the manufacture of vehicle parts was established in Brazil, until in 1957 there were 16 plants for the manufacture of vehicles and 62 for the production of parts. Over 220,000 trucks and automobiles were assembled in 1962, and 1960 saw the production of automobiles with 100 per cent Brazilian-made parts.

The production of electrical and mechanical equipment for heavy industry began about 1955 with the manufacture of small electric motors. By 1958 it had expanded into the production of generators, transformers, and heavy motors, and of machinery for the textile, cellulose, and paper industries.

The development of hydroelectric plants for the production of electric energy is crucial because industry depends on electric energy. As is shown in Table 12, the production of electric energy more than doubled in the 1950–60 decade. In 1961 the capacity of power-generating plants was 5 million kilowatts, and two major hydroelectric plants were in construction. The electric energy capacity of the country is expected to be 8 million kilowatts by 1965, and this rate of increase will barely keep pace with the needs of industry and of home consumption.

A network of first-class motor roads was constructed from 1950 to 1960, connecting Rio, São Paulo, Curitiba, Belo Horizonte, Salvador, Brasília, Recife, and Belém. During the same period there was a substantial increase of railway mileage and of new diesel locomotives and freight and passenger cars. New ships were added to the river and ocean-going fleets.

HUMAN KNOWLEDGE AND SKILLS. Economists have recently recognized the importance of the factors of human knowledge and skill (human capital) and the arts of production in accounting for the rapid growth of production in modern industrial societies.

FIGURE 6

DISTRIBUTION OF NATIONAL INCOME

National income according to economic activities, 1956

(Cr$ 1,000,000,000)

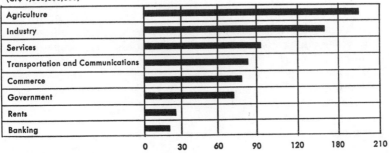

National income distributed among the states, 1956

(Cr$ 1,000,000,000)

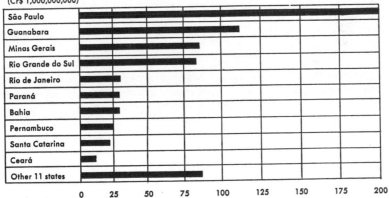

Note: Cr$ 1,000,000,000 were equal to approximately 15.5 million dollars in 1956.

When only the added land, labor, and reproducible capital are taken into account, the total of these three elements falls far short of the actual increase in production. Therefore economists add the other two factors and, under certain circumstances, regard them as having equal or greater importance than one or another of the first three.[1]

In the case of Brazil it is easy to see how the increase of human skill and knowledge is more important to the increase of production than the addition of more unskilled and illiterate workers to the labor force. When a Brazilian farmer buys a tractor he needs to learn how to use and care for the tractor, or to have employees who can do so. For this he needs to be able to read directions, and to learn something about the care and repair of motors and machinery. His employees who have never worked with anything more complex than a hoe and a machete are little use to him in this situation, unless he can train them to use a tractor. Those who get such training become much more productive workers.

Similarly, a sixteen-year-old girl in a county seat in Minas Gerais can earn a little money by sewing or cooking or working in a shop or a restaurant. But if there is a textile factory in town she can learn to operate a weaving machine made in England and become highly productive. At this very simple level, then, a primary school education and a little knowledge about machinery will increase a person's productivity if the machines are there to operate. At a more complex level, men are needed to operate factories and manage banks, to design bridges, survey for highways, fly airplanes.

A society must invest money in the education and training of these people so as to use its machines and factories efficiently. If tractors are run by people who do not know how to look after machinery, the tractors go to pieces. If factory machines are tended by unskilled operators who are supervised by inefficient foremen, the productivity per factory worker is very low. In order to maintain maximum efficiency a growing industrial economy must keep its additions of reproducible capital in step with its additions of human skill and knowledge. This means that it must spend money on education and technical training as an investment in growth.

THE ARTS OF PRODUCTION. The fifth element in economic growth—"know-how" applied to production—is related to university education. The art of running a factory or a farm efficiently is partly a matter of the knowledge and skill of the owner or manager and partly a matter of the state of the productive arts. The development of hybrid corn in the United States represented an increase in the art of agricultural production, just as time and motion studies led to the more skillful design of factory machinery and the more efficient use of manpower by mass-production methods. The arts of production are furthered mainly by research which discovers better methods of production and new products. Money invested in research has paid enormous returns in the growth of modern economies.

Brazil can profit from the arts of production more than some countries because it has such a large population and therefore a large domestic consumption. This demand encourages the devel-opment of efficient mass-production factories.

Brazil's Major Economic Problems

Brazil's recent growth has been spectacular, but the country remains impoverished. Table 14 indicates that its level of development ranks sixth out of twenty Latin American countries. Brazil's improvement has been rapid since 1950–55, the period of Table 14, but its position has probably not changed enough to change its rank order.*

A major problem confronting Brazil is the extreme regional disparity in productivity and per capita income. The problem of the two Brazils is still unsolved. As the more progressive regions move ahead, the distance between them and the backward areas actually increases. Table 15 shows that per capita income in the South and the East has grown more rapidly than in the other regions. While the per capita income of the Northeast increased by a factor of 12 (largely the result of inflation) between 1939 and 1958, that of the more progressive South increased by a factor of 20.

The Northeast, embracing seven states, with a population density of 15 inhabitants per square kilometer, is the poorest area in Brazil, its per capita income being only 36.6 per cent of the Brazilian average, and 27 per cent of the average of the South. The economic recovery of that area is therefore one of the most pressing problems for Brazil, especially since the greater part of the Polygon of Drought coincides with it. In view of the pre-

---

* According to a study made by CEPAL, the Economic Commission for Latin America, the economic growth rate per capita of Brazil between 1955–60 was exceeded only by Venezuela and Guatemala.

TABLE 14

Levels of Development in the Latin American Countries

Country	Demo-economic potential	Income per capita	Level of social well-being	Level of productivity and equipment	Level of development
1. Argentina	100.0	100.0	100.0	94.0	95.8
2. Uruguay	62.5	100.0	100.0	100.0	90.6
3. Chile	75.0	100.0	82.1	95.8	88.2
4. Venezuela	75.0	100.0	75.0	100.0	87.5
5. Cuba	87.5	75.0	93.0	79.2	83.7
6. Brazil	100.0	75.0	64.3	66.7	76.5
7. Colombia	87.5	75.0	67.9	70.8	75.3
8. Mexico	100.0	50.0	64.3	70.8	71.2
9. Panama	37.5	75.0	75.0	79.2	66.7
10. Costa Rica	37.5	75.0	71.4	54.2	59.5
11. Peru	75.0	50.0	53.6	50.0	57.2
12. Ecuador	62.5	50.0	60.7	41.7	53.7
13. Dominican Republic	50.0	25.0	60.7	41.7	44.4
14. Guatemala	50.0	50.0	32.1	29.2	40.3
15. Bolivia	37.5	25.0	25.0	45.8	33.3
16. Honduras	25.0	50.0	28.6	29.2	33.2
17. Paraguay	25.0	25.0	46.4	33.3	32.4
18. Nicaragua	25.0	25.0	50.0	29.2	32.3
19. Salvador	25.0	25.0	32.1	41.7	31.0
20. Haiti	37.5	25.0	25.0	25.0	28.1

Definitions: *Demo-economic potential:* Average of ranks in population and Gross National Product.

Level of social well-being: Average of ranks in life expectancy, infant mortality, number of persons per doctor, number of hospital beds per capita, consumption of food in calories per day, per cent of literacy, per cent of school-age children attending school, newspaper sales per capita.

Level of productivity and equipment: Consumption of steel, cement, and energy per capita, number of motor vehicles per capita, per cent of labor force outside of agriculture, per cent of national product outside of agriculture.

Level of development: The average of the indices in the four preceding columns.

Note: The numbers in the first four columns represent the average of the values for the several indices entering into the columns, with each entry receiving a weight of 100, 75, 50, or 25, depending on its rank by quartile.

Source: Pompeu Accioly Borges, "Levels of Development in Latin America," *Desenvolvimento e Conjuntura*, V, No. 2 (Feb. 1961), 63-85. (Condensed from a Report to the Economic and Social Council of the United Nations.)

carious living conditions in the Northeast, emigration from there to the South and Central West is a constant phenomenon.

It was noted in Chapter I that literacy parallels income level among the regions. So does school attendance. The proportion of children in the age group 7 through 10 who were not attending school in 1958 was 52 per cent in the Northeast, 31 per cent in

TABLE 15

Regional Differences in Per Capita Income, 1939-58

	Northeast	North	Central West	East	South
	(In Cr$, uncorrected for inflation)				
1939	548	669	706	845	1,244
1950	1,985	2,690	2,472	4,241	6,240
1955	3,861	5,715	7,580	9,968	15,375
1958	6,595	10,583	11,974	17,028	24,500

Source: "Diretrizes e Perspectivas da Economia Brasileira," *Desenvolvimento e Conjuntura*, IV (Nov. 1960 [special edition]), 181.

the North, 20 per cent in the Central West, 28 per cent in the East, and 4 per cent in the South.

The North and Central West regions, though showing per capita income higher than that of the Northeast, are low in the scale. The second major problem for Brazil is the more intensive populating of these two vast regions whose area constitutes 64 per cent of the total area of Brazil, but whose population amounts to only 10 per cent of the national total. Although the airplane now serves as the principal means of communication between the interior areas of Brazil and the great industrial and commercial centers, the problem of settlement can ultimately be solved only through railroads and highways.

The transfer of the capital of the Republic to Brasília in the Central West symbolizes the intention to develop the interior of Brazil. Large development corporations acting under government and private funds in the development of the less productive regions. There are corporations for the development of the Northeast, the Amazon region, the valley of the São Francisco, and the southwestern frontier; a government-financed rural credit association; a public service corporation; and a National Bank for Economic Development. Four regional development agencies were assigned 4.5 per cent of the federal government's budget in 1961, and they have borrowed substantial sums from the World Bank and the Interamerican Bank.

A third problem is that of securing sufficient foreign money to finance industrial expansion. Although large amounts of capital from Europe, North America and, more recently, Japan, are being invested in Brazilian industry, the major source of foreign money is the export of coffee, which during the 1950's represented about 45 per cent of Brazilian exports. But prices for Brazilian coffee have dropped sharply as a result of competition from Central America and East Africa. Agreements to restrict coffee exports in order to maintain price levels have been made between Brazil and other coffee-growing countries, but the net result has not been favorable to Brazil. Consequently, Brazil is making major efforts to increase the production of other export products, such as cocoa, sugar, and minerals, the latter being increasingly developed in the 1960–63 period.

Meanwhile, the rise of Brazilian manufacturing for export may be extremely significant. Brazil and other Latin American countries have developed through the Latin American Association for Free Trade economic agreements that will allow each country to export the goods and materials it produces most efficiently without payment of customs duties to the other countries in the agreements. Thus products of Brazilian industry, such as automobiles, rubber products, and electrical goods, will find markets in return for imports of wheat, fertilizer, tin, copper, and other raw materials.

A fourth and all-pervasive problem is that of *technification* of all types of production. The term *technification* is used in preference to *industrialization* because it refers to a process that is broader than the use of machinery. Technification is the use of the most efficient means to reach production goals. While this often means the use of labor-saving machinery, it may also mean the use of scientific information or of a more efficient manual process. For instance, technification of agriculture may take different forms in Brazil than in the United States. In the latter country technification has involved the replacement of the horse and mule by the tractor, as well as the use of better seeds and more efficient methods of fertilizing. This has resulted in an enormous increase of agricultural productivity; the numbers of agricultural workers have decreased, and the excess labor force has transfered to urban industry. However, Brazil, with its large labor force, may find greater economy and efficiency not so much in importing tractors with scarce foreign exchange, as in educating the rural worker in conservation methods and in the use of better seeds and better breeds of animals.

A given amount of money spent on a few agricultural experiment stations and colleges, and on an extension of vocational education in agriculture to schools in rural areas, may result in a greater production increase than would the same amount of money spent on the importation of tractors.

In this respect education has a preponderant role to play. It is possible to improve the existing technology by improving the quality of the work turned out, and this in turn results in increased productivity. In Brazil productivity varies greatly, according to the economic and cultural area. Where the percentage of illiterates is higher, there also the output per worker is lower. For example, São Paulo is the most advanced state in Brazil from the educational standpoint, and the Northeast is the most backward region. Whereas production per industrial worker in São Paulo in 1957 was calculated at 269,000 cruzeiros and that of the rural worker at 75,700, the corresponding figures for the Northeast drop to 139,000 and 24,400 cruzeiros respectively.* Whereas São Paulo had nearly 14 per cent of its population enrolled in schools of all kinds, the Northeast had only 6 per cent of its population attending school. Although swift change in technological facilities may not be possible because of a lack of adequate capital—which may be the actual state of affairs in Brazil at this economic juncture—it is always possible to improve production techniques with the equipment already in existence, provided that men are trained or educated for that purpose.

To a certain extent this is what is taking place in Brazil. During the postwar era rational methods for organizing production were introduced into practically all of the major industries of Rio de Janeiro and São Paulo. The theories of organization and of production originated by Taylor and Fayol have been widely, though gradually, applied in Brazil. The banks, insurance companies, and large business concerns are likewise experimenting with more efficient methods of operation. In agriculture, with government support, experiment stations are being organized for the selection and adaptation of seeds. The Comissão Econômica para o Estado da Produção Agrícola na America Latina (Economic Commission for the State of Agricultural Production in Latin America) indicated that between 1945 and 1955 the per capital productivity of the rural Brazilian worker increased by 39 per cent.[2]

---

* Calculations based on tables relating to employed personnel and the cost of production are from the "Anuário Estatístico do Brasil," 1958, pp. 60, 62, 69, 85, 88—93. It should be made clear that the relation between illiteracy and output per worker is not a simple cause-effect relation. The more productive workers have more and better machines to work with, because they live in areas where there is more capital and better equipment. There is an interaction between amount of education, amount of capital invested in machinery, and production. Each factor influences and is influenced by the other two.

Wasteful agricultural practices, such as clearing the terrain by means of fire and planting on slopes without the proper formation of anti-erosive plateaus, were greatly reduced; and, in addition, the use of animal and chemical fertilizers and artificial irrigation was increased. Skilled personnel in various economic pursuits which in 1940 constituted barely 23 per cent of the Brazilian labor force, rose to 30 per cent in 1950 and to 36 per cent in 1955.

Education and Productivity

Speaking in the 1930's of Brazil's economy, Getúlio Vargas said, "Education is a matter of life and death," and this statement was engraved in stone in the Hall of the Ministry of Education and Culture in Rio de Janeiro. Since that time every Brazilian president has emphasized the truth that economic development required major investment in the education of the people.

But, as we have seen, the needs of the Brazilian economy, like those of every underdeveloped society, are extremely great for physical capital goods to increase production, and for consumers goods to meet the needs of a low-paid labor force. In this situation it is difficult to get money allocated to the education and training of people so as to make them more productive. The government and private business and industry have a certain amount of money to be invested in factors that will cause the economy to grow. Two of these factors, labor and natural resources, are plentiful in Brazil. Thus the country has concentrated on the other three factors—increasing reproducible capital, increasing of human knowledge and skill, and improving the arts of production. When the national government budget is made up, there is competition between the Ministry of Transport and Communications and the Ministry of Education. Some agencies in the government, supported by powerful groups in the society, want the government to spend more money on highways, railways, and power plants. Other agencies and other groups in the society want more money for primary schools, secondary schools, universities, and research institutes. Similarly, in private industry there is competition for the use of growth funds between new machines and new factories, and research and training programs.

A statement published in 1960 by the National Industrial Federation, an organization of businessmen and economists, indicates the belief in the importance of education that is held by many responsible Brazilians. This statement lists some of the principal obstacles to economic development that are to be found in the educational system:

1. A disproportionately low expenditure on education by the government

2. Inequalities in education between the various regions of the country

3. Inequality between urban and rural education

4. A high rate of illiteracy in underdeveloped areas

5. Deficiencies in the school program

6. Inadequacy of technical education for the needs of agriculture, industry, and commerce

7. shortage of teachers, school buildings, and teaching materials

8. Political influence in the field of education [3]

After listing the defects of the primary school system, the statement goes on to say that a secondary education is even worse than primary education. The secondary school is difficult of access to the children of the working class. Furthermore, it pays little attention to the need of the society for vocational training. Only 2.5 per cent of the pupils of secondary schools are taking courses that will make them better industrial or agricultural workers. Furthermore, the universities and other higher institutions are preparing inadequate numbers of engineers, chemists, industrial researchers, economists, and administrators.

This group of business leaders has said, in effect, that the amount of money Brazil is investing in the development of human capital is grossly inadequate for the economic growth of the society. In a later chapter we shall examine this argument in detail. The claims of education as a field of investment for economic growth are stated more explicitly and more urgently in Brazil and in other developing countries than they ever were in the already strongly industrialized nations. The United States and the North European countries had a century in which to become industrialized, a century during which education and technology evolved in step with the economy. It was never quite clear in those countries whether education was a cause or a result of economic development—almost certainly it was both. But the present underdeveloped countries with an industrial potential are trying to get as much economic growth as quickly as possible out of limited investments. For them it is essential to invest their resources wisely, whether in education, research, physical capital, or other means of growth. Brazil is making an experiment, consciously, of investing scarce economic resources in education for the sake of economic growth.

NOTES

1. See, for example, Theodore W. Schultz, "The Economic Test in Latin America," School of Industrial and Labor Relations, Cornell University, Ithaca, New York, *Bulletin 35* (Aug. 1956), and *The Economic Value of Education* (New York, 1963).

2. Brazilian Embassy, *Survey of Brazilian Economy: 1958* (Washington, D.C., 1958), p. 12.

3. National Industrial Federation, "Diretrizes e Perspectivas da Economia Brasileira," *Desenvolvimento e Conjuntura*, IV (Nov. 1960).

7

The
State and
Education

EVERY modern nation supports and administers a national system of public education, as one of its principal functions. The task of administering and of financing the program may be a responsibility of the central national government or of the governments of political subdivisions of the nation, such as provinces states, counties, or local school districts. In every case the state, as the institution for governing and maintaining order in the society, has taken responsibility for the education of the people.

The first truly national systems of state-administered public education were established in the first half of the nineteenth century. These came earliest in the North European and North American countries. At about the same time the Imperial government of Brazil recognized in principle its responsibility for state public schools, but it did not succeed in creating and supporting a comprehensive system. The Republic government made public education one of its principal functions, and after 1900 was able to develop very slowly a system of primary schools which served a majority of the people. Secondary and higher education were developed still more slowly, and it remains a goal for the second half of the twentieth century to make an educational system that is effectively available to all the people.

The system of education that developed during the first half of the twentieth century took as its model the French system of about 1900. Its formal structure is shown in Table 16, with an indication of the ages of the pupils in the various types of schools and of the sources of financial support. Since the federal government and the state and municipal governments all have some educational responsibilities, it is necessary to present a brief sketch of the political structure of present-day Brazil.

135

TABLE 16

The Brazilian Educational System

Level or branch	Subdivisions	Years of study	Age of pupils	Source of support
Elementary	Pre-Primary	2-3	4-6	Mainly private
	Primary	4	7-11	Mainly state & municipal
	Supplementary	2	11-13	Mainly state and munici-pal, with federal aid
Secondary	Ginásio	4	11-14	Mainly private, some state
	Colégio	3	15-18	Mainly private, some state
Normal	Urban	6-7	11-18	State and private
	Rural	4	14-18	State and private
Commercial	Basic	2-4	11-14	Mainly private
	Technical	3	15-18	Mainly private
Industrial	Basic	4	11-14	Mainly federal and state
	Technical	3	15-18	Mainly federal and state
Agricultural	Basic	2 or 3	12-14	Federal and state
	Technical	2 or 3	15-18	Federal and state
Universities and advanced schools	Nearly 25 Schools or faculties & departments, with nearly 60 major or specialized fields of study.	3-1	18 to 25 & over	Mainly federal and private

The United States of Brazil constitute a federal republic of twenty-two states and a Federal District, each possessing a certain measure of autonomy. The latter is limited by the federal government which is comprised as follows: a legislative branch (Chamber of Deputies and Federal Senate), a judicial branch (the Supreme Federal Tribunal), and an executive branch (President of the Republic, departments, and other executive agencies). The state governments are similarly composed of three branches (the Legislative Assembly, the State Tribunal of Justice and a governor, with his auxiliary agencies—secretariats and directorates).

The deputies, senators, the president of the Republic, the governors of the states and the state deputies are all elected directly by the people, and the franchise is extended to all persons aged eighteen and over who demonstrate their ability to read and write. The electorate in 1962 totaled approximately eighteen million.

The federal deputies are elected for a four-year term, the number allotted to each state being proportional to its population. Three senators are elected from each state and from the Federal District, making the total sixty-nine. Senators serve for eight years, the president of the republic for five years. According to the federal constitution adopted in 1946, the immediate re-election of a president of the Republic and of governors is prohibited.

A state is divided into *municípios,* each having a mayor and a city council, both elected directly by the local population. The *município* is the smallest administrative unit in Brazil. There are *municípios* with less than fifty square miles of area, while others are several thousand square miles in size. Some have less than one million cruzeiros income (taxes), others have hundreds of millions. For example, the city of São Paulo, the capital of the state of São Paulo, had nearly ten billion cruzeiros income in the mid-1950's, an income higher than that of several states. There are a total of about three thousand *municípios* in Brazil, of which the state of São Paulo has about five hundred and Minas Gerais about the same number.

The Federal District is regarded as a neutral municipality; it does not belong to any state, it has its own city council elected by the district voters, but its mayor is named by the president of the Republic with approval or ratification by the federal Senate. With the transfer of the capital to Brasília (1960–61), the former *Distrito Federal*—the city of Rio de Janeiro—was converted into the twenty-first state of the Republic, bearing the name of "Estado da Guanabara," as there already existed a state of Rio de Janeiro. The territory of Acre became the twenty-second state in 1962. Besides the twenty-two states and the Federal District, Brazil possesses four territories, three of them in Amazonia, and another made up of the island of Fernando de Noronha. These are administered directly by the federal government.

The Constitution of the Republic and Educational Administration

Education in Brazil is controlled on the administrative level either by the Federal government or else by the state governments, in accordance with the division and limitations of powers stipulated in the constitution. Thus there exist both federal and state systems of education. The former is governed by federal legislation, the latter by laws and regulations of the respective states.

The constitution, which was adopted in 1946, contains the following articles concerning education:

Article 166: All persons shall be entitled to education, which shall be given in the home and in schools and shall be based upon the principles of freedom and the ideals of the brotherhood of man.

Article 167: The various branches of education shall be provided by the public authorities, and may be provided by private persons in accordance with law.

Article 168: Statutes relating to education shall be based on the following principles: (1) Primary education shall be compulsory and shall be given only in the national language. (2) Official (public) primary education shall be given free of charge to all, and official postprimary education to those proving lack or insufficiency of means. (3) Every industrial, commercial, and agricultural undertaking employing more than 100 persons shall be bound to provide free primary education for its employees and their children. (4) Every industrial and commercial undertaking shall be bound to cooperate in providing instruction for its minor employees in the manner required by statute and subject to the rights of teachers. (5) Religious education shall be an optional subject in the curriculum of public schools and shall be given to each pupil in accordance with his religious persuasion as stated by himself if he is of legal age or otherwise by his legal representative or guardian. (6) Teaching posts in official secondary education and in official or private higher education shall be filled competitively according to the formal qualification of candidates and the results of an examination. Teachers so engaged shall be entitled to security of tenure. (7) Academic freedom is hereby guaranteed.

Article 169: Each year the Union shall apply not less than 10 per cent, and every state, the Federal District, and every municipality not less than 20 per cent of its revenue from taxation to the maintenance and development of education.

Article 170: The Union shall organize the Federal system of education and the system to be applied in the territories. The Federal system of education shall be supplementary and only established throughout the country in so far as local provision is inadequate.

Article 171: Each state and the Federal District shall organize its own system of education. The Union shall assist in the development of the aforesaid systems by monetary aid, which in respect of primary education shall be derived from a specific national fund.

Article 172: Every system of education shall be bound to include educational assistance services, which shall provide facilities enabling needy pupils to work efficiently.

Article 173: No restriction may be placed on the teaching of any branch of learning, of letters or the arts.

Article 174: The protection of culture shall be a duty of the state. The foundation of research institutes, preferably in conjunction with establishments of higher education, shall be governed by statute.

In Articles 5 and 6 of the constitution, where the power of the states and of the Union are dealt with, it is stipulated that the Union should legislate concerning "directives and bases of national education," while the states should provide "supplementary and complementary legislation." Since 1947 there has been controversy as to what is meant by "directives and bases of national education." The general consensus is that the constitution should be interpreted to support the following administrative philosophy:

a) Recognition that education takes place in the home and in the school and, consequently, a recognition of the responsibility of the family in any school situation or decision with regard to education.*

b) Regardless of economic, political, or religious status, everyone has the right to all grades or levels of instruction, and it is incumbent upon the state to see to it that this right is in fact assured.

c) Compulsory school attendance applies only to primary education, which may be obtained in public (official) schools or private schools.

d) Only primary, public education is free; in the other levels or grades the state is to assure free tuition only to those who prove they are lacking in resources to pay for their studies.

e) Logically, if the public secondary and advanced schools should prove incapable of extending free tuition to those in need thereof, the state may pay the tuition of such students in private schools.

f) It is also evident that free schooling cannot be provided for all those in need thereof, but only for those who reveal a genuine

---

* This conclusion is warmly defended by the Catholic Church. Some educators of a positivist or pragmatic orientation do not admit the capacity of the family to make all decisions with respect to education. However, there is no doubt that the dominant philosophy is the one indicated above.

capacity for secondary and advanced studies. Free tuition must be subordinated to scholastic capacity.*

g) Pursuant to the provisions of the constitution, it also follows that the rich have no right to free tuition in the schools beyond the primary level, even though this principle is not adhered to by the existing public schools.

h) The constitution excludes the possibility of any kind of state monopoly over education and opens up possibilities for cooperation between government authorities and the management of private schools, with the purpose of providing free tuition for qualified poor students.†

i) While acknowledging freedom of instruction, it is stipulated that private schools must respect the laws that regulate them; in other words, the constitution grants a regulated liberty. In this regard the constitution appears to open the door to two opposite procedures: strangulating regulation or else the simple fixation of minimum conditions to be fulfilled by the private schools. However, since strangulating regulation runs counter to the principal of freedom of instruction, only the second alternative remains.

j) The constitution envisages the existence of a Federal system of education, but this should be supplementary, serving mainly to supply the lacks or deficiencies of the states. Thus the system of public instruction falls primarily within the power of the states, duly aided or supplemented by the Federal Union.

k) The principles cited in i and j demonstrate that the authority delegated by the constitution to the Union to legislate concerning educational bases and standards is not to be confused with the authority to regulate instruction; the latter is free, even though it must conform to certain bases and directives, that is to say, to a general orientation fixed by law, as determined by the representatives of the people in the Chamber of Deputies and in the Senate of the Republic.

l) While legislation is incumbent upon the states, the latter must respect the principle that education is open to private

* The federal government maintains several universities where registration and attendance are completely free, regardless of the economic situation of the student.
† There has been controversy on this point because both the Catholic Church and nonreligious entities are pressing for greater government financial assistance for the schools they have built and are unable to maintain adequately. The opposition group upholds the proposition that "public funds shall be spent only for public, governmental schools."

initiative, and they must heed the consequences implicit in this principle.

m) The one great ideological premise of the constitution supports liberty and human brotherhood; brotherhood implies tolerance and consequently any educational limitation or discrimination is unconstitutional which encourages explicitly or implicitly the struggle of classes or political ideologies. Freedom is limited by the goal of social solidarity, which means that there exists no freedom to destroy solidarity among Brazilians. Furthermore, there must be no discrimination as between public and private instruction; the two complement each other and are united in a single objective, namely, that of providing intellectual, moral, and practical education for Brazilians.

THE LAW OF DIRECTIVES AND BASES OF EDUCATION. The constitution of 1946 called for the formulation by the national congress of a "law of directives and bases of education," which would provide the legal base for the use of public resources in the field of education. About 1948 a report was issued by a commission appointed to propose the content of such a law. The members of this commission represented a group called "Pioneers of the New School." Included in this group were Anísio Teixeira, Fernando de Azevedo, and A. Almeida, Jr. Their report caused a considerable amount of discussion, with some disagreement, and was eventually tabled by congress. After 1956 President Kubitschek appointed a new commission to work out a draft of the law. Its report was discussed over a period of two or three years. Eventually, in 1961, the congress passed a law that was something of a compromise between the proponents of government aid for private schools and those who wanted government support limited to public schools. The law raised the level of federal government support of education from 10 to 12 per cent of the government's income from taxes. There was general approval of the law as it was finally passed, and it was hailed by educators as the magna carta of Brazilian education. Some of the principal features are:

Decentralization of Educational Administration. State and local governments are encouraged to take greater responsibility for the conduct and the financing of education. State councils of education are to be appointed by the governors, to assume responsibility in the states.

Flexible Curriculum. In primary and secondary education, the state councils are expected to provide "a variety of methods of instruction and forms of school activity, related

to the geographical region and the social group being served."
Priority of Public Education. It is provided in the law
that the federal government funds are to be used preferentially
for the system of public-supported education, though the way
is left open for assistance to private institutions. Of the federal
government educational funds, 90 per cent are to be divided
into three equal parts for support of primary, middle, and
higher education, respectively. The law also pays considerable
attention to technical or vocational education at the secondary
level, seeking to guarantee that technical courses will have a
component of liberal education, and that graduates of technical courses will be eligible for entrance to appropriate university faculties and technological institutes.

The State, the Church, and Public Education

Brazil is a Catholic country, but the Roman Catholic church is
not "established," as it is in some countries; nor does the Catholic
church have special rights in the educational field. This situation
has existed since the beginning of the Republic.

Throughout the Colonial period, even during the regime of
the Marques de Pombal, Catholicism was the state religion of the
Kingdom of Portugal and its colonies, with the church controlling
virtually all existing schools. Following the arrival of King João
VI in Brazil, and throughout the era of Brazil's career as an
independent Empire, Catholicism continued to be the established
religion. Even though the schools that began to spring up at that
time were not specifically church schools, the Roman Catholic
church exerted great influence and played an important role in
the orientation of public instruction.

The Republic was proclaimed under the ideological auspices
of a small group of leaders who followed the French school of
philosophical positivism. They set up a secular state and, consequently, the entire system of public instruction, from the primary to the university level, became secular in nature—a condition
that endured until 1934. When, at that time, the Second Republic
constitution was drafted, the Catholics succeeded in having a
provision written into the constitution declaring religious instruction in the public schools optional. By the time the Third
Republic constitution was approved, in 1946, the foregoing provision was amplified and set forth in detail, affirming that religious
instruction is a subject falling within the regular program of
studies, and that it is the responsibility of the parents of the

TABLE 17

Enrollments in Public and Private Educational Institutions
(ratios of public to private institutional enrollments)

Type of institution		1933 Public	1933 Private	1945 Public	1945 Private	1953 Public	1953 Private	1958 Public	1958 Private
Primary schools	Enrollment	1487	307	2313	438	3689	453	5079	723
	Ratio Pub./Priv.	4.85		5.44		8.15		7.03	
Academic secondary	Enrollment	*1938* 40	94	55	185	151	323	251	445
	Ratio	.43		.30		.47		.56	
Commercial	Enrollment							10	127
	Ratio							.08	
Industrial	Enrollment							16	4
	Ratio							4.22	
Normal	Enrollment							38	40
	Ratio							.95	
Universities and higher institutions	Enrollment							47	38
	Ratio							1.24	
All types	Enrollment	*1934* 1763	518	2557	964	*1948* 3568	1149	5441	1377
	Ratio	3.40		2.66		3.22		3.97	

Note: Enrollment figures (in thousands) are those for the last month of the school year.

pupils to decide whether their children should attend classes in religion or not. Instruction in the Catholic religion may be given by priests or nuns or by classroom teachers.

Even though this provision does not grant a monopoly on religious instruction to any one church, Catholicism stands to benefit the most from it, for, though not highly orthodox themselves, the great majority of Brazilians regard themselves as Catholics, and therefore raise no objection against their children receiving a Catholic education. Images of Catholic saints, of the Sacred Heart of Jesus, and of the Virgin hang in Brazilian classrooms and school offices as a manifestation of the Catholic influence on religious education. In the chapter devoted to the primary schools, we shall describe the manner in which this intruction is carried out.

With religious instruction generally available in public schools, the Catholic church has not used many of its resources on the building and maintenance of primary schools, which are 80 per cent public and are maintained by the state and municipal governments. It has displayed a greater interest in establishing church-directed secondary schools and universities. In a survey of secondary education published in 1957,[1] covering 2,321 out of 2,652 institutions of secondary education, it was found that 690 or 30 per cent were operated by Catholic organizations, 59 or 2.5 per cent by other churches, 648 or 28 per cent by government agencies, and 909 or 39 per cent by private, secular organizations or by individuals. In 1959 the percentages of university students in public, Catholic, and other private higher institutions were 55, 18, and 27, respectively. Table 17 shows the enrollment in public and private institutions at various levels. The efforts of the Catholic church appear to be directed at the expansion of its work in the fields of higher education and secondary education.

Since the constitution permits government assistance to private schools, the Catholic church, as well as other churches and groups that operate private, nonprofit schools, has worked hard to obtain government subsidies. The church leaders have taken the position that the state should give full support to church-operated schools. Only in this way, they argue, can parents have full freedom in choosing the kind of school their children shall attend, for they would not have to pay fees for sending the children to a church school, and they could be sure that the church school was as adequately supported as the nonchurch school. Furthermore, the church leaders argue that the state does not need to organize and manage any type of school. It might leave the initiative to parents' groups or other educational organizations, simply offering to pay the cost of nonchurch schools on the same basis as it would pay for the cost of church schools. This type of arrangement exists in Holland, where the population is about evenly divided between Catholic and Protestant, and the major churches operate their own schools with state support.

In the late 1950's possibly as much as 70 per cent of the money granted by the federal, state, and municipal governments to private schools and universities went to Catholic institutions. There was no legal formula for government aid, such as a given amount per pupil or a given proportion of the cost of school buildings. Rather, the decision or allocation was made by the government officials in the ministries and secretariats of education, influenced by important and powerful legislators, church and business leaders, and parents' organizations.*

Federal Government Administration of Education

The federal agency of educational administration in Brazil is the Ministry of Education and Culture, whose minister is appointed by the president of the Republic on the basis of political considerations. The Minister of Education and Culture is assisted by a National Council of Education, composed of twenty-four renowned educators who hold a consultative function in the interpretation and application of educational legislation enacted by the congress.

The principal administrative and technical organs of this ministry are the following:

a) National Department of Education, which is intended to serve as the coordinating agency of the educational programs of the ministry and, in addition, is concerned primarily with the adult education program, extracurricular education, and physical education.

b) Department of Administration, whose principal functions are the personnel and budgetary administration of the ministry.

c) National Institute of Pedagogic Studies (INEP), which carries out the investigation and research necessary for the formulation of the educational policy of the ministry, and administers the National Fund for Primary Education.

---

* These estimates should be read with the fact in mind that about 60 per cent of the federal government subventions for elementary and secondary education went to state and municipal schools.

d) Board of Higher Education, entrusted with the supervision of institutions of higher learning and the application of federal legislation in that area.

e) Board of Secondary Education, entrusted with the supervision of secondary instruction (of the academic, nonvocational secondary education) and the enforcement of federal legislation in that area.

f) Board of Industrial Education, entrusted with the administration of federal technical-industrial schools on the intermediate level and the supervision of nonfederal institutions of the same type.

g) Board of Commercial Education, which supervises commercial schools on the intermediate level and enforces the appropriate federal legislation.

In addition to these main organs of educational administration, the ministry has at its disposal supplementary and temporary agencies that are in charge of specific programs: * Among the latter we may cite:

a) The Brazilian Center for Educational Research, with regional branches in the states of Rio Grande do Sul, São Paulo, Minas Gerais, Bahia, and Pernambuco. These are all engaged in conducting educational and social research, the results of which are utilized by the National Institute of Pedagogic Studies for the formulation of projects, plans, and educational policy of the ministry.

b) The National Campaign for the Improvement of Personnel for Higher Education (CAPES), whose program calls for the improvement in the quality of the teaching staffs in institutions of higher learning. In addition, it administers scholarship funds for postgraduate technological training at home and abroad.

c) The Commission on the Plan for University Institutes (COSUPI), which allocates government funds to support and develop technological institutes and engineering and medical schools.

d) The National Campaign for the Eradication of Illiteracy, which in the late 1950's developed a pilot project in primary education, adult education, and community relations, aiming at

---

* In 1963 all the campaigns and COSUPI were reorganized according to the National Plan of Education approved by the National Council of Education in accordance with the law of directives and bases. The campaigns and COSUPI were abolished as agencies and incorporated into the regular and permanent services of the ministry.

the reduction of illiteracy and the elevation of the cultural level of the people.

e) The National Campaign for Rural Education, whose principal objective is training teachers and leaders for rural areas.

f) The Commission for Educational Planning (COPLED), which was established in 1962 as an agency of the Federal Council on Education to provide the necessary data for the planning of educational development.

In addition to the foregoing administrative agencies, the Ministry of Education and Culture maintains a department of statistics, institutes for publishing books and distributing film projectors and films, and supports the National Library, National Radio, and several museums.

The Federal Government and Primary Education

With regard to the administration of primary education, the function of the Ministry of Education is to collaborate with and aid the states and municípios. The principal agency involved is the Institute of Pedagogic Studies (INEP) which administers the National Fund for Primary Education.

The Institute had developed three principal activities with the aid of this fund: (1) assistance to the states and *municípios* for constructing additional primary school buildings—by 1959 nearly 15,000 classrooms were built in this manner; (2) aid to the states for the construction of teacher-training schools, for training the faculty members of such schools as well as training elementary school principals and counselors; (3) aid to the states for building, equipping, and maintaining "complementary" primary schools, designed to assure a minimum of six years of primary schooling in the cities.

Aside from this broad area of material and technical cooperation with the states in the field of primary education, the Ministry of Education extends its assistance in the investigation of local problems. The state must request this service, and the suggestions made by the ministry on the basis of its investigation may or may not be followed, according to the decision of the state.

The Federal Government and Secondary Education

Until 1930 the development of secondary education in Brazil was slight. Legislation was within the province of the federal government, and supervision was provided by the Ministry of

Education and Culture. However, the government administered only one institution of secondary education, the Colégio Pedro II in Rio, which was maintained as a model school. The state governments maintained one secondary school in each state capital. The leadership in maintaining secondary schools was almost exclusively with the Catholic church; its religious orders supported a small number of schools with academic standards regarded as excellent. After 1930 new legislation encouraged the establishment of private schools by enterprising laymen as well as by the church. There were 100 secondary schools in Brazil in 1929, 717 in 1938, 1,789 in 1950, and 3,027 in 1961.

Federal supervision was exercised by an inspector for each school, whose task was to ascertain the academic qualifications and capacity of the teachers and supervise the examinations, the registration and attendance of the students, the teaching facilities, and the general administration. The federal government issued detailed educational regulations that the schools rigidly obeyed. This situation did not create any special problems, since the schools were located in state capitals, whose economic and cultural patterns were similar to those of Rio and the Colégio Pedro II.

When the Ministry of Education was created, a Board of Secondary Education was established in 1937 to supervise in this area. New schools were springing up in all the cities, large and small, and the old system of supervision through an inspector in each school became too costly. Moreover, it proved difficult to procure competent personnel in sufficient numbers to serve as inspectors in all the secondary schools.

Problems in the secondary schools differed widely from region to region, but the existence of uniform legislation made it necessary for the Ministry of Education and Culture to resort to constant and cumbersome regulations to enforce the laws. The ministerial orders issued between 1937 and 1957 would fill several volumes totaling thousands of printed pages. They dealt with curricula, the official register of teachers, examinations, the fulfillment of school programs, fixing the school term, school vacations, standards for promotion, minimum requirements for teaching facilities—all the administrative problems of secondary education.

As the secondary schools grew in number and enrollment, the ministry was forced to adopt emergency methods of recruiting and training teachers, since the new university faculties of philosophy, letters, and science did not grow rapidly enough to provide more than a few of the new teachers that were needed. Also, the ministry had to fix minimum salaries for teachers in private schools.

In recent years the federal government has found it necessary to take a hand in determining the tuition paid by the students. The National Fund for Secondary Education, whose main aim is to provide free scholarships for poor students, was formed to meet the increasing pressure from the urban population. In order to prevent or reduce future increases in the tuition fees, the fund subsidizes the schools through contributions to the teachers' salaries.

With this growing array of obligations, the task of supervision exercised by the Ministry of Education became extraordinarily involved and voluminous. Sectional inspection offices were established in the various states for the purpose of lightening the administrative burden of the ministry. These are federal organs, subordinate to the Board of Secondary Education, and they do not signify any administrative decentralization, for they do not transfer any authority to local government agencies.

Commercial education on the secondary level is administered in the same fashion. Within the Ministry of Education the Board of Commercial Education is charged with the enforcement of the federal laws in this field. In this sector likewise, private initiative is predominant, but it, too, is subject to federal regulation. A corps of inspectors enforces compliance with federal laws.

With regard to industrial training the situation is somewhat different. In this area private initiative plays a minor role. The industrial schools are generally attended by young people from all social classes, many of whom are unable to pay tuition, and the equipment for such schools is very expensive. Thus the Ministry of Education defrays most of the costs of industrial training. A Board of Industrial Education in the ministry is entrusted with not only the legal control of the schools but also with their administrative supervision and the preparation of plans for their facilities. Recently several states, especially those which are more highly developed economically, have begun to concern themselves with industrial education, and a network of state schools devoted to industrial training is developing in present-day Brazil.

In this chapter devoted to secondary education we shall de-

scribe the system of schools maintained by the National Bureau
of Industrial Apprenticeship (SENAI), affiliated with the associations of industrialists, and the system supported by the
National Bureau of Commercial Apprenticeship (SENAC), affiliated with the associations of commerce. Although these
bureaus are the result of a federal law, they are not subject to
government control, being maintained exclusively by contributions from manufacturers and merchants.

Agricultural training on the secondary level is entirely controlled by the Ministry of Agriculture. This is done in order
to give the Agricultural Ministry power and responsibility for
the program of furthering rural production.

The Federal Government and Higher Education

The federal government keeps a closer control over higher
education than over the other levels, and pays a larger proportion of the cost. Within the Ministry of Education and Culture
the Board for Higher Education is entrusted with the enforcement of federal laws and regulations. It concerns itself chiefly
with the organization of all institutions of higher learning,
federal, state, or private in character.

There are thirty-two universities in Brazil, and the majority
of these are federal sponsored. In addition there are over
two hundred other higher institutions, federal, state and private,
not combined into universities but giving university-level education. A variety of summer courses and noncredit courses given
through extension departments are supported by non-university
organizations, sometimes using university facilities.

The federal laws relating to higher education allow little
autonomy. The universities' authority is confined to such routine
responsibilities as the organization of programs, the establishment of student schedules and standards for credits, and—in
the case of federal or state universities—the disbursement of the
funds allocated to them.

The public universities do not even have the right to choose
their major professors. These appointments are made by the
government in accordance with regulations fixed by law. Although the universities are empowered to conduct competitive
examinations to which candidates for a university chair must
submit, the competitive examinations may be canceled by the
federal government. Also, if a university desires to introduce a
new academic department or course of studies leading to a

diploma or degree, it must submit this to the government for approval, in order that the diplomas may have legal standing.

Every university is administered by a rector assisted by a council comprised of full professors, and, similarly, every institute of higher learning is headed by a director and a council of professors. The university rector and the director of a higher institute are both chosen by the government (in the case of public institutions) from a list of three names submitted by the university council in the case of the rector, or by the faculty in the case of an institute director.

The private universities and institutes enjoy more freedom in this respect. They choose their professors and directors without interference from the government, conforming only with minimal legal requirements. On the other hand, they possess less autonomy in the organization of school programs, being entirely subjected to governmental standards.

No diploma or higher degree issued by an institution of advanced learnings possesses legal standing or confers the right to practice a learned profession unless it is registered with the Board of Higher Education of the Ministry of Education and Culture. Since this board must ascertain whether the requisite legal regulations have been complied with, it frequently happens that more than twelve months must elapse before a graduate acquires legal status and is able to practice his chosen profession. This means that no Brazilian school of university level is able to guarantee that its graduates will enjoy specific professional rights. The Ministry of Education and Culture has the last word on the validity of the training received by the graduate.

Responsibility of States and Municípios for Primary Education

Responsibility for the organization and administration of primary schools is in the hands of the state governments, though most *municípios* have supplemented the state system of primary schools with a municipal system. Thus there are actually three sets of primary schools—the state administered, the *município* administered, and the private schools that come under state inspection. The states themselves differ in their forms of administration, some having a central administration operating from the state capital, and others having a decentralized administrative system.

No doubt the present chaotic administration of the primary schools will be replaced by a simpler and more rational system as more money becomes available for the support of primary education. It remains to be seen whether the administrative and financial responsibility for primary education will be centered in the state capitals or decentralized to the municipal level. There is much discussion of the desirability of decentralization, but the process has not gone very far.

At present each State Department of Education attempts to satisfy the constitutional requirement of free, compulsory education at the primary level by maintaining a four-year primary school and attempting to get and keep all children in school for at least four years, generally between the ages of 7 and 11. This program has met varying degrees of success, depending on the wealth of the state and on its distribution of population.

A system of supervision is also maintained by each State Department of Education. The trend is to broaden the functions of the school inspector so that he does more than collect school statistics and certify compliance or noncompliance with the laws. He is expected to give advice and assistance to the school directors and to help them do a better job of supervising and improving the work of their classroom teachers. In the richer states, especially Rio Grande do Sul, São Paulo, Guanabara and Paraná, inspectors are carefully selected and well trained. Here there is a tendency to build up regional offices for supervision, with a staff of specialists under the direction of a general inspector.

Financing Education in Brazil

About 80 per cent of the total cost of education is paid by the government in Brazil. Private support, through payment of tuition fees and gifts to schools and colleges, amounted to approximately 23 per cent of the total in 1956, and has probably continued at that level. Most of the private support is applied to secondary education, but there is an increasing amount of private expenditure on higher education.

Tables 18 and 19 show how the various levels of government and private sources have supported education. The federal government has spent most of its effort on higher education, the states and municípios have put their major emphasis on primary education, while secondary education has been supported relatively heavily by private funds. However, as seen in Table 18A, the actual expenditures of the federal government, states, and

TABLE 18

Financing Education in Brazil, 1951, 1956, and 1959

A. Relative Expenditures on Education by Various Government Levels and Private Sources

| | Percentage distribution of expenditures by source | | | | | | | | | | | |
| | Primary education | | | Secondary education | | | Higher education | | | Total educational expenditures | | |
Source	1951	56	59	1951	56	59	1951	56	59	1951	56	59
Union	5	7	18	12	20	32	55	54	55	16	25	33
States	77	71	61	49	46	32	40	15	18	61	46	39
Município	14	15	15	1	2	1	—	—	—	7	6	7
Private	4	7	6	38	32	35	5	31	27	16	23	21
Total	100	100	100	100	100	100	100	100	100	100	100	100

B. Expenditures on Education According to Level of Education

| | Percentage distribution of expenditures by level | | | | | | | | | | | |
| | Primary education | | | Secondary education | | | Higher education | | | Total educational expenditures | | |
Source	1951	56	59	1951	56	59	1951	56	59	1951	56	59
Union	14	10	22	26	27	28	60	63	50	100	100	100
States	61	55	62	28	35	24	11	10	14	100	100	100
Município	94	85	93	5	14	5	1	1	2	100	100	100
Private	11	12	12	84	49	49	5	39	39	100	100	100
Total educational expenditures	48	36	41	35	35	29	17	29	30	100	100	100

Note: This table differs slightly in its 1956 figures from those given by Oliveira and Carvalho, and follows the estimates of private expenditure for education made by J. Roberto Moreira. For 1959, Moreira's estimates for 1957 are used as a basis of estimating private educational expenditures. Some simplifying assumptions are made in categorizing educational expenditures reported for 1959 under "other expenses." The estimates for private expenditures are reasonable ones, based on information concerning fees paid by students in 1957 and on information concerning private gifts to private universities.

Sources: Ministério de Educação e Cultura, *Estatística Das Despesas Com o Ensino e Cultura, 1959-60*; Américo Barbosa de Oliveira and José Zacarias sa Carvalho, *A Formação de Pessoal de Nível Superior e o Desenvolvimento Econômico* (Rio de Janeiro: CAPES, Ministério de Educação e Cultura, 1960).

TABLE 19

Government Expenditure for Education, 1955-57
(percentage distribution)

Purpose	Federal government	States	Municípios	Total
Salaries of teachers and administrators	35	66	47	53
New buildings	21	8	30	15
Equipment and furniture	10	3	6	5
Subsidies to private schools for physical plant	5	1	0.8	2.4
Repairs and conservation	2	0.7	1.5	1.3
Subsidies to private schools for current expenses	9	10	8	10
Supplies consumed	13	8	3	9
Social service payments (mainly tuition grants)	6	4	4	5
Totals	100	100	100	100
Primary education	3	63	94	45
Secondary education	38	31	5	33
Higher education	59	6	1	22

private sources are now about equal in the field of secondary education. During the 1950-60 decade relative expenditures on primary education decreased, while those on higher education increased. However, federal expenditures on primary and secondary education show a relative increase in the early years of the 1960 decade.

It will be recalled that the law of 1961 requires the Union to spend 12 per cent of its tax income on education and the states and *municípios* to spend 20 per cent of their tax income on education. There is some doubt as to whether the Union and the *municípios* are meeting their obligations, though the question is difficult to answer, due to complexity of government accounts and the shifting value of the cruzeiro.

In 1957 the public expenditures for education at all levels were 1.7 per cent of the gross national product, and the private educational expenditures added another 0.4 per cent, making the total educational outlay about 2.1 per cent of the national product. A study made by the National Council on Development calculates that the proportion of the national product spent by government agencies on education during the period 1952–56 varied between 1.5 and 2.3 per cent annually, averaging about 2.0 per cent.[2]

The annual cost of education in the United States was about 5 per cent of the national product in 1959. Russia was spending more than this proportion of her national product on education, and the countries of North Europe were spending about 3 per cent. Relative to many other countries, Brazil's expenditure of public funds is substantial, but these countries support education more liberally from private funds.

Calculating the cost per student per year at the various educational levels in 1957, taking into account both public and private contributions, Brazil's cost of education amounted to the following: (1) Primary school—1,600 cruzeiros, or about $25.00 (U.S.) at the prevailing rate of exchange; (2) Secondary school—10,500 cruzeiros, or $162.00 (U.S.); (3) University—76,000 cruzeiros, or $1,170.00 (U.S.). This calculation is crude, but it is certainly accurate within a range of 10 per cent. A similar calculation made for the year 1959 shows the costs per pupil in primary school, secondary school, and university to be in a proportion of 1 to 7 to 50; that is, it cost fifty times as much to educate a university student for a year as it cost for a primary school pupil. This is a remarkable difference. The university cost of about $1,170.00 is not far from the cost per year for American students in the United States at the same date. But the cost of $25.00 per primary school pupil is less than one-tenth of the cost per pupil in the primary schools of the United States. The cost per pupil in United States primary and secondary schools combined was $388.00 in 1956, and $476.00 in 1960.

NOTES

1. Conselho Nacional de Estatística, *Estatística do Ensino Medio: 1956* (Rio de Janeiro: Ministério da Educação e Cultura, Serviço de Estatística da Educação e Cultura, 1957).

2. Conselho Nacional de Desenvolvimento, "Análise do Esfôrço Financeiro do Poder Público com a Educação: 1948–1956," *Desenvolvimento e Conjuntura,* I (Sept.-Dec. 1957).

8

Primary
and Fundamental
Education

THE administration and organization of the primary schools and the institutions for training primary school teachers fall under the jurisdiction of the states. Each state has a department of education, whose head is appointed by the governor. The state government makes laws concerning the primary educational system of the state, and the State Department of Education enforces these laws, with a system of supervisors and inspectors that varies greatly in size and competence from one state to another. The state government receives some financial support from the federal government for primary schools, and uses most of this money for new school buildings. In 1959 about 46 per cent of the total public expenditure on education went to the support of primary education, this money being provided by the states, federal government, and the *municipios* in the ratios of 67, 21, and 12, respectively.

There are three general types of primary schools. The most common is the state school, supported and administered by the state. Next in order of enrollment is the municipal school, maintained by the *municipio* under the general supervision of the State Department of Education. Third is the private school, which may be church supported or secular, and is supervised to some extent by the State Department of Education, particularly to see that it complies with the state educational laws and, if it receives public funds, that it uses the money wisely. Enrollments in the three types of primary schools in 1958 were 57 per cent in state schools, 30 per cent in municipal schools, and 13 per cent in private schools.

The municipal schools are in a sense supplementary to the state schools. The *municipio* tends to build and maintain schools

156

in places where they are needed and where the state has not taken the responsibility. The great majority of rural schools are maintained by *municípios,* and there are also municipal schools in the towns and cities. Municipal schools are generally poorer than state schools, a condition reflected in the fact that few municipal teachers have had a normal school training, and many of them have merely graduated from a primary school. It is not surprising, therefore, that they are paid about a third as much as state school teachers.

There are three types of primary school buildings, and corresponding school organizations. Many rural schools have only a single room and a single class which may contain pupils in all four primary grades. A second type of school building has two or three classrooms, with one teacher in charge of each. For example, there may be one first grade, one second grade, and a combined third and fourth grades. When the enrollment is heavy those in the first and second grades may attend in the morning, and those in the third and fourth grades may attend in the afternoon. There is no principal or director in such a school, but one of the teachers receives a small additional payment for taking administrative responsibility. A third type of school, called the *grupo escolar,* has four or more classrooms, with separate classes for each grade, and usually with a principal or a director in addition to the classroom teachers. This type of school, found in towns of more than ten thousand population, generally engages specialized teachers for instruction in music, fine arts, woodworking, sewing, and physical education.*

Most urban schools operate for eight and a half months, with two semesters separated by a thirty day vacation in July and a ten-week summer vacation from December to March.

---

* In 1958 there were 83,000 primary schools in Brazil with 183,000 teachers. Forty-one thousand of the schools were municipal, with 52,000 teachers. Clearly, most of these were rural schools with one teacher. Thirty-three thousand schools were maintained by the states with 105,000 teachers, and 9,000 were private schools, with 25,000 teachers. At the same time there were 3,750 secondary schools, with 73,000 teachers. In the United States at this time there were 104,000 public elementary schools with 900,000 teachers and 26,000 public secondary schools with 600,000 teachers. A comparison of these figures indicates (a) the relatively underdeveloped state of secondary education in Brazil, and (b) the relatively large extent of primary education, the great majority of the primary schools being small rural schools. In the United States the one-room rural school is disappearing, and consequently the number of primary schools is decreasing.

Schools sometimes meet six days a week, but five sessions is more common. The school day is generally four and a half hours, but may go to six hours in some schools, and may be as little as three hours in others. This variance depends to some extent on the pressure of enrollment. When the cities grew rapidly after 1930, there was a severe shortage of school buildings and practically all city schools went on a two-shift basis. Even this did not supply enough classrooms in larger cities, and some schools went to three daily shifts of three hours each. Teachers generally teach one shift of four and a half hours, but sometimes a teacher will teach two three-hour shifts. Other emergency solutions have been adopted by some of the rapidly growing cities. Thus, São Paulo and Pôrto Alegre have built temporary wooden buildings, or simple open-air shelters with wooden roofs.

The primary school is essentially a four-year institution, with the normal age for admission seven or eight in the urban areas and eight or nine in rural areas, where children may have to travel long distances to get to school. Table 20 gives the age distribution of the pupils in the primary schools in 1959. Education is compulsory by law only for the four primary grades. A child who goes to school for four years has met the legal requirement, whether or not he has been promoted beyond the first grade.

TABLE 20

Age Distribution of Pupils in Primary Schools, 1959

Age	—7	7	8	9	10	11	12	13	14	15+
Enrollment	83	722	989	1,044	1,015	830	650	405	218	151

Note: Enrollment (in thousands) in the last month of the school year.

Before 1935 there was a development of "complementary" primary schools of two or three years, designed to give the pupil more general knowledge and mental skill as well as some simple job training. These schools were partially abandoned during the period from 1935 to 1950, under the pressure of increased enrollment in the four primary grades, and only in the late 1950's did they begin to be restored, sometimes as annexes to existing schools and sometimes in separate buildings to serve the districts with two or more primary schools. Also, a fifth grade was added to many four-year schools. This serves as a year of preparation for the entrance examination to secondary schools, and is attended by pupils who expect to go on to secondary school.

The towns and cities with greater resources offer kindergarten for children of four to six years, sometimes in conjunction with primary schools and sometimes in separate buildings. There were 200,000 children in more than 3,000 such schools in 1957, more than half of them in the states of São Paulo and Guanabara. Many of them are private schools.

TABLE 21

Enrollment in Various Types of Primary School
(percentage distribution)

Year	State	Municipal	Private
1933	67	16	17
1934	63	20	17
1935	61	23	16
1940	59	23	18
1945	60	24	16
1950	57	30	13
1953	61	28	11
1957	59	29	12
1958	57	30	13

We have already mentioned that the primary school system suffered during the 1930's and 1940's as the demand for schools and the cost of education increased. This is reflected in the increase in the proportion of pupils in municipal schools, which was 16 per cent of the total in 1933 and 30 per cent of the total in 1950, and was still at this level in 1958, as can be seen in Table 21. This increase of municipal school enrollment indicates a decline in quality of education. For a municipal school system to match the state system it would be necessary for the *município* to spend much more money on schools than it has been, to pay teachers much more, and to develop a system of professional administration and supervision.

A municipal school might gain strength from the active interest and support of the people in the local community. For example, the common schools of the United States are believed to be strengthened because the local community is responsible for most of their financial support and for their administration, while the state gives supplementary financial support, a minimum of inspection and supervision, and licenses the teachers. However, Brazil has a tradition of strong federal and state government, and weak local government, in contrast to the United

FIGURE 7

POPULATION GROWTH AS COMPARED WITH ENROLLMENT
GROWTH IN ELEMENTARY SCHOOLS, 1870-1950

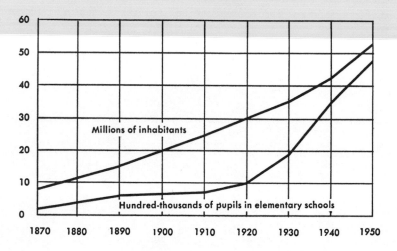

States' tradition of responsible local government at the city or
county level. Also, although there are regional differences, as
well as differences in standard of living among communities
within a state in the United States, these differences are not
so great as in Brazil. Some *municípios* are extremely poor and
backward in comparison with others, and cannot take responsibility for an efficient school system.

Who Goes to Primary School—How Long and How Far?

In 1958 the enrollment in Brazilian primary schools during
the last month of the school year was 5,802,000. At that time,
the boys and girls in the four-year age group 8 through 11 numbered approximately 6,200,000. Thus if all children stayed
four years in school—no more and no less—it might be concluded
that 94 per cent of school-age children were in school during
that year. However, the situation is more complicated than this.
Some children never attended school, possibly 5 to 10 per cent
of the age group. A great many children attended for only a

year or so. Others attended primary school for five or even six or seven years. Table 20 shows that there were children under age 7 and over age 15 in the primary schools in that year, though the ages of maximum enrollment were 8 through 11. Table 22 shows that some 47 per cent of the children were in the first grade and only 10 per cent were in the fourth grade.

In order to see more clearly what happens to boys and girls in the primary school, it is useful to follow a group that enters school in a given year. This was done by the statistician Moyses Kessel for the group who entered the first grade for the first time in 1945.[1] The result of his study is shown in Table 23. Data for the years after the primary school have been added by the authors.

TABLE 22

Regional Differences in Enrollment in Primary School Grades, 1957
(percentage distribution)

Region	Total number	First grade	Second grade	Third grade	Fourth grade	Fifth grade or first completed
Brazil	5,901,000	47	24	18	10	1
North	191,000	51	25	15	8	1
Northeast	971,000	54	23	14	8	1
East	2,036,000	52	22	16	9	1
South	2,505,000	38	25	22	13	2
Central West	198,000	52	25	14	8	1

In 1945 there were about 1,280,000 boys and girls who became seven years old. During that year, 1,204,000 children entered school for the first time. Seventy-six thousand, or about 6 per cent of this group, did not enter school. Of those who began school in 1945, 104,000 did not stay through the year; 1,100,000 finished the first year of school, though many of them did not succeed in passing into the second grade. Some of this group never passed out of the first grade, though they may have stayed in school four or more years. About 26 per cent finished a fourth year of school, though probably less than 20 per cent actually passed the fourth grade. The table goes on to show what percentages entered secondary school, graduated from secondary school, entered a university, and graduated from a university.

From this table we can see that the median child who

TABLE 23

Progress Through the Educational System
The Educational History of the Age-group Who Were Aged 7 in 1945

Number of children aged 7 in 1945 = 1,280,000
Number of children who entered school for first time in 1945 = 1,204,000

Year	Approximate age			No. per 10,000 who:	
				reached this level of education	completed formal education at this point or before
		Did not enter school at all, or did not stay in school through first year	180,000	1,400	1,400
1945	7	Finished a first year of school*	1,100,000	8,600	5,340
1946	8	Finished a second year of school	593,000	4,660	6,550
1947	9	Finished a third year of school	441,000	3,450	7,420
1948	10	Finished a fourth year of school	330,000	2,580	8,540
1949	11	Finished a fifth year of school	186,000	1,460	8,754
1950	12	In first year of secondary school	158,000	1,246	9,448
1953	15	Completed fourth year of secondary school	70,000	552	9,608
1956	18	Graduated from secondary school	47,500	392	9,808
1957	19	First year of university	23,000	192	9,808
1960	22	Graduated from university	16,000	133	10,000

* "Finishing" a year does not mean that this number passed the grade referred to. Some of them failed one or more times.

Principal Source: Moyses Kessel, "A Evasão Escolar no Ensino Primário," *Revista Brasileira de Estudos Pedagógicos*. XXII, No. 56 (Oct.-Nov. 1954), 52-72. Other sources are annual statistical reports of the Ministério de Educação e Cultura.

entered school in the 1940's stayed in school about two years. The median child of the group that entered school in 1950 stayed about three years, and 37 per cent finished a fourth year of school. For the year 1960 it is likely that 50 per cent of children finished a fourth year of school.

When the data on school attendance are examined for regional differences and for rural-urban differences, as in Table 22, it is clear that the failure to attend school for four years is largely a phenomenon of rural areas, especially in the Northeast. It is also a phenomenon of sócial class.

SOCIAL CLASS AND SCHOOL ATTENDANCE. The following sketches of three classrooms in the primary schools of three small or medium-sized cities in different parts of Brazil will reveal something of the relationship between social class and what the child learns at school.

School A. Dona Clementina lined up her pupils outside the entrance to the school, then marched them into the building, up the stairway, and into the classroom. Hers was the third year Group B of School J. S. of Joinville, in the state of Santa Catarina.

With each pupil standing beside his own desk, she led the class in singing the hymn to the flag, marking time with her hands. She told the class to sit down, and called the roll. Of thirty-six pupils only two were absent. Perhaps they were sick or possibly they had to stay home to help their parents. Dona Clementina could not imagine that any of her pupils might be truant.

She knew her class very well now, in the middle of the school year. All the children came from the south end of Joinville, and, having passed the first and second grades, could read and write fluently. Some were children of German stock, others of rural people recently come to the town from the area of Parati, and still others came from families of workers who had lived all their lives in the city. A number were Protestant, but the majority were Roman Catholic.

While the class was doing written work, Dona Clementina walked up and down the aisles, looking to see who needed help. She stopped beside Murilo, the elder son of a bookkeeper for the firm of Meyerle. She looked at his arithmetic lesson, carefully written in orderly lines. His clean white cotton shirt, his neatly trimmed nails, his carefully combed hair, all revealed the training he had at home. He was a joy as a pupil, though at times he had difficulty grasping some of the more complex elements of grammar.

Over there was Artur, who had been born in Germany and had recently arrived in Brazil with his parents. He still had trouble with language, and misspelled words frequently. A lonesome boy, "picked on" by the others, he seemed suspicious even of his teacher. His father worked in a machine shop and his mother as a seamstress. But Artur was learning, getting average grades, and taking pleasure in answering correctly after someone else had made a mistake.

In the first row sat Maria, daughter of a widow who was employed in a factory. She made slow progress with her school work, but spent a good deal of time helping out at home and taking care of her little sister. She had repeated the second grade and might have to repeat the third. She seldom played games with the other girls, acting as though games were not made for her. But she liked to talk with her neighbors, and sometimes forgot that the classroom is not a place for conversation. Certainly Maria would not go beyond the fourth grade, which she would reach at about the age of fourteen. Then she would get a job in the factory where her mother worked.

Dona Clementina returned to the front of the room and stood by her desk, looking at her pupils and thinking how different they were: children of factory workers, of farm workers recently come to the city, of bookkeepers, sales clerks, and small business people; some with clean uniforms, others carelessly dressed, and even dirty; some who came to school barefooted. Most of them had little chance of going to secondary school, but all of them could and probably would finish the primary school and then go to work.

School B. Dona Helena was proud to see her class, lined up with the others in the recreation area waiting to enter their classroom. The children wore clean, well-made uniforms and shoes; they carried leather or plastic briefcases. There were no children "of the people" to interfere with the schooling of the middle-class children in the "Number One" school of Leopoldina. The pupils were well-behaved and interested in their schoolwork. It was easy to see that they came from good families.

The class marked time with the right foot and at a signal marched into the school. No one spoke. Each student was serious, conscious of his duties and obligations. In the classroom, Dona Helena led them in the morning prayer—an Ave Maria recited in unison. Then they sang the hymn to the flag, and seated themselves to begin the work of the day.

They were all there, from the son of the judge to the son of the factory owner. Their fathers had the most important positions in the town. Dona Helena knew that it was a good school to work in. The principal could have anything she asked for in the way of supplies. Dona Helena felt that her work was appreciated and well received. In the last three years none of her pupils had failed. Their examinations were well-written, without errors or erasures.

It is true that three children from a nearby working-class area had enrolled at the beginning of the school year, at the suggestion of the school inspector. But after a few weeks they had decided to leave, because they did not feel at home. They would do better in another school.

Dona Helena looked over the class. In the front desk, center row was Marly, daughter of the owner of a stationery store. She was a careful student who wanted to become a secondary-school teacher. Therefore she would have to graduate from secondary school and go to the university. Marly certainly would succeed, for she was studious and intelligent.

Just behind her was Edite, also a good girl, a little careless but clever. Up to now she had no definite plans for the future. She said she wanted to be like her mother, who was often at school, working on projects of the association of parents and teachers.

First in another row was Roberto, son of a judge. He was a silent boy, not very studious but not troublesome to Dona Helena. He was proud of his father and said he wanted to become a judge. Though weak in arithmetic, he did well in geography and history, and his compositions were written clearly, with some originality.

So it was with the others. There were no bad pupils. Some had difficulty with one or another subject, but they would work hard to be able to pass at the close of the year.

While the pupils worked on their arithmetic, Dona Helena looked over their language homework. This was her chance to pick out mistakes and to find out what she should explain again to the class. After arithmetic the class would rehearse for the spring play.

Just then the director entered the classroom. She came to ask the pupils to make a special contribution to the school fund for this particular month. They would need to buy some things for the spring festival. The school fund in this school did not help needy pupils, since no pupils were in need; it was used to buy materials that the State Department of Education did not furnish.

Dona Helena listened to the director talking to the class. It was a pleasure to be with such children, to visit in their homes, and to feel that the work of a teacher was so much appreciated in the community.

School C. Seated at her desk, Dona Maria do Carmo waited for the remainder of her pupils. There were no paved roads in that part of Timbaúba, and the children had arrived with mud up to their knees. Only eight of the forty had been on time. They were muddy, wet, shivering with cold, wearing only cotton shirts or pants or dresses. At this time of year the attendance was irregular. Probably no more than twenty would attend school today.

Dona Maria gave the children newspapers to clean their legs and feet, then led them in singing, so that they might get warm. Afterward she would give them hot milk.

The school was in a new building, certainly the finest structure in this poor part of town. Timbaúba, in the backcountry of the state of Pernambuco, had a population consisting largely of farmers from the surrounding rural areas; poor people with no experience of towns. Most of the fathers of these children had only intermittent employment and earned just enough for subsistence. Clearly, the pupils could not buy uniforms and school materials; they could not even bring a lunch to school. The director of the school appealed everywhere for money to provide some material assistance to the pupils: to the municipal council, to local businessmen, to the state and federal governments. With the small amounts so obtained she was able to help the most needy.

The eight who had already arrived were the better pupils. They were seldom absent, and only for a very good reason. They were interested in their studies and even dreamed of going beyond the primary school. Jaquinha, the smartest, could speak correctly, read fluently, and liked to write imaginative compositions. He was a lively boy, though thin and pale. Marilyn was the hardest worker and got the best grades in the class. She stayed regularly after school was out, to study. Too bad that she was so small. Dona Maria do Carmo had visited her several times when she was sick. She had arranged for the girl to be given a month's careful treatment in the hospital, where she improved; but now she was losing ground again, and the rings under her eyes were very dark. Dona Maria always gave her fruit and two glasses of milk during the school lunch hour.

Almost all of the pupils were thin, sickly, and with distended stomachs. They were quiet children and seldom made trouble. When they were given attention they seemed to enjoy school, but their attendance was irregular, either because of illness or because they found small jobs in the town or in the marketplace. They seemed to be condemned to malnutrition, illness, and poverty.

At times Dona Maria became discouraged. Perhaps she should apply for a position in the bigger school in the center of town, where children of the "better" families attended. The work would be easier, and she could obtain more results from her efforts; promotion would be more rapid. But there was competition for those posts, and it would be difficult to get a transfer. When she thought about this, Dona Maria saw her poor little pupils almost as enemies.

And their number was increasing. In its first year the school had only 200 pupils, but now, in its second year, there were more than 400. Already the school operated in two shifts, and next year three might be necessary. The number of rural migrants into Timbaúba increased from year to year, even though work was scarce.

With a mixture of devotion to duty, yet discouragement, love, and dedication, yet hostility, Dona Maria taught her classes, and visited the homes of her pupils, helping them to get whatever social assistance was available from the *município*.

SOCIAL CLASS AND SCHOOL ACHIEVEMENT IN RIO DE JANEIRO. The foregoing sketches illustrate the differences that can be found in almost every town and city of Brazil in the school experiences and attitudes of children of different social classes. These differences have been examined more scientifically in a study of promotion and failure in the primary schools of Rio de Janeiro, which is summarized in Table 24.

TABLE 24

Factors Affecting Primary School Performance in Rio De Janeiro

Socioeco-nomic status	First grade		Second grade		Fourth grade	
	% of pupils	% passing	% of pupils	% passing	% of pupils	% passing
Medium	28	73	38	94	53	82
Poor	72	48	62	76	47	67
Color						
White	61	63	75	87	77	79
Mixed	25	49	17	78	18	53
Black	14	34	8	71	5	73

No. of times the first grade was repeated, by those who failed at least once

Socioeco-nomic status	1	2	3	4	
Medium	100	0	0	0	Percent of those who failed
Poor	63	32	3	2	Percent of those who failed

Extent to which the city was known by the pupils: per cent who were acquainted with all sections of the city and its suburbs

Socioeco-nomic status	I (high)	II	III	IV	V (low)
	83	82	50	12	11

Source: Roger Seguin, *Promoção e Aprendizagem Escolar no Ensino Primário* (Rio de Janeiro: Centro Brasileiro de Pesquisas Educacionais, Ministério de Educação e Cultura, 1959).

There is obviously a close relation between the socioeconomic status of a child's family and his success in school. Color, being related to social status, is also related to school performance. Those of higher social status score higher on the tests of intelligence and of scholastic achievement. However, the qualitative differences between children of the higher and lower social status decreases from the first to the fourth grades, indicating that the school was promoting selectively, to keep the brighter children of lower class and of colored families in school to the fourth grade. It is natural that families in the high socioeconomic level can and do provide a variety of physical, social, emotional, and intellectual experiences for their children, which expand their personal worlds and develop their intellectual capacities outside of the classroom. And it likewise follows that families in the low socioeconomic level do not provide these experiences of the wider social, intellectual, and emotional world, and their children generally remain unaware of their intellectual capacities.

Characteristics of the Primary School Program

The primary school curriculum and the methods used in the individual school are similar throughout Brazil, even though the state is the responsible governmental unit, and, in theory, there might be considerable variation from one state to another. In general all authorities require a pupil who passes the first grade to read short passages, to compose sentences or phrases, and to do easy exercises in each of the four fundamental operations of arithmetic.

In the second year a start is made with dictation and short written compositions, and pupils are taught to solve simple arithmetical problems involving ordinary fractions and decimals and calling for an elementary understanding of the metric system of weights and measures. The pupil also starts to read short and fairly simply-phrased extracts from literature, including complete stories or tales.

In the third year the use of fractions is developed more systematically, and pupils are set more complicated problems in arithmetic requiring the handling of fractional quantities related to the metric system of weights and measures. The style of compositions becomes less descriptive and more narrative and imaginary, and pupils write short family letters. The degree of poetry reading, which started in the second grade, is widened.

In the fourth grade the arithmetic includes elementary proportion and interest. Pupils now have to write paraphrases, short explanations of simple poems, and more advanced letters.

Along with this syllabus, which is considered basic, other subjects are studied. Geography starts in the first grade with the position of the classroom in the building and of the building in the town, and proceeds through the fourth grade to the study of the *município*, the state, and Brazil itself.

History is taught in the same way, starting with the school, the town, the *município,* and the state, and going on to the principal events in Brazilian history. The natural sciences are studied by object lessons intended to give the children an understanding of the life of the plants and of the more common animals. The time devoted to science also includes certain fundamental rules of hygiene. Drawing and handwork occupy a small part of the weekly timetable. Physical education, school games, and school festivals and celebrations complete a general outline of the curriculum.

Instruction in the various aspects of the language and in arithmetic generally occupies the first 90 minutes of the school day, the remainder of the program being allotted about 180 minutes a day, including 30 minutes for recreation and lunch. In the following pages the school day is described systematically for several typical urban schools, with stress on their differences.*

Before School. The pupils use the common means of transportation to get to school, which is generally on foot. They delay their entry into the school grounds as long as possible, remaining in the vicinity of the school building in small groups. They do not form into a crowd, for this would not be permitted by the school. Five to ten minutes before the bell is rung to announce the beginning of the classes, the pupils enter the school grounds to await their entrance to the classrooms.

As a rule, in the playgrounds the pupils group themselves according to the grade or school year to which they belong. Groups of friends form among pupils in the same class, and occasionally there are groups composed of pupils from different classes.

Both in the schools in the Northeast as well as those in the South, the sexes sometimes group themselves in different *patios* (courtyards), and sometimes mingle in a common one. In all cases, however, groups engaged in sports or games consist of boys or girls only. This is explained naturally by the differ-

---

* Observations made by J. Roberto Moreira and his assistants, in Paraná, Santa Cafarina, Rio Grande do Sul, São Paulo, and Pernambuco, 1934, 1954, and 1956.

ences in athletic and playing interests among boys and girls of seven to fourteen years. The children of an earlier age generally play together, regardless of sex.

The teachers arrive at the school ten to fifteen minutes before classtime, put away their personal effects, don their *guarda pó* (smocks), and go out to the courtyard where they come in contact with the students. Generally they do not join the pupils of their own classes in a body; they come in contact with a relatively smaller group. The first effective contact between teachers and their pupils during the school day occurs inside the classroom when the former assume the responsibility for class management.

In Brazil the mingling of teachers with pupils is virtually nonexistent except in the strictly formal aspects of school activity: children and adults lead their lives separately, even during periods of close physical proximity, before the formal teaching process begins as prescribed by the school. Thus within the school itself the two generations are more or less segregated.

The bell rings signaling the beginning of the school day. The reaction to this signal varies from one school to another. In some there ensues a general tumult, as if the pupils are not very enthusiastic over the beginning of classes, since they have to give up the games or sports in which they are engaged. In other schools the signal seems to have an almost magic effect on putting an end to the noises.

Thus the schoolday is marked by something that sharply separates the natural and spontaneous life of the child from his school activity and the duties pertaining thereto. The bell or gong has the power to transform the child who was gamboling spontaneously or engaging in some sport or game, almost into an automaton—a being who reacts to certain fixed signals in a single, stereotyped, invariable pattern.

Activities Inside the Classroom. The formalism established at the beginning of the school day does not continue. Once they are in their seats the pupils gradually break through the artificial barrier; then, from time to time, the teacher deviates from her teaching tasks to appeal for order or silence. There is a murmuring, restlessness, and stirring in the classroom, increasing in volume until a certain spontaneity is established.

Some schools have established another ceremony; they begin proceedings with a patriotic or children's song. Rarely, the day is started with a prayer or an Ave Maria.

Religious instruction is given during school hours, although it is not compulsory. It may be given by the teachers themselves or by representatives from the churches. For the small numbers of Protestants, the children of several classes may be grouped together for religion.

The roll call is a regular event. Since the teacher must bend over the register and read the names, the responses of the pupils are often accompanied by some silent prank. While in certain respects rigidity of behavior is required for the children, on the other hand the pupil invents a thousand tricks, takes advantage of every possible opening to counteract such demands made upon him by the school.

A general idea of the pedagogic method can be obtained from the following example of what was done in a fourth grade class in a school in Santa Catarina. It was on a day preceding September 7, the "Independence Day" of Brazil. The observer describes the sessions of that day as follows:

As it was just prior to September 7, the teacher took advantage of the occasion to launch the language lesson with a copy of the Independence Anthem. This was designed also to further oral language study, since the anthem in question was to be read by the pupils. Of the difficult words which appeared in the song the students were given the necessary explanation; their attention was also drawn to the words in which frequent errors were committed. The teacher then turned her attention to the poetry which was to be recited on the seventh. The words which were poorly pronounced were to be repeated correctly as indicated by the teacher, precisely when the mistake was made. She then called attention to the punctuation which was to be heeded in the course of the oral presentation. The arithmetic session then followed, consisting of a review of how to find the highest common divisor and the lowest common denominator. The teacher had the pupils solve some problems entailing these arithmetic principles. This was followed by the lessons in science and in history. The latter had nothing to do with September 7, because the pupils were already studying the War with Paraguay. The science session dealt with measles; also with sound—how it was produced, its velocity and its transmission.

In the science and history classes, the teacher began with an oral exposition, and then asked questions. If the pupils did not know how to answer, she would formulate the answer and have the pupils repeat it two to five times so as to memorize it. This went on until the entire lesson had been assimilated. In the language classes she explained, asked questions, and required that the pupils give correct answers, having them repeat till the answers were on the tips of their tongues. Written exercises were also utilized, and these kept the pupils occupied mechanically. In the arithmetic lessons the exercises were as much on the blackboard as in the notebooks. On the blackboard one pupil would work out the exercise, with possible help from classmates who had been paying attention. The oral computations were regarded of great importance by the teacher, because they made it easier to solve problems. When the exercises had been copied in the notebooks, each one solved the problems by himself, with corrections being made afterwards by the teacher, who would mark with a "c" the correct answers and with an "e" those that were wrong. A half hour before the session ended, the teacher began to give out the homework. At the beginning of the day or else at the beginning of each lesson she marked *visto* [seen] on the exercises done at home. The teacher merely gave her *visto*. For that reason many pupils did not do them well. Still they might be surprised. From time to time the teacher would decide to read the exercises, and then the erring pupil was punished by forfeiting his recreation period or by being kept a half hour or more after school.[2]

Corporal punishment is prohibited in the Brazilian schools. How then can the teacher induce the children to submit to a rigid formalism which they might be expected naturally to resist? The school has at its disposal other coercive devices than corporal punishment. Such as loss of the recreation period and being kept in after school. Some teachers dominate the class by their severity, by keeping the students at a distance, by their capacity to enforce their authority by speaking in a loud voice, or through some other mode of punishment which, while not physical, exposes the pupils to something disagreeable and distasteful to the transgressor. For example, to have to go to the office of the principal who might in turn report the misbehavior of the pupil to his parents, who are not inhibited from inflicting corporal punishment, can be most effective. Furthermore, the punishment may assume the form of social disapproval from his comrades as well as from the adults in his environment, if his behavior results in low grades and failure at the end of the year.

STRESS ON VERBAL INTELLIGENCE. Possibly related to the formalism and the emphasis on memorizing in the schools is the tendency in Brazilian schools to place a premium on the verbal aspect of intelligence. The teachers who were observed in action tended to favor pupils who could speak and write easily and who had good memories for language. Pupils who are quick-witted and fertile-minded but lack verbal facility are not valued highly. Those who can use their hands skilfully may find the teacher saying, "You loafer! You are only good for becoming a teamster! You are no good for studying!" This is in keeping with the generally low value placed on manual work.

When teachers speak about great men or successful men to their pupils, they tend to use examples of the liberal professions—the lawyer, the physician, the university professor. One of the most highly honored heroes of Brazil in the third and fourth grade curriculum is Ruy Barbosa, and the things about him which are stressed are his intellectuality, his easy eloquence with words, his ability to discourse brilliantly on many and varied topics. His other great qualities are seldom mentioned—his political and social philosophy and his worth as a man of action in a time when his country needed deeds more than words.

SOCIAL RELATIONS AMONG PUPILS. The relations between adults and children in the school are rigidly formal; likewise the methods of teaching do not encourage cooperation or any other kind of social interaction among pupils. Yet social relations do exist, as they must in any society. These social relations do not have great educative value because the teachers do not use them for this purpose, and the school program is not designed to encourage or to profit from socially organized effort on the part of the pupils.

There are several types of social relations in the Brazilian schools, none of which is officially recognized or deliberately cultivated. One such group is the neighborhood group of children who live in the same small area. They come to school and go home together, playing on the way. They have a range of ages, and they tend to be homogeneous in social class. This group exists independently of the school, and is relatively un-affected by it.

An informal and almost embryonic kind of group is the "rivalry group." In a class there may be two or more groups of the brighter students, who tend to compete with each other for the teacher's attention. Each group tends to throw its resources behind one or two leaders who are expected to know all the right answers. This results in a kind of cooperation which the teacher cannot tolerate. The members of a group help their champion if he needs help. They come to his aid in the case of an oral examination, or when he is reprimanded by the teacher. At such times one becomes aware of a curious activity, accompanied by a more or less subdued commotion among the children, who, with notebook or textbook hidden under the desk, try to whisper the answers to their leader. On the other hand, a rival group may denounce these actions to the teacher. Thus it becomes a kind of game which the children play with each other and with the teachers, and which is limited to the classroom. These intellectual champions may have no prestige at all on the playground or in the going-home and coming-to-school activities.

Another type of social relation is organized around the *amiguinhos* or teachers' pets. These pupils enjoy special privileges from the teacher, for any of a variety of reasons. They make it a point to accompany her when she comes to school or on her way home from school. They bask in the sunshine of her smile, despite the criticism of the other children. When their teacher is absent these children are forlorn, until they can establish such a relationship with the new teacher.

Still another type of social role which the school seems to engender is that of the *bagunceiro*, the trouble-maker. These children exist in almost all classrooms. They are not easy to talk with because they are suspicious and timid with strangers. Often they are an active, restless type, and sometimes they lack adequate affection and attention at home. Generally they are no better than average in their school work, and if they have manual skills, such as designing or modeling, these are not highly valued in the school. They may be good at sports, and they often get some reluctant admiration from their classmates through their pranks and their clowning.

Finally, there are small upper-class groups of children, who dress better than the others and have manners that suggest social superiority. They always have money in their pockets which they spend in the school canteen. This group is generally accepted by the other children without resentment, and their gifts of candy and paper and pencils are gratefully received.

PRIMARY EDUCATION IN THE STATE OF SÃO PAULO. This description of primary schools will be concluded with a summary of a survey made by Professor Renato Jardim Moreira of the primary schools of the state of São Paulo, where primary education is more widespread than in any other state.[3]

About 1920, the authorities of the state of São Paulo decided to attempt to offer primary school education to all children. At that time, 26 per cent of children aged 7 through 14 were in primary school; this percentage increased to 67 by 1958, which meant that all children attended school, and the vast majority attended for at least four years. Most of the increase was taken up by public schools, which gained 600 per cent while private schools increased only 64 per cent. Private primary schools almost disappeared in the rural areas during this period. The rapid increase in enrollment resulted in overcrowded schools. To meet the demand for classrooms, in 1928 one school was placed on a double shift, and this "emergency action" soon became customary for practically all urban schools, as can be seen in Table 25. Half of the urban state schools gave the pupils three hours or less of schooling per day. In the private and municipal schools of the city of São Paulo, between 20 and 25 per cent of the pupils had three hours or less per school day. The median number of pupils per class in state schools increased from 25.5 in 1935 to 38.1 in 1959.

TABLE 25

Number of Shifts or School Groups Per Day in Urban Schools in the State of São Paulo

Schools with:	1 or 2 shifts	3 shifts	4 shifts
1936	525	102	1
1957	1,007	472	30

Even today equipment for the schools is scanty. Audio-visual aids are almost unknown and textbooks are uninteresting.

The director of the school may be responsible for the work of twenty, thirty, or even fifty classroom teachers. The state

TABLE 26

Distribution of Primary School Pupils Among the Four Grades in the State of São Paulo

Grade		Enrollments	
		1934	1959
1	Absolute No.	208,105	480,748
	Relative No.	100	100
2		49	78
3		27	57
4		16	38

school inspectors generally have to supervise the work of about two hundred teachers, working in more than a hundred different schools in three counties.

Still the schools have improved their record of holding and of promoting pupils as can be seen in Table 26. They need new buildings, a program of active supervision to stimulate and assist the classroom teachers, and an integrated program of education for the state, based on studies of the needs of the state for urban and rural schools, primary and secondary.

The Functions of Primary Schools

As stated by the Congress of 1946, the functions of the primary schools are (1) to initiate all persons into the life of the nation and the practice of the moral and civic virtues by which the national life is maintained; (2) to give all children between the ages of 7 and 12 an opportunity for a balanced mental training and personality development; and (3) to teach knowledge that will improve family life, individual health, and occupational competence.

This Congress also established that basic primary education be governed by the following principles: (a) it should develop systematically and gradually in accordance with the natural interests of childhood; (b) its teaching should be based on the pupil's own activities; (c) it should be related to the realities of the environment in which it is given, so that it may assist pupils to appreciate that environment more fully and to use it more profitably; (d) it should cultivate the spirit of cooperation and the sentiment of social brotherhood; (e) it should reveal the individual bents and aptitudes of pupils and contribute to the better use of these for the good of the individual and of society; (f) it should be governed in all its aspects by the principle of national unity and the brotherhood of man.

Brazil regards primary education as an experience that is good for the individual and the society. Literacy is seen as having good consequences beyond that of making the individual a more productive worker. Combined with knowledge about history, literature, health, and geography, literacy should make the Brazilian a better family member and a better citizen.

Still, there are certainly important economic consequences of literacy, and Brazil is seeking to improve itself economically through the spread of literacy. Among the countries that are in the process of industrialization and urbanization, there is a close relation between literacy and economic production. For example, a study of seventy countries with 85 per cent of the world's population showed a correlation coefficient of .84 between the degree of literacy and the per capita income.[4] The same kind of computation for the Latin American countries shows a correlation coefficient of .75.

The major criticism of Brazilian primary education is that it has not been effectively universal either in its goal of making the society completely literate or in its goal of teaching to all people the knowledge necessary for good citizenship, good health, and good family life. Although by the middle of the current century the primary school was enrolling all but the most isolated children (geographically or culturally), the majority of these children were not going beyond the second grade. They could hardly be said to be literate.

Anísio Teixeira has pointed out that the Brazilian primary school is a *selective* institution, rather than a *comprehensive* one. The primary school is conducted as if its principal task were to screen the intellectual elite and to pass them on through the primary grades to the secondary school, while keeping large numbers of other students in the first grade for all of their school life, as a sign that they have not been "chosen." Teixeira and other educational leaders have argued for some such procedure as a grouping of children in school by chronological age, or by number of years in school, perhaps with subgroups based on achievement in school subjects. They propose a kind of automatic promotion, or at least a far more generous system of promotion, which would reduce the number of failures and repetitions of a grade to somewhere between 10–20 per cent of an age group. They argue that children will learn more if the teachers and the schools take it as their job to succeed in teaching the children in accord with their abilities rather than to select only a few for the symbol of success and to treat the others as though they were useless. To the criticism that this proposal is a "lowering of standards," Teixeira and his allies argue that the bright children can learn as much or more than they do now, while the average and slow children will learn more if they are treated as persons who can learn. Thus, they claim, the standards of pupil achievement will actually be raised.

DEVELOPMENT OF PRIMARY EDUCATION IN THE 1960's. At the beginning of the decade of the 1960's, a policy for the expansion of primary education was formulated, and by the end of 1962 substantial efforts were being made to put this policy into effect. The major element in the new policy was the entension of the primary schools to five and eventually to six years. As new buildings became available, the new classes were added and the fifth year was made obligatory. The sixth year is to become the equivalent of the first year of the seven-year secondary school. Thus the basis is being laid for a 6–3–3 plan of school education. The Ministry of Education announced that the goal for 1970 was to get 100 per cent of the children aged 12 to 14 into the fifth and sixth grades of the primary school or into the first two years of the secondary school.

Rural Schools and Fundamental Education

We have already seen that the rural Brazil is, for the most part, backward educationally. Even in the areas where there is agricultural wealth—in sugar, coffee, cattle, wine, and grain-producing areas—the agricultural economy generally consists of large estates with poorly-paid and illiterate workers. The rural workers live in isolated houses or possibly in collections of twenty to fifty houses on a fazenda. If there is a school for their children, it is usually one room in which pupils of all ages and grades are taught by a single teacher. The rural schools are generally municipal schools, which means that they are ill equipped, with inferior teachers who are poorly paid (see p. 157). Most of the pupils come from very poor homes, their parents are illiterate, and they get very little educational stimulation from their homes, either by example or by precept.

There are exceptions to these general statements. In some areas of relatively prosperous single-family farms, generally in the southern states, the parents are comparatively well educated and the rural schools are fairly good. Sometimes the wife or daughter of a plantation owner teaches in the school where the employees' children go, and she may do a better job than the average city teacher. And there are sure to be a few children in every school who learn quickly and well, even with poor teaching.

Secondary schools are almost nonexistent in the rural areas. A rural child might have to travel as far as fifty miles to get to the nearest secondary school. Although a few children live close to the other towns where schools are located, in most cases the only rural children who get to secondary school are those who can live with relatives in town or those whose parents can transport them every day to the town. There are no systems of free transportation to school for rural youth.

THE NEED FOR AGRARIAN REFORM. Brazilian educators have concluded that the rural primary schools cannot be basically improved until the standard of living in rural Brazil is substantially raised. They believe that agrarian reform is essential to achieve this goal. Agrarian reform in Brazil would include the breaking up of many large estates, the selling of land to individual farmers, and the assisting of these farmers to use more productive methods. These changes would end the vicious circle in which the rural laborers and the Brazilian economy are caught. Twenty million rural people live on a mere subsistence level; they produce little, sell little, buy little, and take little part in the national economy. If they can produce more, they can sell more and buy more, and thus enlarge the market for Brazilian manufacturers, while at the same time producing more raw materials for the manufacturers and providing more food for the expanding city population.

A North American rural sociologist, T. Lynn Smith, has described Brazil's need for agrarian reform and its relation to education as follows:

Explicitly or implicitly, or so it seems to the writer, three broad and basic objectives seem to be involved in most proposals and programs of agrarian reform. These may be stated rather simply as follows: (1) A genuine agrarian reform should effect substantial improvement in the abilities, capacities, and performances of those who cultivate the land to bring them more in line with human potentialities. (2) Any worth-while agrarian reform should result in a substantial increase in the amount of agricultural and livestock products secured from a given amount of land and the efforts of those who work it. (3) A real agrarian reform should result in the replacement of wasteful, inefficient, bemeaning, and stultifying ways of producing agricultural and livestock products by methods of agriculture that are efficient, that husband human energy, and that may be considered as uplifting, dignifying, or ennobling to those engaged in agriculture and stock raising.

.   .   .   .

Through education, training, and experience, the ordinary man who works the land must be developed into a person who is capable of exercising with considerable facility the functions of the manager or entrepreneur and those of the capitalist or property owner, as well as those of the agricultural laborer. Each farmer must come to combine in his own personality all the attitudes, skills, and habits that go with the performance of the three basic economic functions of which the economist writes, namely that of the capitalist, that of the manager, and that of the laborer. In brief, this means teaching, encouraging and enabling each future agriculturist to develop all the qualities, skills, characteristics, attitudes, and habits of the middle-class farmer.

.   .   .   .

It is just as simple as that—these agriculturists need to learn how to farm. And this can come about only if there is throughout a country a far greater emphasis upon education in general and agricultural and mechanical training in particular than generally has been true throughout the past. Changes are involved that will result in a much more sparing use of labor in the productive process, a far greater use of draft animals and machinery, and, probably most important of all, far more extensive and effective applications of managerial skills in the conduct of the ordinary farm business. The primitive and abhorrently wasteful system of *derrubadas e queimadas* which is employed throughout most of Brazil, and the labor-devouring hoe culture which is the main reliance in most of the zones of commercial production, must be replaced by ways of farming in which the labor of the ordinary man enters into a more fruitful combination. This means the universal use of considerable horsepower and well-designed implements in preparing the seedbed, planting the crops, controlling the weeds, gathering the harvest, processing the products, and transporting the farm produce to market. Brazil and most of the other countries can and should improve the efficiency of their rural labor forces to the point at which no more than 40 per cent of a nation's population is needed to produce the food, fiber, and raw materials needed by her entire population plus a substantial volume for export.

.   .   .   .

. . . each *município*, or county, in order to retain status as such, and each new one established subsequently, should be required to maintain at least one publicly supported secondary school with a minimum of five full-time teachers. Such schools should offer instruction in the usual subjects, such as language, literature, mathematics, geography, and history; and, in addition, they should provide elementary courses in general agriculture, mechanics, and home economics. It definitely [is] not intended to establish agricultural and mechanical schools in which the instruction would be widely different from that in other secondary schools, and whose graduates would be ineligible to enter universities for further training . . . . it [is] intended that instruction in agriculture, mechanics, and home economics be accepted as a part of the general education needed by the ordinary citizen.[5]

Something like the proposal just cited is being started by the Banco de Nordeste, in cooperation with the United Nations

Food and Agriculture Organization. It is a supervised loan and socioeconomic service to middle-sized and small landowners in the Northeast. ANCAR (Northeast Association for Rural Credit and Social Service) helps the farmer study the soil and the potentialities of his land, offers him a bank loan to cover the costs of a reasonable program of improvement, gives technical advice on the program, and offers social services to help the farmer's family improve its home situation. The loan and the interest are repaid as the land increases its productivity, and the cost of technical advice and social services is paid from state and federal subsidies and from small fees paid by the farmers. ANCAR has also encouraged the organization of producers' cooperatives to facilitate the purchase of seeds, fertilizers, machinery, and fuel.

It is estimated that in 1958 330 million acres out of 530 million of productive land in Brazil were under private ownership but were not being used for cultivation. Thus it appears that 5 to 10 million farmers could be provided with land in units sufficient to guarantee them a reasonable living if a program of agrarian reform were carried out.

Education alone will not do much for rural life; rather it may serve to denude the rural areas of population. Allied with an educational program must be a program to increase rural productivity and to improve the economic and cultural opportunities of rural life.

CAMPAIGNS AGAINST ILLITERACY. Since the 1950 census, which revealed that half of the adult population was illiterate, Brazil has been officially committed to incessant campaigns for the extension of literacy. The first major campaign, mounted in 1947, with the title "Campanha de Educação de Adultos," took the form of appeals to organizations in local communities to start schools for adults, with the promise that the Ministry of Education would provide teaching materials and technical advice. Eventually some 17,200 evening schools were established. Slide projectors and filmstrips were distributed, together with simple reading material for adults.

The name of this program was changed to "Campaign for Education of Adolescents and Adults," and it was continued throughout the 1950's. However, a critical evaluation in 1957 indicated that it had gradually lost much of its drive. At that time the program was reorganized with an emphasis on work in communities with more than 5,000 population, while the "Na-

tional Campaign for Rural Education" took over the responsibility for literacy teaching in rural areas. Between 1956 and 1960
the reports of the Campaign for Education of Adolescents and
Adults show an average of 113,000 people were taught to read
each year.

Another program has been promoted largely by the Roman
Catholic bishops under the name "Movement for Basic Education." With support from the Ministry of Education and from
private sources, the bishops have shown imagination and energy
in working with rural people. One aspect of this movement
has involved the use of radio programs to teach illiterates. Bishop
Dom Eugenio Sales of Rio Grande do Norte has established a
program known as "Serviço de Asistencia Rural" which broad-
casts a variety of educational and religious programs during the
daytime, and after five o'clock in the afternoon gives a series of
three or four lessons graded for reading ability. The essential
element in this program is the small study group consisting of
ten to twenty persons led by a monitor, who gather in a home
or other suitable place for their class meeting. The monitor has
a small blackboard and a few simple teaching materials, including readers. The group listens to the lesson broadcast by an
experienced teacher; they work the exercises under the supervision of the monitor, and eventually they take examinations to
test their proficiency in relation to what the public schools
expect at the end of the first, second, third, and fourth years of
primary school. The monitor is usually a young woman who
hopes to attend a normal school and become a teacher. Her
group consists mainly of young people aged 13 to 25. They form
a social group as well as a school class, and thus they stimulate
one another to attend regularly and to do their school work.

Each new president seems to feel the necessity of starting a
campaign against illiteracy, giving it a new name to distinguish it
from that of his predecessor. Thus, President Janio Quadros,
only a week before his resignation, ceremonially launched the
"Mobilização Nacional Contra a Analfabetismo," in the presence
of ten state governors, the mayor of Brasília, and the archbishop
of Rio de Janeiro.

Just five years earlier, President Juscelino Kubitschek had
asked the Ministry of Education to set up a program to eradicate
illiteracy. The committee working in the ministry reported that
educational procedures alone could not remove the social and
economic causes of illiteracy, but they drew up plans for an

experimental program of intensive education in several pilot projects, and these projects were started in 1958 with the title, "National Campaign to Eradicate Illiteracy." The Director of the project was J. Roberto Moreira.

Three areas were selected for pilot projects: Leopoldina in the state of Minas Gerais (East), Timbaúba in the state of Pernambuco (Northeast), and Catalão in the state of Goiás (Central West). Each area was a municipal center together with its rural district. The three areas had about the same population, but the rural and urban elements were differently distributed. Leopoldina is more industrialized and its rural areas are more developed. Timbaúba has a very large poor urban area, a sizeable marginal population, and the beginnings of industrialization; its rural area has many sugar cane plantations. Catalão is more agricultural, being the municipal center and mainly a small marketplace of a rural district; but its future seems to be excellent because it is not far from Brasília, the new capital of Brazil.

The project first made a rapid and complete survey of the area, with emphasis on economic activities, labor possibilities and trends, social structure and stratification, cultural patterns, and educational facilities. It then initiated a campaign to get the support of the local people and to help them accept the responsibility of making decisions about the proposed plans. After establishing the main lines of the project in accordance with the opinions and choices of local people, it made objective checks on the experiment in order to evaluate results and in order to correct mistakes, readjust methods, and forecast further consequences. In all three areas it appeared necessary:

1. To enlarge the existent elementary school system in order to enroll all the population from 7 to 12 years of age in an elementary school of five grades, and to provide emergency classrooms and emergency education for youth of more than 12 and less than 16 years of age who had had no opportunity to attend school.

2. To organize the elementary schools in such a way that all pupils, even the most retarded ones, would progress from grade to grade without the failure and repetition that has been so common in Brazil.

3. To reconstruct the elementary school curriculum in terms of local conditions and possibilities, changing the abstractness of the teaching into a more concrete set of activities incorporating local facts and local meanings.

4. To provide complementary prevocational schools both in rural and urban areas.

5. To change as far as possible the rural schools into social centers, where not only children but all local people could have a place for meetings to study and discuss their problems.

6. To organize a system of basic adult education, capable of leading the rural people to accept and practice more productive agricultural and cattle raising activities.

7. To provide places and means for training rural teachers, selected from the rural population, and to equip them with knowledge and skills to lead rural people toward improved health conditions, home economics, and work conditions.

8. To cooperate so far as possible with rural organizations and to seek technical assistance from the Ministry of Agriculture in the program of basic education.

9. Wherever possible to organize special classes for illiterate adults, and to search for appropriate teaching methods for these classes.

10. To make full use of parent-teacher associations, clubs, recreational organizations, and a citizenship education program.

The projects were pushed ahead with considerable enthusiasm by the people in the towns and rural areas. The expanded school system was popular, and the teachers improved greatly as a result of a simple in-service educational program.

Though a definitive evaluation of these projects has not yet been completed, it appears clear that the projects succeeded in encouraging local people to care about education and take responsibility for making choices and decisions concerning an educational program. However, a major reservation remains concerning the results of this program in improving the conditions of rural life. The gains there were probably not sufficient enough to make life in these communities attractive enough to prevent people who had made educational progress from migrating to urban areas—to a higher economic life and better living conditions.

While slow progress is being made toward the reduction of illiteracy, it seems doubtful that an educational program alone will accomplish much in this direction. Illiteracy is a part of a complex of rural poverty and backwardness that can be resolved only by economic changes that make literacy valuable to rural people.

NOTES

1. Moyses Kessel, "A Evasão Escolar no Ensino Primário," *Revista Brasileira de Estudos Pedagógicos*, XXII, No. 56 (Oct.-Nov. 1954), 52–72.

2. J. Roberto Moreira, unpublished notes.

3. Renato Jardim Moreira, "O Ensino Primário Paulista," *Revista Brasileira de Estudos Pedagógicos*, XXIV, No. 80 (Oct.-Dec. 1960), 219–31.

4. Hilda Hertz Golden, "Literacy and Social Change in Underdeveloped Countries," *Rural Sociology*, XX (Mar. 1955), 1–7.

5. T. Lynn Smith, *Current Trends and Problems in Latin America*, Latin American Monographs, No. 1 (Gainesville, Florida, 1957), pp. 34–40. Quoted by permission of the publishers, University of Florida Press.

9

Secondary
and Higher Education
and their
Functions

THE most striking educational development in Brazil since 1930 has been the creation and the growth of a system of secondary and higher education. Thus, while Brazil still has the uncompleted task of developing a primary school system to make the nation literate, it works at the same time through its secondary schools and universities to make the nation more politically competent and economically productive. Table 27 shows that secondary schools multiplied their enrollments by ten, between 1930 and 1960, while universities and other higher institutions multiplied five- to sixfold.

TABLE 27

Secondary School and Higher Education Enrollments in Relation to Total Population and to Population of Appropriate Age

Year	Secondary Education			Higher Education		
	Enroll-ment in all second-ary schools	Number enrolled per 1,000 population	Number enrolled per 1,000 aged 11-17	Enroll-ment in higher institutions	Number enrolled per 1,000 population	Number enrolled per 1,000 aged 18-21
1910	—			8,000	0.35	4.4
1930	90,000	2.7	17	17,000	0.51	6.3
1940	227,000	5.5	35	19,000	0.45	5.8
1950	493,000	9.5	60	45,000	0.87	10.7
1959	980,000	14.6	90	87,000	1.30	16.7
1960	1,050,000	15.3	96	95,000	1.37	17.4
1961	1,220,000	17.2	109	102,000	1.44	18.1
1962	1,460,000	19.5	130	—	—	—

Note: Enrollment figures are those for the last month of the school year.

We have already seen that Brazil's middle class has grown rapidly during the twentieth century, as the society became more urbanized and industrialized. The expansion of secondary and higher education was both a result and a cause of this transformation in the society.

Social Functions of Secondary Education

During the Imperial and early Republican periods, secondary education in Brazil had two principal and related functions. It gave the members of the elite a humanistic education which helped them carry on their role of leadership in the social and political life of the nation; and it gave them a means of maintaining the social status into which they were born. A secondary education was a mark of a gentleman—a symbol of upper- or at least upper middle-class status. It assisted the upper and upper middle class families to raise their children "properly" and pass their social status on to the children.

As the society became industrialized, secondary education was called upon to perform two other societal functions: (1) to give young people the general knowledge and technical skills they would need to become productive members of a technological society; and (2) to prepare a substantial group of lower-class and lower-middle-class youth for positions in the rapidly expanding middle classes. An illustration of the joint working of these two functions can be seen in the story of a working-class girl from the South.*

Alicia attracted the attention of her teachers because she was a serious and hard-working girl of fifteen years. She was obviously from a poor home, for she wore the same dress to school, night after night. Her father worked intermittently at unskilled labor, and drank too much. Her mother was in poor health. The large family lived in a hovel next to the railroad. Their main source of income were Alicia's wages as a factory worker and those of her sister.

---

* From an account written by Dalilla C. Sperb, Executive Secretary of the Centro Regional de Pesquisas Educacionais in Pôrto Alegre, who founded an evening secondary school in a small industrial city. The school functioned for thirteen years, when the city finally obtained a state-supported school. During these years, among the graduates of the night school were a medical doctor, two lawyers, eleven primary school teachers and a number of bank employees.

Working eight hours a day and attending secondary school three hours in the evening, Alicia completed the three-year course in two years. With the assistance of the school, she changed from her factory job to one in an office; and shortly afterward she began work in a bank. She succeeded in her new jobs—partly because in school she had learned to dress better and to get along socially with her teachers and colleagues. She became an attractive and outgoing young woman.

At the age of eighteen Alicia passed a difficult examination for entrance to a higher commercial school in a large city nearby. She completed this course and then qualified for a job with good pay in the government of her home town. Her first act was to move her family into a comfortable apartment in a good part of the town, giving the younger children a chance to attend better schools. Success in secondary school and then in a school of commerce gave Alicia a self-assurance that enabled her to move easily among middle-class people.

Although Alicia's experience has been repeated thousands of times, it has been limited because educational opportunity is scarce and educational performance is low in the lower class of Brazil. Alicia is one of a minority of lower-class children who succeeded in primary school and were lucky enough and ambitious enough to get into a secondary school.

The social class composition of secondary school students is not known with much certainty, but in 1960 only 20 per cent of an age cohort were entering secondary schools and only 4 per cent were graduating, which indicates that secondary school students are a select group, and probably a select group on the basis of socioeconomic status. One factor that tends to assure socioeconomic selectivity in secondary schools is the requirement of passing an entrance examination. The fourth grade of the primary school does not prepare a child very well for this examination. Normally, a pupil who expects to go on to secondary school will continue through the fifth grade (but many schools do not offer a fifth grade) , or will have a private tutor or attend private class to assist him in preparing for the examination. Furthermore, public secondary schools are often not available, and the government grants for tuition fees for poor but able students went to only 40,000 boys and girls in 1960.

One study indicates that only 8 per cent of a sample of students in the fourth year of the *ginásio* were from working-class homes.

These were day students in seventeen of the eighty-seven secondary schools existing in the city of São Paulo in 1948, when the study was made. The sampling was intended to be representative of São Paulo schools, but the study did not cover night schools, which enroll many working-class youth. Also, there are probably more working-class youth in the academic secondary school at present, since the secondary school enrollment has grown substantially since 1948.[1]

About 1930, when the secondary school system began to grow rapidly, there were two possibilities for its development. One was for the traditional school to continue with enough modification and adaptation to serve the new societal functions fairly well, though not as well as the proponents of educational reform would wish. The alternative was to create one or more new types of secondary schools. Both possibilities have been tried, and the result is the present system of secondary education.

Present Structure of Secondary Education

The main body of pupils enter the *ginásio* at the age of 11 to 14, the most frequent age being 12. The *ginásio*, with a four-year course, and the colégio which follows with a three-year course, make up what is called the secondary school, while the other middle-level schools supplement the traditional secondary school to make up *ensino médio*. The two sexes are approximately equal in numbers. Table 28 compares the enrollments in the various schools and shows how enrollment falls off with the increasing age of the students. This drop in enrollment is especially marked between the fourth and the fifth years, in the regular secondary school, and is caused partly by a substantial shift of pupils from the *ginásio* to one of the vocational schools. Thus the secondary schools with an explicit vocational orientation have a majority of the students from the fifth year on.

The commercial schools prepare students for white-collar jobs and for certain trades. There are schools of stenography, radio electronics, elevator maintenance, sewing and dressmaking, commercial Portuguese, English, secretarial work, and others emphasizing specific skills. Most of them are in private hands and many are maintained by philanthropic or religious organizations. Tuition fees are generally moderate. These schools are found in all cities with a population of 20,000 or more.

Few official statistics are available concerning these schools, but a survey of two Rio de Janeiro newspapers published in July

TABLE 28

Distribution of Students in *Various Types of Secondary Schools*
(beginning with a group aged twelve years)

	Total no. of children in group in year	Passed fourth or fifth grade	Entered a secondary school [a]	Graduated from a four-year course	Entered second cycle of secondary school [b]	Graduated from secondary cycle	Entered a university	Graduated from a university
	1950	1948 or 1949	1950	1953	1954	1956	1957	1960
	1,260,000	228,000	158,000	70,000	83,000	47,500	23,000	16,000
Type of secondary school — Academic			126,000	58,000	36,000	17,300		
Commercial			16,000*	5,500	22,000	13,200		
Normal			10,000*	4,000*	23,500	16,500		
Industrial			5,000*	2,000*	1,200*	480		
Agricultural			500	300	130	—		
	1952	1950 or 1951	1952	1955	1956 [b]	1958	1959	
	1,320,000	254,000	183,000	81,000	89,000	53,200	25,700	
Type of secondary school — Academic			150,000	68,600	38,400	19,200		
Commercial			17,500*	6,600	26,300	15,300		
Normal			10,000*	4,000*	22,200	18,100		
Industrial			5,000*	2,100	1,400	600		
Agricultural •			500	300	180	600		

[a] A number of children entered secondary schools without formally passing fourth or fifth grades of primary school.

[b] A number of students dropped out of the academic secondary school and entered either commercial or normal school. This number also includes some students who were repeating the first year of the second cycle.

• Agricultural school has a duration of five years.

* Estimated; actual data not available.

1958 showed that 218 such schools or practical courses were advertised. These may be grouped under five categories: (1) commercial training schools (30 per cent); (2) trade schools (20 per cent); (3) those specializing in training for small industry and business services (10 per cent); instruction in business Portuguese and English (25 per cent); and secretarial training (15 per cent). In 1954 a similar survey, involving three newspapers in Porto Alegre, capital of Rio Grande do Sul, found 112 such practical courses advertised.

Normal schools are especially popular for girls, and are found in close connection with regular secondary schools in many municipal centers with a population of 5,000 to 50,000. The normal school is a secondary school with two cycles, parallel to the two cycles of the *ginásio* and colégio; but many students transfer from the *ginásio* to the second cycle of the normal school. In some states the normal school consists of one three-year cycle which follows the *ginásio*. In addition to preparing a person for a position as a primary school teacher, the normal school satisfies one of the entrance requirements to a university and thus has a double advantage for a middle-class girl or one who aspires to middle-class position: she can go to work at the end of the normal school or she can continue her studies in a university. The normal school probably should be classed with the academic secondary school, being more general and humanistic in its curriculum than the vocational school.

The industrial secondary school has made relatively little headway in Brazil. Its expensive equipment has discouraged private enterprise from entering this field. Since there is a need for technicians the government has encouraged industrial schools, and they exist in the major cities, supported by the state or federal government; but they have not proved popular.

However, as a means of meeting the manpower needs of a growing economy, Brazilian industry and business support and administer a type of technical school outside of the regular system. Such schools were provided for by a clause in the constitution of 1946 which requires industrial and commercial enterprises employing more than a hundred persons to provide schooling for their employees and the employees' children. These enterprises must pay a special tax into a fund administered by the National Federation of Industry and by the National Federation of Commerce.

Two administrative services were set up to conduct schools

for these organizations—Serviço Nacional de Aprendizagem Industrial (or Comercial) —generally known as SENAI and SENAC. The schools organized by these services are located in the major cities and smaller industrial towns. They provide courses for employees of local industry and business, and for adolescents, the latter serving a type of apprenticeship. Under this program young people aged 14 to 18 alternate between school and work. In 1949 about 40,000 students were enrolled in these schools. By 1955 the number had grown to 60,000 and in 1959 to 80,000.

Thus it appears that when the official school system does not meet certain needs for economic development, society can create new types of education outside the system. Meanwhile, the official policy of the Brazilian government continues to be directed toward expansion of industrial schools at the secondary level.

Secondary schools for training agricultural technicians have been in existence since about 1940. They parallel the regular secondary schools and are maintained by the federal or state government, generally as residential institutions. In 1960 there were fifty such schools, with a capacity of about 20,000 students,

TABLE 29

Growth of Enrollments in Secondary Schools

Year		Academic secondary	Commercial	Normal	Industrial	Agricultural	Total
		Enrollments (1950 = 100)					
1931		12	25	51	—	—	—
1935		23	30	66	16	—	—
1940		42	63	63	25	—	—
1945		63	110	58	86	—	—
1950	Absolute No.	407,000	76,000	33,000	19,000	4,500	540,000
	Relative No.	100	100	100	100	100	100
1951		108	108	113	97	88	108
1952		115	113	127	95	86	114
1953		126	125	146	97	105	126
1954		137	138	165	100	113	137
1955		148	154	180	103	109	149
1956		159	170	195	102	80	160
1957		171	189	230	109	98	174
1958		181	204	233	106	98	184
1959		195	225	244	115	127	199
1960		213	245	275	113	149	218
1961		237	274	300	158	150	242

Note: Figures are for *matricula inicial,* the total number of names on the school records at the beginning of the year.

but an enrollment of only about 6,000. These schools appeal to the interests of a few progressive farmers and middle-class residents in the rural districts who see a chance for their sons to get employment as agricultural technicians on large, modernized farms. But the curriculum of the ordinary secondary school in a rural area offers nothing to teach sons and daughters of farmers the techniques of becoming better farmers; there is no instruction in agriculture or home-management.

The system of secondary education, as shown in Table 29, continues to be dominated by the academic secondary school, with some students moving out of the general courses into occupational-training courses as they reach their middle teens. However, the more popular schools with an occupational training value are the normal and commercial schools which lead to a white-collar job or on to the university.

The secondary schools perform four functions: (1) they give boys and girls the knowledge and attitudes that will make them better members of society; (2) they give them the knowledge and skills that will make them more productive workers; (3) they help middle- and upper-class youth maintain their social status; and (4) they enable a growing minority of working-class and lower-middle-class youth to move up in the social scale.

The Future Shape of Secondary Education in Brazil

By 1960 the great majority of pupils who continued beyond the primary school entered the *ginásio* at the age of 12 to 14, and stayed there either for the full four-year course or dropped out of school. At about the age of 16 the decision about choosing a vocation became pressing enough to move a substantial group out of the general academic course to one of the vocationally-oriented courses that led toward a job but kept the way open to the continuation of studies in the university. This alternative was a good temporary solution of the problem of secondary education, since only about 20 per cent of youth were entering secondary school and only 4 per cent were graduating. They would be absorbed by the labor force which was thirsty for any kind of educated manpower.

But the society could use at least twice this number of secondary school graduates, and the economic development of Brazil calls for a doubling of the secondary enrollment. Although any effort to increase the enrollment of industrial and agricultural schools will probably meet the same cold reception that was evident between 1950 and 1960, the number of sons of workers and farmers entering the secondary school will increase sub-stantially. From them may come many of the students who want a secondary education with an industrial emphasis.

Yet it seems likely that the traditional academic secondary school, with some modifications, will continue to be the major element in secondary education. This will meet with approval in Brazil for several reasons. Because of the prevailing prejudice against manual labor, most people prefer the academic school to a school for training in technology or manual skill. The traditional secondary school has the function of maintaining middle- and upper-class status, and working-class youth who wish to move up the social scale believe that such a course, if it is good for the elite of the society, will be useful to them in their effort to im-prove their social status. Also, in the near future, parents will want their eleven and twelve-year-old children to enter the aca-demic secondary school because this will not commit them to an early decision about a career; they will be free to wait at least until the age of fifteen or sixteen before making a decision. Another consideration is that employers favor the humanistic, academic-type of secondary school on the ground that successful mastery of the curriculum indicates a "good mind" and good mental habits, and therefore is a good predictor of success on a job. And, finally, those who think of the possibility of attending a university will continue to choose an academic secondary school.

This analysis of the Brazilian attitudes toward secondary schools is supported by a study of the type of occupation parents desire for their children. In a sample of parents from all social classes, both urban and rural, in the state of Rio de Janeiro, 38 per cent expressed a preference for the liberal professions, and only 9 per cent for office, technical, or manual work; 21 per cent expressed a preference for a government job, teaching, or a military career; another 16 per cent thought the children them-selves should decide; and 12 per cent had no definite preference. Thus, the vast majority of those who had a definite opinion about the future occupation of their children expressed a preference for careers based on an academic secondary school education.

It seems likely that the *ginásio*, or the unit of the secondary school for ages 11 or 12 to 15 or 16, will become standard for almost all students in Brazil. Its curriculum content may be modified to reduce some of the emphasis on literature and language and to make it a more "active" and exploratory type of educational experience. There may be more emphasis on the teaching of the natural sciences and the social studies.

One evidence that change may come about in the *ginásio* is the effort begun in 1961 to establish with federal financial support a new type of junior secondary school known as the *ginásio industrial*, a four-year school with required courses in Portuguese, mathematics, general science, English, history and geography of Brazil, drawing, and six to ten hours a week of shop work. If this type of school should receive substantial government support, it might rival the *ginásio humanístico*, and it might also become accepted, without Latin, as a prerequisite to the scientific course in the colégio, and thus permit a student to qualify for university entrance without studying the classics.

The period immediately after passage of the Educational Foundations Law in 1961 has seen several types of experimentation with the curriculum, especially at the *ginásio* level and also at the colégio level, since the law permits a variety of curricula. Some curricula do not require Latin. Some have moved in the direction of the "activity" curriculum found in many North American schools, with units of study dealing with the local community, the nation, Latin America, and world affairs. The current experimentation in North America and in Europe is being adapted to the new curricula, especially in the areas of mathematics and natural science.

The second cycle of the secondary school, the "senior high school," will probably have a variety of programs, as it has today; and these programs may develop as part of a single comprehensive school, rather than as separate schools. This change would allow secondary school students a better opportunity to try themselves out in the various courses and to transfer from one to another. It would also bring all types of pupils, from all social classes and with a variety of vocational goals, together in a single democratic educational institution.

Higher Education

Higher education in Brazil began only in the nineteenth century, with the establishment of some isolated higher schools or faculties—a law school in one place, a medical school in another, and an engineering school in a third (see p. 61). Instruction in these professional schools was generally given by members of the profession in their spare time, primarily as a means of achieving prestige. The schools were far below the levels of universities in Europe and North America. Young men who wished to become scholars went abroad for university training.

After about 1910 the number of higher institutions began to increase rapidly, as can be seen in Table 30. Some were started at the instigation of state governments; others were initiated by local groups of professional men and operated privately, not so much for profit as for the cultural values they would bring to a city or state. This proliferation of institutes of higher education continued until in 1961 there were 447 establishments with 1,236 entities, such as schools or faculties giving programs of instruction, or courses of several years duration leading to a bachelor's degree.

Meanwhile a university system had come into existence, and it combined many of these higher schools or faculties into loosely federated universities. The first university, established in Rio de Janeiro in 1920, combined the existing law school, medical school, and engineering school. The federal government provided by law for giving charters to universities, both public and private in their administrative relation to the government.

Between 1920 and 1940 the universities developed slowly. In 1938 the University of Rio de Janeiro was absorbed into the University of Brazil, and in 1934 the University of São Paulo was organized through a combination of existing faculties. It was provided with a charter by the state of São Paulo. Although São Paulo charters its own universities, they also receive federal support. Even the privately administered universities receive subsidies from the federal government.

By 1961 there were thirty-two universities, of which twenty-two were public institutions supported by the federal government; three were state universities; six were Roman Catholic; and one was private and nonchurch administered (Mackenzie University in São Paulo). All but five have been established since 1946. These figures omit the more than four hundred unaffiliated institutions.

Higher education enrollment grew from 21,000 in 1939, to 38,000 in 1949, to 102,000 in 1961. Of these students, 44 per cent were in private institutions in 1960, 38 per cent in federal government-supported institutions, and 17 and 1 percent in state and municipal institutions, respectively.

RESEARCH INSTITUTES. Institutes for research have been developed on a growing scale since 1951, when the National Research Council was created by the federal government. The Council has government funds to support scientific and technological research, to pay foreign professors and scientists for work in Brazil, and to pay stipends to postgraduate research scholars. There are several outstanding institutes, including the Agricultural Research Institute at Campinas, São Paulo, the Engineering Research Institute in the city of São Paulo, and the Technological Institute of Aeronautics in the state of São Paulo, patterned after the Massachusetts Institute of Technology in the United States.

The American educator Richard Smith, who assisted in the formation of the Aeronautics Institute, reported that the technological situation of Brazil was like that of the United States in 1890. But by that year the United States already had six hundred engineers per million inhabitants, whereas Brazil in 1946 had barely two hundred for the same number of inhabitants. A similar situation existed in the fields of medicine, chemistry, physics, and agriculture. Trained technical personnel in Brazil in 1946 were not more than one-third the number available in the United States in 1890.

The effort to master this problem of development continues. In 1958 measures were taken to widen and to stimulate technical education on the secondary level, with a view toward increasing registrations in the engineering schools. Fourteen new institutes for research and training of specialized personnel were established. Furthermore, the resources of the "National Campaign for Improvement in Personnel on the Higher Level" (CAPES), have been expanded. The objectives of CAPES are to assure the availability of the specialized personnel needed to meet the needs of public and private undertakings contributing to the social and economic progress of Brazil, and to enable the better qualified individuals lacking the requisite financial resources to pursue their post-graduate studies and training.

More specifically devoted to the development of education and research in technology at the higher level is the Commission on Technological Institutes (COSUPI), which dispenses federal funds to universities and technological institutes for new buildings, increased faculty salaries, and student stipends in engineering, agriculture, and other branches of technology.

Several of the higher institutions are supported by federal agencies other than the Ministry of Education. Thus, the Ministry of Agriculture supports agricultural universities, and the air force supports the Institute of Aeronautical Engineering at São José dos Campos in São Paulo, even though this institute gives training in several branches of engineering and enrolls very few students from the air force.

Operating also in the area of higher education is the Getúlio Vargas Foundation, set up by the federal government to give instruction and to support research in the areas of economics and public and private administration.

UNIVERSITY OF BRASÍLIA. Shortly after the new capital was created, a commission of educators was appointed by the President to design a modern and efficient university at Brasília. The commission has proposed a basic introductory course that will be common to the entire university and will advance the general intellectual competence of all students before they enter their respective fields of specialization. This course will give instruction in such basic subjects as mathematics, chemistry, physics, and Portuguese, and thus avoid the costly overlapping of instruction in basic courses as they are ordinarily given by the separate faculties. During their introductory year in the university students will have the time and opportunity to select their fields of specialization, with the help of vocational guidance based on aptitude and interest tests. The new university is also provided with a number of institutes for post-graduate work, including the first graduate school of education in the country.

Functions of Higher Education

During the hundred years from 1810 to 1910, the institutions of higher education had two functions: to train practitioners of the liberal professions, especially law and medicine; and to enable sons of high-status families to maintain their status. Most of the young men who only wanted a status-giving degree took a law course, the successful completion of which entitled a person to use the title of "doctor." On the other hand, many able and ambitious young men studied law in order to practice it or to go into public life. The law schools gave the broadest kind of education available.

These functions are still important in Brazilian higher education, but others have been added to them. One of the new functions is the training of people for technical work in industry and business; for this the schools of engineering and economic sciences are most important, and have been growing rapidly in enrollment. The other new function is the training of people for secondary school teaching, for the rapid growth of secondary education since 1930 has created a demand for large numbers of teachers. This is the responsibility of the faculty of philosophy, sciences and letters, which is somewhat like the North American college of liberal arts. Thus higher education in Brazil has become more "functional" in the sense of preparing people explicitly for the work that they will perform as adults, rather than giving them a degree which they will regard largely as a symbol of status and which they may or may not use professionally.

In the same period there has been an increase in the enrollment of sons and daughters of working-class and of lower-middle-class families; they use the university as an avenue of upward social mobility. Further, there has been a relatively large increase in the enrollment of women, though they are still outnumbered by men 3 to 1. Almost half of the women are in the faculties of philosophy, usually indicating either that they expect to teach or that they have no definite vocational objective, but higher education does give them the opportunity for pursuing a career outside of the home.

TABLE 30

Enrollments in Universities and Higher Institutions by Faculty

Year	Total enroll-ment	Per cent of total enrollment					
		Philos-ophy, Science, Letters	Law	Economic Sciences	Medicine, Dentistry, Pharmacy	Engi-neering	Agri-culture, Veterinary Medicine
1907	6,000	—	41	—	48	7.0	2.5
1912	10,000	0.5	27	—	48	12.8	11.2
1928	14,000	0.4	19	—	54	14.5	5.4
1933	24,000	1.3	33	1.0	46	8.5	5.4
1938	24,000	5.7	32	2.0	38	8.4	6.3
1943	27,000	13	22	9.0	30	11	4.8
1948	38,000	11	23	5.6	31	15	3.7
1953	65,000	15	26	6.0	25	14	2.7
1958	84,500	18	26	7.6	20	14	2.8
1960	95,700	22	25	8.3	19	12	2.8
1961	101,600	23	24	9.1	18	12	2.8

Source: *Sinopse Retrospectiva do Ensino no Brasil*, 1958, and *Sinopse Estatístico do Ensino Superior*, 1960 (Rio de Janeiro: Serviço de Estatística de Educação e Cultura, Ministério de Educação e Cultura).

Table 30 shows how these new functions are reflected in the enrollments of higher institutions. In the last thirty years, the percentage of university students enrolled in medicine and related areas has dropped from 50 to 20, while the percentage enrolled in law has remained fairly constant. The great increases have come in the faculties of philosophy, science and letters (liberal arts), and the economic sciences. Engineering has increased in absolute numbers but not much in relative proportion, and agriculture and veterinary medicine have decreased their relative numbers. The regional distribution of higher institutions and their students (Table 31) follows the tendencies already described for economic development and educational achievement.

TABLE 31

Number of Professors and Students in Higher Education, 1958

States	Regions	Professors	Totals	Students	Totals
Amazonas	North	70	367	206	1,377
Pará		297		1,171	
Maranhão		163		494	
Piauí		30		214	
Ceará		337		1,586	
Rio Grande do Norte	Northeast	96	2,028	340	9,260
Paraíba		239		851	
Pernambuco		990		4,904	
Alagoas		173		871	
Sergipe		106		335	
Bahia		620		3,392	
Minas Gerais	East	1,431	5,278	7,896	35,959
Espírito Santo		149		835	
Rio de Janeiro		472		4,466	
Guanabara		2,500		19,035	
São Paulo		2,704		22,943	
Paraná		733		5,132	
Santa Catarina	South	94	5,320	727	36,508
Rio Grande do Sul		1,789		7,706	
Mato Grosso	Central West	10	242	126	1,377
Goiás		232		1,251	
		13,235		84,481	

Education and Economic Growth: Present-Day Brazil

In this survey it has become clear that the rapid growth of secondary and higher education since 1930 has been closely related to industrialization, urbanization, and the growth of the middle classes in Brazil. The economic and political leaders of Brazil have become convinced that a major investment in human capital, through more secondary and higher education for more people, is a necessary element in the economic development of the society. Consequently they have made large increases in the public expenditure on education, especially for secondary schools and universities. Perhaps they have not made enough of an investment, as was suggested in the Chapter VII, but they have adopted a policy of supporting a major expansion of education.

At this point it is useful to discuss systematically the relations between education and economic growth. Education contributes to the economic development of a society in several ways. Most directly, it can give people the knowledge and skill they need to become efficient workers—whether this be at the level of mere literacy, so that an unskilled worker can read directions, or at the level of highly technical work, such as programming an electronic computer.

It also helps to make or to maintain a fluid social structure. By giving economic opportunity to children, regardless of the social class of their families, education encourages social mobility. Such mobility is generally regarded as conducive to economic growth, since it continually brings poor but able people into positions where they can benefit themselves by making the economy more productive. Their economic welfare contributes to the economic growth of the society. On the other hand, if the society were rigidly stratified the families with wealth and power could hand these on to their children without the pressure of competition, and their children would not be under much compulsion to make the economy more productive. When Brazil was an aristocratic, agricultural society, the wealthy landowning classes had little or no incentive to increase their economic efficiency.

Education has already contributed to the economic growth of Brazil by helping the nation to achieve two of the six conditions defined by Oliveira as necessary: a technological tradition and a technical ideology (see p. 80). While North Europe slowly accumulated a technical tradition over a period of a thousand years preceding the Industrial Revolution and then passed it on to the United States, South Europe had much less of this tradition of inventions and labor-saving devices, and Brazil received little from its southern European settlers. This lack of technical tradition combined with a prejudice against manual work, in the case of Brazil, and constituted a considerable barrier against industrial development. The educational system traditionally emphasized the verbal and academic type of study, with a neglect of practical application. Oliveira and other educators who are interested in technological development believe that the primary and secondary school curriculum should be modified (1) to increase the amount of positive or favorable attention given to technology in the school books of history, geography, and social sciences, and (2) to increase the amount of attention given to pure and applied science in the school curriculum, with more emphasis on student work in the laboratory and the school shop.

ECONOMIC VALUE OF HIGHER EDUCATION. While the economic values of a technological tradition, a technological ideology, and an open social structure cannot be computed in terms of money, the economic values of education can and have been computed. Economists have found that a person's earning power is increased by education, and therefore the earning power of a society, which is a measure of its productivity, is increased by education—at least within broad limits. A study published by CAPES attempts to show how much increase in income the society will receive for a certain investment in the education of more people at the university level.[2] The report begins with an analysis of the census data on the numbers of people with a university preparation and their distribution among three regions of the country. Region A consists of eight states: those of the South plus Minas Gerais, Guanabara, Rio de Janeiro, and Espírito Santo. Region B consists of eight states in the Northeast including Bahia and Sergipe, and excluding Maranhão. Region C consists of five states: Maranhão, Pará, Amazonas, Goiás, and Mato Grosso.

TABLE 32

Regional Distribution of Specialists of University Level, and Related Data

Region	Professionals of university level per million population 1950	University enrollment 1958	% of national product 1957	% of labor force 1950
A	3,701	64,700	81	60
B	936	12,200	14	31
C	968	3,000	5	10

Source: Oliveira and Carvalho, A Formação de Pessoal de Nível Superior e o Desenvolvimento Econômico, pp. 12, 15, 41.

Table 32 shows data concerning the distribution in 1950 of the university-trained professional group. It is clear that the regions with greatest per capita income also have the greatest numbers of university graduates in relation to the population, and the greatest numbers of university students. Thus it seems that economic growth will involve, possibly as cause and possibly as effect, or both, an increase in the relative numbers of university-trained professionals.

The numbers of new professionals likely to be produced during the decade 1960–70 can be conservatively estimated by using as a base the numbers of university students in the period 1956–59, and assuming a modest increase in enrollment of about 5 per cent per year (see Table 33). To recruit and train this number would require an expansion of higher education of about 65 per cent between 1960 and 1970, which is about the same rate that was realized in the 1950–60 decade.

The amount of the investment in each individual can be com-

TABLE 33

University-Trained Specialists, 1950, 1959, and 1970

Type	1950 Census	1959 Estimated	1970 Projected
Agronomists	5,784	7,431	11,529
Veterinarians	1,663	2,535	4,525
Architects	1,636	3,788	8,132
Engineers	20,403	28,241	51,690
Chemists	3,493	3,702	3,715
Medical Doctors	25,752	35,227	52,368
Dentists	17,277	26,241	41,919
Pharmacists	11,226	13,814	19,223
Lawyers	31,233	52,518	108,195
Economists	5,516	11,740	35,953
Teachers—secondary school and university; research specialists	8,052	20,849	64,815
Total	132,035	206,086	402,064

Source: Oliveira and Carvalho, *A Formação de Pessoal de Nível Superior e o Desenvolvimento Econômico,* Table 60, p. 180.

puted approximately. It consists of two parts: the cost of instruction and the cost of keeping him out of the labor force during his period of preparation (the salary he could have earned if he had gone to work and had not used the time for study).

The estimated cost per person in each of five educational levels is shown in Table 34, together with the estimated lifetime earnings of this person, both in cruzeiros of 1959.

These figures show that it is "good business" for Brazil to continue to expand its system of secondary and higher education, at least at the present rate of development. In a more fully-developed country there might be some danger of producing so

TABLE 34

The Educational Investment in a Person, and His Resultant Earning Power
(Cr$ of 1959)

Category	Investment in this person: instruction, income foregone	Income received during active life
Illiterate or semi-illiterate	—	1,500,000
Primary school course (4 years)	3,200	4,600,000
Secondary school course	210,000	7,000,000
University course	1,275,000	10,000,000
Post graduate course of 2 years	1,900,000	12,000,000

Source: Oliveira and Carvalho, *A Formação de Pessoal de Nível Superior e o Desenvolvimento Econômico,* p. 162. (The numbers are rough estimates, but are certainly reasonably close to the facts, which could only be obtained by a long, drawn-out field research.)

many university graduates that they could not all be profitably employed, but Brazil would profit from educating more graduates than can be produced in the next decade.

A Policy of Education for Economic Development

The authors of the CAPES report conclude with a statement of recommended policy which indicates that Brazil should give priority to investment in education. The present investment of about 2 per cent of the national income in education should be increased somewhat, but it is equally important to correct the errors in the present system. Among educators and sociologists there is quasi-unanimous agreement that the present system of education was designed in the interests of a social group (the nineteenth-century agricultural aristocracy) that has lost power and ability to improve the economic condition of the country. The two systems of education are clearly opposed, the old one being a form of conspicuous consumption pertaining to a particular social class and the new one being a form of investment of resources of state, private industry, and the individual, which will produce profits for all.

Educational policy should include expansion of primary, secondary, and intermediate schools (especially of the industrial type); and it should involve expansion of higher education, particularly in the technological fields. There should be special emphasis on increasing the supply of agronomists and specialists in veterinary medicine, through scholarship aid to students and through salary increases to government employees in these areas, since most of these specialists are employed by the government. Private industry and the government should cooperate to support the proposed expansion and to direct its flow into the channels that will count the most for economic productivity.

NOTES

1. Juarez Rubens Brandão Lopes, "Escolha Ocupacional e Origem Social de Ginasianos em São Paulo," *Educação e Ciências Sociais,* I, No. 2 (Aug. 1956), 48.

2. Américo Barbosa de Oliveira and José Zacarias sa Carvalho, *A Formação de Pessoal de Nível Superior e o Desenvolvimento Econômico* (Rio de Janeiro: CAPES, 1960).

10

The Family and Education

THE family is the fundamental educational agent in every society. It educates the emotions of the child; it teaches him a set of basic attitudes toward the world; it gives him the physical and emotional security that he needs while growing toward maturity; it gives him models of masculine and feminine behavior and a moral code; it continues to educate him throughout his life, as he becomes a father or mother, husband or wife, grandfather or grandmother.

When a society becomes complex enough to require a school to assist in the education of its children, the school inevitably depends on the family. The family presents children to the school, already partly formed, with potentialities and limitations. The family explicitly or implicitly delegates some tasks to the school.

Brazil has only recently gone into the process of delegating major responsibilites for the rearing of children to its educational system. This fact alone makes it necessary to study the Brazilian family in order to understand Brazilian education. And the modern Brazilian family is still very much influenced by the patterns and mores of family life that developed during the colonial period. For this reason it is of more than historical interest to look at the family life of the colonial period, and to ask how it educated children.

The Colonial Family

Colonial Brazil consisted of a number of large families living more or less distant from each other in a vast area of country. The state was weak—it had little apparatus for government. The church was loosely organized, and locally it was structured around the

207

large family unit. The economy was a loose collection of family units dealing with individual traders and moneylenders and with the government tax collectors. There were no strong banks, trading companies, or other economic agencies with an organization and structure in which people could invest their energy and discover careers for themselves. Thus the Brazilian family took to itself most of the functions of a variety of institutions that exist in a more complex society, including educational functions.

Based on agriculture, and generally on a single crop agriculture, with slave labor and plentiful land, the family became a large social unit—a little kingdom—with many people of various statuses and functions to make it up. It was an extended family, including not only blood relatives but also a variety of dependents, both free and slave. This extended family included three groups of people. First, there was the nucleus of blood relatives—the man and his wife, their children and grandchildren, and the cousins and uncles and aunts and nephews and nieces. Second, were the *agregados*—free people who worked on the fazenda as managers, stewards, and retainers of various types, including illegitimate children of the patriarch, the issue of his sexual intercourse with light-colored and attractive female slaves, or even free women, the daughters or relatives of the retainers. These children, when baptized by the patriarch, became his godchildren and acquired an intermediate status. A great many of the priests and scholars of Imperial Brazil stemmed from these illegitimate children or godchildren. For the patriarch would often send a bright boy to the secondary and advanced schools of the period. The third group were the slaves, who also belonged to the family in their way.

The relation of *compadresco* or godparent and godchild was an important factor in cementing the extended family together. Children of upper-status families generally had godparents who were related to them. But the father or mother of low status would seek a godfather or godmother who could help the child by giving him work or educating him. The godparent was obliged to take the place of the father whenever necessary, and to help with material goods, such as presents of cattle; the godchild, in turn, gave whatever aid he could to the godparent and often took the name of his family.

Since the relationship on the maternal side was as valid and important as that on the paternal side, godparents might be chosen from either side of the family. This custom served to extend the family even further. The system of names, so puzzling to Anglo-Saxons, was related both to the equivalance of the two lines in the family and to the system of *compadresco*. Daughters tended to take the mother's surname, whereas sons took either that of the father or mother. Sometimes they took the names of grandparents or other relatives. Thus the name expresses not the child-parent relationship, but participation in a vast kinship system. Antonio Candido cites the seventeenth-cenutry marriage of Tomé de Lara e Almeida with Dona Maria de Almeida Pimentel (the pair having one name in common), to them were born: Fernando Paes de Barros, Antonio de Almeida Lara, José Pompeu Ordonho, Lucrecia Pedroso de Barros, Maria de Almeida Lara, Sebastina de Almeida, Branca de Almeida, Inácia de Almeida, Luzia Leme, and Maria de Almeida Lara Pimentel.[1]

There was a tendency to marry within the extended family, in order to keep family property and possessions together. Marriages between cousins were common. "From a good stock cannot come a bad thing" was the common attitude. The new family added to the strength of the existing extended family. This family could organize itself for economic and political purposes, and it did so quite effectively until well into the twentieth century, when the agricultural oligarchies finally lost their hold on Brazilian politics.

Relationships among relatives were ritualized by forms of address which excluded the intimate terms that have come into use in the current century. The man called the father *Senhor pai* and the mother *Senhora mae* (father, my lord, and mother, my lady) and addressed them as *Vossa Mercé* (your worship). The children asked the parents' blessing at morning, at night, and always when they met. The parents also addressed the children as *senhor* or *senhora*, often making the form more familiar by shortening it to *nho* or *nhá*, or *vossemece*. A cousin was addressed as *Senhor* Cousin and an uncle or aunt as *Senhor* Uncle or *Senhora* Aunt.

There were two groups of women, both subordinated to the men of the nuclear family. One group consisted of African slaves, and earlier of Indian women who were taken formerly by the Portuguese colonists as concubines. Later, there was some marriage of white men with mulatto or mestizo women, but this was rare on the part of high-status men. The other group of women were those of Portuguese extraction, who eventually appeared in large enough numbers to provide wives for the Portuguese colonists.

The tradition was one of authority of the man over the woman, as well as the authority of the patriarch over the entire family. By the end of the eighteenth century this tradition was already losing ground. Antonio Candido quotes the following lines of a Portuguese or Luso-Brazilian poet who wrote prior to 1780:

When the twisted mustache lent a fierce and fiery look to the wise old Portuguese,
When his hair was untamed by oil or scissors, and tied in a rough knot,
When the woman trembled at the shadow of her husband,
While prudent custom isolated her sex from the clamorous world;
Then how innocent and happy was the Lusitanian kingdom,
Alas! lost happy day! forever past.[2]

The Brazilian wife of a land owner was traditionally idle, frail, submissive, and secluded. Writers describing the woman of that period, especially in the Northeast, depict her as indolent, like a hothouse flower, lolling in a hammock and abusing the Negroes, while her husband ruled the household and took his slave concubines in full view of his wife. However, the wife was mistress of the large household. She directed the work of the slaves in the house, as well as their spinning, weaving, lace-making, and making of clothes for the family and for themselves. She had to manage the vegetable and fruit and flower gardening because generally the men did not like this task.

Girls learned these things from their mothers. As soon as they reached the age of twelve or thirteen they began, with the help and instigation of their mothers and slave-maids, to prepare themselves for marriage. They might learn some of the domestic arts or even how to play a musical instrument. They lived secluded in the large house, their innocence and virginity supposedly preserved until the time came for them to marry the man picked out for them by their father.

Boys were reared much more freely, after they reached the age of seven or eight. They seldom had schooling of a regular sort, and were not given prescribed tasks or obligations. "In our backland districts," a traveling Catholic priest of that day commented, "the upbringing of the young is lamentable." [3] As soon as the boy reached the age of puberty he was given sexual liberty with the women slaves. Often wild and wicked, he owed obedience only to his father. The latter would decide, when the time came, whether the boy should remain on the fazenda or be sent off to a colégio, to become a priest or a scholar. Later, the father would arrange the marriage of his son.

While the writers of colonial history do not deal fully with other groups of people, it is clear that there were increasing numbers of "common people," who were legally free and did not live on the fazendas. Some of them were manual workers in the towns and cities, with or without a trade. Apparently they were poor people whose forebears had somehow dropped out of or been cast out of the extended families of the fazendas. If they did not maintain relations with an extended family or fazenda, they had very little structural support for their lives. Antonio Candido comments, "They reproduced themselves haphazardly and lived without regular norms of conduct." [4] Other town and city dwellers of higher social status were members of the agricultural families and maintained economic, social, and political ties with them until the twentieth century.

Clearly, the colonial family was a powerful organization for economic and political purposes and served as the elemental unit of the society. It had very little use for formal schooling, though occasionally a priest acted both as chaplain and school teacher on a large fazenda and taught the children to read and write. The poor people who were outside the extended family structure were also outside the social structure. They simply existed, and society did nothing to educate their children.

The Nineteenth-Century Family

By the time the Empire came into being, Brazil had become socially and economically complex enough to produce a greater variety of family life, and also to require some education outside of the family for a considerable number of children. There were two main causes of the changes in family life. One was urbanization and the beginning of industrial system; the other was immigration from central and southern Europe.

The Imperial division of the country into provinces, each with its own capital and legislative assembly, assisted the development of regional centers which were growing in economic significance. By the middle of the nineteenth century, when the railroads and the first textile mills were built, there was a substantial number of urban people whose family structure was different from that of the fazenda.

Meanwhile the sons of the plantation owners, pursuing their studies in Recife, Salvador, Rio, or São Paulo, were no longer attracted back to the bucolic life of the fazenda, preferring the social life, the political activity, the literary circles, and the business ventures of the cities. Thus the family patriarch found himself unable to decide the marriage-choice and the career of his son. If he would cut off the young man's allowance, the latter would generally become self-supporting by entering one of the liberal professions, such as journalism, or get a job in a bank or business office. Some of these young men joined forces with the newly emerging upper-middle class which grew out of the administrative organization of the Empire and the development of substantial business and industrial organizations. Yet they were products of the old-family organization, and they made of themselves a vital link between the old family and the emergent new middle-class family.

Meanwhile the same political and economic factors were drawing toward the cities the masters of the *casas grandes*. Isolation on their rural estates was making it difficult for them to defend their economic interests and to promote their political purposes. Hence they began to build a second home in the city and to live there during a period of the year when they could leave the management of the fazenda to a foreman or a relative. In Rio de Janeiro, Recife, São Paulo, they built their particular style of house, called a *sobrado*, which was a two-story mansion set in a landscaped property with flower beds, orchards, and vegetable gardens. They walled themselves off from the street, and built verandas and garden bowers for their comfort on the warm days.

Outside the iron portals the streets were given over to the common people—Negroes on sundry errands, colored boys carrying parrots, women of the street. Any boy from a *sobrado* playing on the street was likely to fall into bad company; a girl venturing out alone could be suspected of being a streetwalker. The proper place for a boy to play was in the courtyard of the residence; the proper place for a girl of good family was the living room or, at the most, the veranda or the window.

Still, the city life encroached inexorably on the ways of the rural aristocracy. During parties and receptions the rural patriarch had to open his doors to the upper-middle class of the city. The intellectuals and politically ambitious young men thus became acquainted with his daughters; and his sons who were in the colégio or in one of the higher schools invited their city friends.

At the same time the upper-middle class people were building their houses near to the *sobrados*, and more open to the public— Swiss-style chalets and other forms that later came into style. These homes gave easy access to visitors. Social contacts, self-initiated by young people, became the rule. The educated man, white or mulatto, regardless of social origin, could move in the "best" social circles and might gain admission to the "best" families by marriage. And the attractive and well-bred girl living in a middle-class chalet could capture a young man of the upper or upper-middle class without depending on her father, and sometimes in spite of him.

In the smaller cities of 5,000 to 50,000, which did not know "high society" and were largely bypassed by the rural aristocracy as the latter concentrated attention on their fazendas or on life in the capital, there developed a middle-class family life much influenced by tradition but not structured so much along patriarchal and extended family lines.

Children of the middle class in the municipal centers had a more extensive relationship with their own age group than did those growing up on a fazenda. They attended the local primary school. By the end of the nineteenth century they were developing modes of recreation and of courting that involved much more direct and unsupervised social contacts than had been the rule. Dances and movies were to come in the twentieth century, but the "footing" became institutionalized at this time. This was a custom of walking around the town plaza in the evening, girls in one direction and boys in the other. Girls walked in pairs or groups, and so did the boys, and thus each sex encountered the other, face to face, and every boy could see every girl several times during the course of the evening. Each social class had its own area within the plaza. Visual encounters might lead to conversation, and the latter to acquaintance.

Thus the concept of marriage as an arrangement between two families was gradually replaced by a concept of an arrangement between two individuals, motivated by romantic love. This led, eventually and not until the twentieth century, to the practice of dating and to the custom of a boy or a girl having a series of light love affairs, some approved by the parents and others unknown to them.

Children of the working class were generally more free in their social contacts, though they certainly were not without rules or norms of conduct. Relations between the sexes were less closely supervised than in the case of the middle class, and marriage was less formal, often taking the form of "living together" after the birth of children signified that a family had come into existence. As the working-class group moved up the social scale and up the scale of standard of living, the upper working class took on some of the middle-class ways. For instance, the institution of the "footing" seems to have been maintained by working-class youth after the middle of the twentieth century, while middle-class youth took up a more sophisticated social life, with parties and dances and informal meetings in the afternoon and evening in favorite tearooms or *confeiterias*.

THE EUROPEAN IMMIGRANT FAMILY IN THE SOUTH. While the extended family system originating on the plantations of the Northeast and East was going through an evolution, an entirely new type of family system was developing in the South, among the immigrants from Germany, Italy, and Poland. These people came in large enough numbers to Rio Grande do Sul and to Santa Catarina to form entire new settlements, in which they were the only or at least the dominant cultural group. Thus they did not become assimilated in a preexisting culture; they formed their own culture. Their towns, often with European names such as Nova Hamburgo, Blumenau, and Joinville, looked like towns of Central Europe. Many Germans were Protestants. With agricultural techniques and with handicrafts that were superior to those of Brazil, some of these people emerged as middle-class business men and small factory operators. The majority of them became small independent farmers in the hilly and rainy country between the coast and the interior highlands.

The family structure of these immigrants was simpler than that of the extended family of the northern states, as was their social structure. Generally they formed local communities for cooperation in building schools and churches, employing teachers and pastors, and enforcing law and order. This they had to do because the state and the church were not active enough to do it for them. Thus they developed a kind of hybrid culture, combining their European heritage with the elements of the Brazilian that they found available. They generally adopted the language, and made substantial use of the existing educational facilities. This immigrant culture was a base for an emerging middle class of small nuclear families, without slaves and without much use of the *compadresco* so important in other parts of the country.

EDUCATION AND THE NINETEENTH-CENTURY FAMILY. By the end of the nineteenth century the Brazilian family was allowing its children a considerable degree of autonomy in choice of career and of spouse. Even a girl in an upper- or middle-class family could attend a secondary school and then teach in a primary school, thus gaining considerable freedom of movement, social and physical, outside of the home. Young men of the upper and middle classes were attending secondary schools and universities and thus gaining autonomy in the choice of an occupation. Children of lower-middle-class families and even occasionally of working-class families were rising in the social scale by means of education and leaving their families behind.

The Twentieth-Century Family

Family structure in the twentieth century changed slowly but inevitably under the impact of industrialization and urbanization. Its adaptation to new conditions as well as its tenacious hold on tradition have been described by Emílio Willems as follows:

THE UPPER- AND MIDDLE-CLASS FAMILY

The upper- and middle-class family of Brazil may be interpreted as a dialectic structure based upon asymmetric roles ascribed to males and females. The female role is centered in a cluster of values which may be characterized as a virginity complex. The belief that the virginity of unmarried females ought to be preserved at any cost has so far tenaciously resisted change. Such institutional arrangements as segregation of the sexes, chaperonage, and family-controlled courtship, which are to be regarded as component traits of the virginity complex, have undergone so many changes, at least in the larger cities of Brazil, that the original pattern is hardly recognizable. However, under the somewhat deceiving appearance of changing intersexual relationships and vanishing family controls, the old rule that females should abstain from premarital sexual experiences has been rigidly maintained. Carefully conducted interviews carried out over a period of nearly twelve years showed that even the most liberal-minded men were apt to become suddenly intransigent if asked what they thought of the prospect of marrying somebody with premarital sexual experience.

.   .   .   .

Despite the fact that women may now choose among many different occupational prospects, there are as yet very few career women in Brazil. Those who study or work are apt to regard this as an interlude which by no means is thought of as precluding or even postponing marriage. Consequently, adjustments to changing social conditions are made in such a way as to avoid forms of behavior which might possibly spoil or reduce the chances for marriage. Under the closest scrutiny of an androcentric society, under the pressure of gossip and slanderous interpretation of inadvertent actions, the Brazilian girl is forced to protect her reputation under conditions which make efficient protection increasingly difficult. Small wonder then that wherever women appear in public they tend to stick together, to form at least groups of two or three and to avoid places and hours which may cast suspicion on their behavior. To be seen in the company of different men, and under circumstances suggesting intimacy, would be extremely damaging to a girl's reputation.

As it is now practiced in the larger cities of Brazil, dating is rather "monogamous" and noncompetitive. Obviously it does not serve the selective function that has been attributed to it in the United States. The male companion is not supposed to assume definite obligations toward the girl as long as he does not visit her parents' home. Unchaperoned dates of this kind are increasingly tolerated by urban parents, but single dates are still frowned upon and usually concealed from the girl's family.

.   .   .   .

Up to this point it has already become clear that the role of the Brazilian male is antithetic to that of the woman. His is a markedly androcentric society, which encourages almost everything denied to women. The male role is centered in a set of values which may properly be called a virility complex. A young Brazilian is expected to get actively interested in sex at the age of puberty. Even before puberty the average boy becomes used to the sexual bravado of older companions. He learns that regular sexual intercourse is not only believed to be physically healthy, but above all an essential attribute of manhood. There is a generally accepted opinion that early and frequent sexual intercourse is stimulated by peculiar racial and the physiological effects of a tropical climate.

.   .   .   .

At first glance it may seem improbable that these antithetic roles, which largely determine husband-wife, father-daughter, and brother-sister relationships, should be integrated into such a closely knit group as the Brazilian family. Actually these roles are adjusted to each other with a minimum of friction or conflict. There is a strict separation between the sex-ridden, overbearing, and irresponsible Brazilian male as he likes to appear to his companions outside his home, and the devoted father and provider as he appears to the members of his family. Typically, Brazilian men have a highly developed sense of honor and respectability with regard to their families, and they endeavor to bring up their children in accordance with the austere rules of tradition. Thus, whatever his conduct outside the family, a Brazilian husband and father is apt to assume his role of guardian of strict morality toward his family.

.   .   .   .

Although urbanization and industrialization have so far been unable to change the antithetic positions of the sexes, peripheral changes in the family structure have been numerous. Under increasing economic pressure many middle-class husbands do not object any more to their wives' holding other than teaching jobs, and unmarried daughters are not only allowed, but in most cases are even expected, to work. There is little doubt that these changes relieve fathers and brothers of a great deal of their former controls, but hasty conclusions should not be drawn as to the freedom Brazilian women are supposed to enjoy, or as to their desire to enjoy the degree of freedom which is taken for granted elsewhere.

To what degree is the Brazilian family still an extended family? If the term is taken in the sense of joint resistance, it must be said that, except for the *famille-souche* type, the extended family is rapidly disappearing. However, in the sense of solidary groups of related nuclear families residing in the same locality, the extended family is far from being extinct. Despite huge internal migrations and what might be called atomistic aggregation of migrants in urban centers, existing family ties are frequently strong enough to resist even the diluting influences of metropolitan centers like São Paulo and Rio de Janeiro. Residents of São Paulo City who could be interviewed were able to distinguish between thirty and five hundred relatives, a considerable part of whom lived in the same city. It is taken for granted that one may expect protection and aid even from distant "cousins" whom one may never have met before. In the cities of northeastern Brazil, a young relative from the interior may suddenly come to visit his uncle and stay for several years. During that time, the uncle is expected to feed him and take care of his education.

The fact that in southern Brazil hardly anybody would expect this kind of aid from relatives other than his own parents indicates regional differences that are not necessarily those between city and rural areas. However, there are forms of aid and protection that, in any part of Brazil, may reasonably be expected from a relative. Individuals holding an important job are likely to become employment agencies for their kinfolk. Large kinship groups are extremely valuable to those who are running for office; in such cases electoral support is taken for granted.

.   .   .   .

THE LOWER-CLASS FAMILY

In the light of the rather limited information available, the structure of the lower-class family seems to be quite different.

There is hardly anything to which the term courtship may properly be applied. After a young man has achieved some understanding with a girl, he seeks to obtain the consent of his prospective father-in-law, which is rarely denied. As there are no property arrangements to be made, marriage follows immediately. Most girls marry at an age which varies between 14 and 17. As to the form of marriage, the church ceremony certainly is the preferential pattern; but in localities that are seldom visited by Catholic priests, people are quite tolerant with regard to common-law marriages. Civil marriage, however, is not only expensive but meaningless as well. This attitude toward civil marriage has doubtless historical roots. During the Empire (1822–89) the religious marriage ceremony performed in a Catholic church by an ordained priest was not only legally recognized but also the only form of marriage with religious and legal effects. Separation of church and state led to a distinct civil marriage procedure. Since then, the religious marriage ceremony has been regarded as the act by which social and supernatural sanctions may be obtained, while the civil procedure has been accepted as an indispensable legal formality, chiefly by the middle and upper classes. To lower-class rural people, however, who do not have to worry about property and inheritance, the civil procedure adds nothing to the religious sanction, except fees.

Recently, separation between civil and ecclesiastical marriage has been somewhat reduced by a law providing for ecclesiastical marriage with legal effects. Prior to the church ceremony a legal document may be obtained which states that the marriage will be performed in such and such a church by such and such a priest. Otherwise the separation persists. Children whose parents are not married according to canon law are illegitimate in the eyes of the church. And those whose parents are married only according to canon law are illegitimate so far as the legal authorities are concerned. Thus official data on illegitimacy are misleading. However, by legally recognizing their "illegitimate" offspring, parents are allowed to equalize the status of their children with those born out of a legal marriage.

Among the rural and urban lower classes there seems to be no perceptible discrimination between sexually inexperienced women and those who have previously indulged in sexual intercourse. Thus female virginity is not regarded as a prerequisite for a stable union, and consequently the rules of chaperonage and segregation of sexes are far less elaborate.

.   .   .   .

CHILD TRAINING

By European standards parents are overindulgent toward their infant children, and there is hardly any attempt to enforce a rigid discipline. Usually infant training follows the patterns of traditional lore rather than the standards of modern psychology and medicine. Parents seeking advice of social workers and physicians still constitute a small minority. Where scientific facilities are available, it has been a problem to induce parents to utilize them.

The tightly knit extended family of the upper strata must of course be considered as a far more effective training agency than the somewhat amorphous, loosely integrated family of the lower classes. In the middle and upper classes the child is not only trained by the family but also predominantly for the family. Very early it receives the indelible family stamp and learns to think in terms of family relation-ships. That particular way of life, which has been named youth culture, and which consists of a peculiar mixture of irresponsible play and responsible learning, must still be considered largely as a privilege of the middle and upper strata. In the lower classes, however, empha-sis is laid on early breadwinning, and youth culture remains con-spicuously absent, especially among the rural populations where the social status of the youth, boy or girl, is measured by his or her capac-ity of performing the normal tasks of an adult.[5]

Facts About the Twentieth-Century Family

The difference between the ages of husband and wife is less than in earlier days, when girls married young and men relatively late. In a study of marriage records in the São Paulo *município* of Itapetininga, Orácy Nogueira found that, in 1875, 83 per cent of the recorded marriages showed the men to be older than the women with a median difference of ten years. Many of the girls at this time were married at the age of 14 or 15. In 1955, the same type of records showed 84 per cent of the men to be older than the women, with a median difference of two to three years.[6] Other recent studies of age of marriage show that the median age of marriage of women is about 20, and of men about 24, which is not far different from the situation in the United States.

The rural Brazilian family is getting smaller, though it is still large in comparison to families in urban and industrial societies. It is particularly the urban family and the middle-class family that are growing smaller. Thus in 1950 the average rural family consisted of seven persons; this was the number of people living under one roof, and dependent on the head of the family. The average urban family was five persons. Of the total number of people in the rural family 8.5 per cent were neither head of family, wife, or child; they were grandchildren, parents of the family head, grandparents, other relatives, and godchildren or godparents of the head of the family. But in Rio de Janeiro the number of people not in the nuclear family was 2 per cent, and in the city of São Paulo, 1 per cent.

Furthermore, people of high socioeconomic status have fewer children than those of lower status. In the city of Sao Paulo in 1950, men aged 50 to 59 reported 2.9 children per person and 3.7 children per father in the professions, while those in manu-facturing industries reported 4.8 and 5.6 children respectively.[7] Outside of the city of São Paulo families were larger, but the same socioeconomic differential existed. There were 4.1 children per man and 5.0 children per father in the liberal professions, and 6.2 children per man and 7.0 per father in the manufacturing industries.

Bertram Hutchinson found that the number of births per married woman aged 47 to 66 was 4.9 for women without schooling, 3.5 for women with primary school education only, and 2.2 for women with a secondary school education.[8] J. V. D. Saunders found that in the state of São Paulo, the numbers of children residing with their parents were smallest among the liberal professions and increased according to the following order: banking and finance, government and military service, factory workers, employees in business, transportation workers, agriculturists.[9]

While the family has been going through these changes, the place of women in the society has changed considerably. Many more women are now employed outside of the home. In 1940, 17 per cent of the urban labor force was women; this figure moved to 26 per cent in 1950, but was only 12 per cent in 1920. Middle-class women are now to be found in large numbers in banks, stores, and business offices, and also in the social service field, whereas they were just beginning to get into the schools as teachers in 1900. Working-class women are factory operatives, clerks in small stores, or domestic servants.

The old patriarchal family has been greatly reduced in numbers, though many of its characteristics remain in the families of the fazendas of Bahia, Minas Gerais, and São Paulo. In its place has come the modern, small conjugal family. This family usually exists in the cities, large or small, and is characterized by the wife's freedom to have a job or to lead an active life outside of her home; the sharing of responsibility by husband and wife for maintenance of the home; a smaller number of children—often three or four; the responsibility of the family for the support of children's education through secondary school (middle class) or primary school (working class); the children's greater freedom during adolescence; the limited kinship obligations outside of the nuclear family; the absence of the children from home when they are in school or at play; a rise in the rate of divorces and legal separations (*desquites*); an increase in remarriages by divorced or separated people.

At the same time, a new form of conjugal or nuclear family is coming into existence, the *amigação* or "friendly agreement" family. There are two forms of this type of family. The middle-

and upper-class form is an informal marriage between divorced or legally separated people (*desquitados*), who cannot, according to Brazilian law, be remarried, because the law does not recognize divorce, and *desquites* are not grounds for remarriage, only for separation of a married couple. These people attempt to re-organize their marital and family lives by friendly agreements concerning responsibility for children. About three-fourths of the separations are by agreement and are not contested in the court. When people who have been separated wish to marry other people informally, they sometimes draw up a legal contract for reciprocal services that has the function of a marriage contract. There are not a large number of *desquitados*. The 1950 census reported only 23,000 separated women, and the number of new legal separations averaged about 2,700 per year during the 1950's, compared with over 600,000 marriages per year.

Among the working classes, and especially in the rural areas, there are many families based upon common-law unions. A man and woman live together, they have children, and eventually come to think of themselves as a family, though there has been no formal wedding. Sometimes they ask a visiting Catholic priest or missionary to marry them. Civil marriage has no particular significance to them. Illegitimacy has never been regarded in Brazil as a major disgrace, and in cases such as this it is only a technicality. In the 1950 census, 727,000 women reported them-selves as unmarried with children, and they had an average of about 2.5 children apiece. Clearly, most of these were living in *amigacao* families.

Education and the Contemporary Family

As the Brazilian family has lost many of its economic and political functions in a world of growing complexity, it has naturally turned over many of its earlier educational responsi-bilities to the schools. Compared with colonial times, the modern school:

1. Gives mental skills essential in contemporary society
2. Teaches knowledge and attitudes for citizenship
3. Gives orientation concerning possible vocations
4. Gives knowledge and skills necessary for an occupation
5. Gives knowledge and experience leading to autonomy.

And as the Brazilian family has lost so much of its extension in social space, its political function, and its activity as an economic institution, it has likely increased its effectiveness as an agency for molding a complex personality for a complex world. It now has the clear-cut function of forming the child's personality. The twentieth-century Brazilian is different from the Brazilian of the nineteenth century, or of colonial times, partly because the family is different, partly because the economy and the state are different, and partly because he has gone to school.

We might say that the school system, after being created by the Brazilian society to serve some of the child-rearing functions formerly handled by the family, has formed an uneasy alliance with the various kinds of families whose children it receives, and the terms of this alliance are continually being negotiated and renegotiated.

NOTES

1. Antônio Cândido de Mello e Souza, "The Brazilian Family," in *Brazil: Portrait of Half a Continent,* ed. T. Lynn Amith and Alexander Marchant (New York, 1951), p. 299.

2. Tomás Antônio Gonzaga, *Marília de Dirceu e mais Poesias* (Lisbon, 1937), cited in Cândido, p. 292.

3. Freyre, *The Masters and the Slaves,* p. 394.

4. Cândido, p. 304.

5. Emílio Willems, "Brazil," in *The Institutions of Advanced Societies,* ed. Arnold M. Rose (Minneapolis, 1958), pp. 564–72. Copyright 1958, University of Minnesota. Quoted by permission of the publishers, University of Minnesota Press.

6. Orácy Nogueira, "A Organização de Familia no Município de Itapetininga," *Educação e Ciências, Sociais,* V, No. 11 (Aug. 1959), 61–112.

7. Christopher Tietze, "Human Fertility in Latin America," in *A Crowding Hemisphere: Population Change in the Americas, Annals of the American Academy of Political and Social Science,* CCCXVI (Mar. 1958).

8. Bertram Hutchinson, "Analfebetismo em São Paulo," *Educação e Ciências Sociais,* III, No. 7 (Apr. 1958), 51–70.

9. J. V. D. Saunders, *Differential Fertility in Brazil* (Gainesville, Florida, 1958).

11

The
Church and
Education

IN the development of Western Europe the church was the first great agent of formal education. As an offshoot of Western Christendom in the sixteenth century, colonial Brazil depended on the church almost entirely for schools and colleges, even after the nationalistic movement in Europe had created state-supported schools. Before describing the system of church schools that grew up in Brazil, it will be useful to describe the political relation between church, state, and education that exists in Brazil today, and to show how Brazil differs from other countries in this respect. There are three types of relationships between church and state in Latin America, with respect to the conduct of education:

1. The Roman Catholic church has a legal right and responsibility for making educational policy, and is consulted in all matters pertaining to education. Colombia is the chief example of this type of relationship. In 1887 a concordat was negotiated with the Vatican in which the church was recognized as "an essential element of the social order." Education at the several levels was to be "organized and directed in conformity with the dogmas and morals of the Catholic religion."

2. A dual system of schools and other educational institutions, with public and private schools, and with one or more churches conducting some of the private schools. Religious instruction is given in the schools. Government support is given partially to church-directed schools. Examples of this type are Chile, Brazil, Peru, and Costa Rica.

3. Education at the primary and secondary levels is exclusively a function of the state, and the church is barred from conducting schools. Higher institutions may be conducted by

the church, under strict government supervision. Mexico is an example of this type of organization, though actually the church has been informally allowed greater educational activity in recent years.

In Brazil the Roman Catholic church was "established" and supported by the state during the Empire as during colonial times. The government nominated candidates for the major church positions, and the church received an appropriation from the state. With the coming of the Republic, however, church was separated from state. Instruction in the public schools was made secular. But the constitutions of 1934 and 1946 declared that religious instruction should be offered in the primary schools, with parents having the right to choose among various forms of religion or to exclude their children from the religious classes.

The Catholic Church and Education in Colonial Times

When the Jesuit missionaries found that the Indians, whom they had hoped to educate, were disappearing from the Atlantic seaboard, they established a set of secondary schools for instructing the sons of colonists in the liberal arts. They had eighteen colleges and seminaries in 1759, the year of their expulsion from Brazil, and they provided the only systematic schooling to be found. Supplementing their efforts and operating in a haphazard way, the priest-chaplains of the great plantations developed local primary schools for teaching the children of the masters and their retainers, and even some of the slave children.

After the expulsion of the Jesuits, the Franciscans opened a variety of schools which were in agreement with the reform principles of the Marques de Pombal. Then, in 1798–1800, Bishop Azaredo Coutinho established the seminary at Olinda, near Recife, which trained priests and laymen at the secondary level.

Thus the education provided by the church during colonial times was essentially an education for the upper class and served to inculcate the knowledge and ideology of Western Europe in the minds of a small number. For another half century, as the Empire was created and made its start, there was only the beginning of a state system of education. For almost three centuries the Roman Catholic church had a major responsibility for whatever formal education was given in Brazil.

Catholicism in Brazil was not the same thing as Catholicism in Europe or even in Spanish America. Nor was it a single, simple entity in Brazil. Roger Bastide has described three forms of Catholicism that existed in Brazil, side by side, engaged in a perennial conflict which still goes on. One was Portuguese Catholicism.

This never assumed the tragic aspect of Spanish Catholicism, brutal or mystical and inclined always toward death or ecstacy. It was a softer and more human Catholicism, whether that of the peasants captivated by village feasts in honor of saints who were protectors of love or harvests, or that of city dwellers saluting with a thousand rockets and firecrackers the baroque processions coming out of their churches that recalled the sea, decorated with stone seaweed and shells.

This type became the familial Catholicism of the plantation, which was often opposed by the more Roman and universalist Catholicism of the religious orders, and especially of the Jesuits.

Familial Catholicism possessed neither inflexibility of dogma nor puritanism of conduct. It was all indulgence, softened by the heat of the tropics and by the sensuality of the Negro women. It let itself be contaminated by the superstitions of the Indians and the religions of the Africans, beliefs in forest spirits, water mothers, love potions. It did not prevent the cruelty of the masters toward their slaves, nor the polygyny of the whites, nor the sadism of the mother of the family, jealous of her husband's colored mistresses. In a word, it was a Catholicism that was more a climate of feeling than an education for the spiritual life.

.   .   .   .

Custom also required that the young girls who did not marry should shut themselves up in convents, but these convents were no mystic cloisters. There they made preserves and candies, received visitors, gossiped, and acted in comedies. All the foreign travelers who went to Brazil were struck by this festive atmosphere in the female convents, where the inmates played ball with the images of the saints.

Another Catholicism was that of the religious orders, especially that of the Jesuits. The Jesuits did all they could to defend the morality of the Roman church and to extend its ideologies. They influenced the women through the confessional and the boys through schools which taught them to respect the rules of the church. Thus the bishops and the Jesuit fathers defended European culture and Roman Catholic morality against the turbulence of the lords of the plantation, the polygyny of the whites, and the rural superstitions. They succeeded in creating a small elite of educated men who were closer to the interests and ideals of the mother country than to those of the colony and who helped in what little progress Brazil made during the colonial era toward urbanization and becoming part of Western Christendom.

The third Catholicism was created by the African slaves out of their tribal beliefs and their contacts with Christianity on the plantations.

The African was baptized, either on his departure or his disembarkation. He learned the Credo and the Ave Maria, genuflexion before the altar and the sign of the cross, but slavery placed a barrier between the blacks and the whites. On the *engenho,* mass was not said at the same hour for the masters and for the Africans, or, if there was but one mass, the blacks remained on the porch outside and took part in the divine mystery only through the open door. The social structure thus modified Christian egalitarianism. The blacks provided for themselves black saints, Saint Efigênia, Saint Benedito, patrons of their race, protectors of their misfortunes. In the towns they created private brotherhoods, those of the Rosary of the Black People, with their rules and privileges, their Kings and Queens, and incorporated several of their dances, modified and controlled by the Church. As in the United States there were two Protestantisms, so Catholicism here also, under the effect of slavery, tended to a dualism that followed the color line. Sometimes there was even a pluralism, for the brotherhoods of creole Negroes refused to mingle with those of imported Negroes and the brotherhoods of the mulattoes refused to mix with either.[1]

Bastide concludes that the church began to reflect Brazilian society when the sons of colonists became priests, and the colony was no longer dependent on clergy sent over from Portugal. The priest was active in political, economic, and intellectual fields. He was relatively liberal and also nationalistic. He entered into conspiracies and secret societies aimed at gaining political and economic independence. Under the Empire, priests were members of the Chamber of Deputies and were cabinet ministers or members of the opposition. Thus Brazilian Catholicism appeared more social than religious, more directed toward things of the Brazilian earth than toward the supernatural.

The church served as a channel of social mobility for mulattoes and poor whites. The former were permitted to enter the religious orders at the close of the seventeenth century. At first the orders received the sons of priests by Negro women for whom the fathers wished to provide a situation, and later the children of legitimate origin were recruited, provided they could learn well in school. Men of humble origin were more apt to listen to orders from Rome than would the sons of plantation owners. They were more careful of morality, more rigid in dogma, and more faithful to the Pope. They were important figures in the reformation that occurred within the church at the close of the Empire.

Church and Education in the Twentieth Century

During the middle years of the nineteenth century there ensued a struggle within the church for control of Brazil. On one side was the Vatican with its desire to purify the clergy and through them to bring the practices of the Brazilian church more in accord with universal Catholic practice, and on the other side were the freethinking Brazilian church leaders, who at one time proposed to break with Rome and to found a national church something like the Church of England.

The victory of the Roman or universalist policy at the end of the nineteenth century was partially caused by the fact that the upper-class Brazilian families had reduced the numbers of their sons going into the priesthood. The church recruited from working-class and middle-class Brazilian families, and it brought in foreign religious orders—the Dominicans of Toulouse; German, Italian, or Belgian Benedictines; and German Franciscans. Even in the twentieth century the clergy were recruited more from the sons of immigrant Italians and Spaniards than from the old Brazilian families. The foreigners and the upward mobile Brazilians were bound more closely to Rome than to the ruling class in Brazil.

In making itself more Roman the church made itself less Brazilian:

The Catholic clergy became remarkable for its orthodox Catholicism, its lofty morality; but what it gained here, did it not lose otherwise, by becoming more a foreign body in the bosom of a population that remained nostalgically turned toward a more Lusitanian and festive Catholicism? In becoming Roman, the Church denationalized itself.

There remained thus a final task to be performed: that is, to keep all that the Church had gained in religious depth and moral authority but to reintegrate it in the national community. . . . The Church attempted to reconquer the world, but without abdicating any part of its Roman character, and without making any compromise with the popular Catholicism of the people. It created confessional schools and organized a press of its own. It interested itself anew in politics and did not hesitate to recommend certain names or parties to the electors, even sending some of its members to hold seats in the Chamber of Deputies. . . . In order to bring laymen under the direction of the clergy, it founded Catholic Action for groups of men, the Women's

League for women, the *Juventude Universitária Católica* for students, and the *Juventude Operária Católica* for working youth. . . . It attacked the solution of social problems, many of which exist in Brazil: gambling, the family instability among the well-to-do, the poor housing, nutrition and hygiene among the poor classes.[2]

This policy of the church led it into the field of education at all levels, and it continues to follow this course. Its Catholic Action is a form of adult education. Its work in the *favelas* of Rio is another form of adult education. Its work with university students is increasing, both in the Catholic and the state universities. In 1961, for example, the University Student Movement to Eliminate Slums gained its main strength in the Catholic universities. In the same year one-third of the secondary schools of the country were conducted by Catholic organizations, and about one-third of the academic secondary school students were attending such schools.

The Church is using its political influence to get more government financial support for private schools, which would permit it to expand its network of schools, particularly at the primary school level. Religious instruction is provided in all primary schools, but the scarcity of priests and teaching monks is so great that the church generally relies upon the regular classroom teachers to give these lessons.

According to the 1950 census, 93.5 percent of Brazilians are Roman Catholics. It is often said that the majority of Brazilian Catholics are only nominally so. There are various ways of estimating the number of "devout Catholics." For instance, one may assume that a practicing Catholic will take at least one communion a month. According to church statistics, the number of communions in 1959 was 135 million, or a few more than 10 million a month. This would suggest that about ten million people are devout. The number of Catholic church marriages in 1959 was 423,000, which is about two-thirds of the number of marriages of that year. The number of baptisms was 2,722,000 which corresponded to about 94 per cent of the newborns of that year, although Catholic baptism is a social event, and does not imply devoutness on the part of the family. There were 8,722 parish priests, or about one to 7,000 nominal Catholics. Perhaps one might conclude that one-third of Brazilian adults are fairly devout Catholics. Perhaps one-tenth are active enough to belong to a church association (there were 4 million members of 33,868 church associations in 1959.)

Protestant Churches

Protestant missionaries came to Brazil as early as 1819. Though started as a missionary venture, Brazilian Protestantism soon organized national churches with theological schools and Brazilian pastors. By 1900 the number of Protestants was about 40,000 and in 1959 it was 1,750,000 with 6,570 churches and 6,800 clergymen. Protestants are strongest in the South and East, but between 1940 and 1950 they grew more rapidly in numbers in the Northeast than in any other region. As in North America, the Protestant churches are related to social class. The Anglicans, Evangelicals, and Methodists are strongest in the middle class, with Baptists drawing heavily from the lower-middle class. The Pentecostals appeal to the working class, and one can find Assembly of God chapels in the *favelas* of Rio.

Education has been a major activity of the Protestant churches. In the South the German Lutherans built secondary schools and rural schools. The North American churches started schools, generally secondary schools, which have had some influence on the development of Brazilian education. Mackenzie College, started by the Presbyterians in São Paulo, is influential both as a secondary school and a university. Bennett College, a Methodist school in Rio, is also well known.

Spiritualism

The third church in size is the Spiritualist, with 636,000 members in 1958, 1,286 church buildings, and 1,022 other meeting rooms. Starting in Brazil in 1865, soon after they began to flourish in Europe, at first the Spiritualist groups regarded themselves as good Catholics, and their centers had a Catholic altar. Later they were disapproved by the Catholic clergy.

According to Bastide there are three types of Spiritualists, separated from one another by social class lines. At the top is a form of belief and practice called scientific, cultivated by middle-class intellectuals, which is concerned with metaphysical phenomena. Below this level are the followers of the Frenchman Alan Kardec, who organized the practice and the dogma of Spiritualism in Europe in the mid-nineteenth century. These people are mainly of the lower-middle and upper working class—medium-level government officials, skilled workers, and commercial employees. They have a number of imposing temples in the larger cities. Their services include prayer, confession of sins, reading Kardec's writings, and seances in which the spirits

TABLE 35

Religious Affiliation

Religion according to statements by those interviewed (1950)

(in thousands)

People who have stated their religion: 51,944,397

Religions	North	North-East	East	South	West-Central	Brazil Numbers	%
Catholic	1,783	12,212	17,833	15,118	1,614	48,559	93.50
Protestant	36	176	475	1,018	37	1,741	3.30
Spiritualist	5	34	336	392	58	825	1.60
Buddhist	—	—	2	149	1	153	0.30
Jewish	2	2	30	36	—	70	0.13
Orthodox Church	—	—	6	34	1	41	0.08
Mahometan	—	—	1	2	—	3	0.007
Other religions	11	10	44	67	7	120	0.23
Without religion	8	59	166	159	20	412	0.79

Source: Census of 1950, *Censo Demografico do Brasil* (Rio de Janeiro: Instituto Brasileiro de Geografia e Estatistica).

of the dead take possession of the mediums and answer questions and give advice. Finally, there is "low Spritualism" or the Spiritualism of *Umbanda*, which is practiced by the lower classes, including many Negroes. This form has a strong mixture of *macumba*, the African-Amerindian religion of the Northeast. It employs dances, chanting, animal sacrifices, and spectacular trances.

Conclusions

Since schooling is needed for so many purposes in modern Brazil, formal education has marked out its own field of action which overlaps the fields of the basic social institutions—the state, the church, the family, and the economic organizations. No one of them has created an education that meets the needs of the society, as it was possible for the church to do in the rough and simple colonial period.

Today the public educational system stands by itself. However, in trying to accomplish its functions in society, the church finds schools indispensable. When directed by the more aggressive and single-minded elements in its leadership, the church attempts to make its own educational system serve all or nearly all of the educational needs of the society. From this point of view society would need no other schools than those maintained by the church. Thus there is competition between the proponents of public education and of church-directed education, with the two groups fairly evenly matched.

NOTES

1. Roger Bastide, "Religion and the Church in Brazil," in *Brazil, Portrait of Half a Continent,* pp. 334–37.
2. Ibid., pp. 342–43.

12

Teachers
and the Teaching
Profession

TEACHERS are the largest group among the people practicing the professions. There were in 1960 approximately 290,000 teachers, out of a total of about 700,000 men and women engaged in the professions and what the Brazilian census called "social service activities," which include teaching, social work, nursing, and the religious professions. Teachers made up about 1 per cent of the adult population between the ages of 20 and 65, and about 2 per cent of the employed adult population. They were distributed as follows over the three levels in 1960: primary school teachers, 200,000; secondary school teachers, 73,000; and university teachers, 19,000.

In 1933 the total number of teachers was 71,000, and in 1940 the number was about 105,000. The growth has been especially rapid since 1940, due to sharp increases in secondary school and university enrollments, together with steady increase in primary school pupils.

Social Status of Teachers

Teachers range in social status from upper class to lower-middle class. The occupation itself is ranked by Brazilians, according to Hutchinson's study, at the middle-class level, below medicine and law. The primary school teacher is ranked above an "owner of a small commercial establishment" and above a "public official of middle grade," but below a journalist. A university professor would be rated substantially higher than a primary school teacher, with the secondary school teacher between.[1] However, there is no distinction in title within the broad limits of the profession. Every teacher is a *professor* or a *professora*, regardless of the extent and quality of his professional preparation and the character of his teaching position. All people with a degree in higher education are by common consent called "doctor," and this title is preferable to that of *professor*. The holder of an M.D. or a Ph.D. degree does not have a special title. The university professor who occupies a chair as head of a department is sometimes addressed as *professor catedrático*.

The actual social status of a particular teacher depends on several factors in addition to his occupation. One of these is his family background. Many primary school teachers are upper-class people because their family is upper class and has been so for several generations. On the other hand, some university professors are accorded upper-middle-class status if their families were middle or lower class. Another element in social status is the membership of the teacher in social clubs and organizations. A person active in certain exclusive charitable organizations is likely to be upper-middle or upper class. In the smaller cities a teacher's social status is often related to the status of the local social club to which he belongs; if he does not belong to a social club and does not come from an upper-class family, he is likely to be seen by other people as a lower-middle-class person.

The Normal School

The first normal school of Brazil was founded in Niteroi (capital of the state of Rio de Janeiro) in 1835, and by 1900 there were eleven such schools, all in state capitals. These schools were operated at the secondary level, with courses lasting various numbers of years. Then with the coming of the reform wave in the 1920's and the early 1930's, efforts were made to improve teacher training. Laboratory schools—schools for practice teaching—were added, and the course was extended for one or two years.

After the mid-1930's the normal school fell into a pattern that persisted through the 1950's. There were two normal school courses. The shorter one, given in the regional normal schools, was a four-year course for graduates of primary schools, who must be at least 13 years of age to enter the course. Graduates of this course were called Regentes de Ensino, and were expected to teach in rural schools. The other course, given in the Escola Normal, was a three-year course at the level of the colégio and for entrance required a diploma from a *ginásio* as well as a minimum age of 15. The course for Regentes de Ensino is much smaller than the normal school course, having 3,900 graduates in

1960 compared with 19,000 graduates from the normal school course.

Finally, each state has in its capital and sometimes elsewhere an Instituto de Educação which gives the regular normal school course and also advanced courses of one or two years' duration for the training of primary school directors, supervisors, and technicians in tests, measurements, and educational records. The state of São Paulo has a system of thirty-four institutions of this type.

TABLE 36

Types of Institutions Training Primary School Teachers

| | Numbers of school units | | | | | |
| | 1956 | | 1960 | | 1961 | |
	Regional Normal (Ginásio)	Normal School (Colégio)	Regional Normal	Normal School	Regional Normal	Normal School
Public	134	221	213	305	222	320
Private	78	495	134	586	143	634

Source: *Sinopse Estatístico de Ensino Médio*, (Rio de Janeiro: Serviço de Estatística de Educação e Cultura, Ministerio de Educação e Cultura [for 1956, 1960, 1961]).

There were 1,319 schools for teachers in 1961, distributed as shown in Table 36. Many of these normal schools are quite small. Half of them had less than sixty students for a three-year course in 1960, or, on the average, less than twenty per grade.

An example of the curriculum of a three-year normal school is given below, for the state of Rio Grande do Sul, which established this program in 1955. The first year is given almost entirely to courses of general cultural value, while the second and third years include courses that are primarily professional in content. Finally, there is a six-month probationary period, during which the new teacher, under supervision, takes charge of a class.

First Year—14 units	units
Language and Literature	3
Mathematics and Natural Sciences	3
Social Science	2
Health and Hygiene	1
Design and Applied Arts	2

Music and Recreation	1
Home Economics and Practical Arts	2

Second Year and Third Year—28 units
Fundamentals of Education	
(Philosophical, Psychological, Sociological)	12
Methods and Curriculum	14
School and Class Administration	2

The Primary School Teacher

In speaking of the Brazilian primary school teacher it is justifiable to use the pronoun "she," because 93 per cent were females in 1958. This percentage of female primary school teachers represents an increase over 1933 and 1940, in which the percentages were 85 and 90, respectively. There is general acceptance of married women as teachers, and the four and one-half hour school day makes it relatively easy for a housewife and mother to look after her home and family and to teach at the same time.

TABLE 37

Social Class Backgrounds of Teachers
(percentage distribution)

Social class	State of Rio de Janeiro		Normal school students in the states of São Paulo and Minas Gerais	Normal school students in Rio de Janeiro
	Primary school teachers	Secondary school teachers		
Upper and upper-middle	26	40	25	24
Lower-middle	53	56	57	58
Working class	20	3	19	18
Number in sample	160	122	1,441	263

Sources: For teachers: Aparecida Joly Gouveia, "Professores do Estado do Rio," *Revista Brasileira de Estudos Pedagógicos*, XXVIII (July-Sept. 1957), 30-63.

For Normal School students: Aparecida Joly Gouveia, *Working Paper for Study of Normal School Students*, (unpublished paper, Rio de Janeiro: Centro Brasileiro de Pesquisas Educacionais, INEP, 1961).

For Normal School students in Rio de Janeiro: Riva Bauzer and Iva Waisberg Bonow, *Caraterísticos da Adolescente do Instituto de Educação* Rio de Janeiro: Instituto de Educação, 1961).

The primary school teachers come from a wide range of socioeconomic status, slightly more than half of them having been reared in lower-middle-class families. The data in Table 37 do not come from a national sample, but they are representative of teachers in the state of Rio de Janeiro in the 1950's, and of normal school students in Minas Gerais and São Paulo in 1960. These two separate studies show substantial agreement. They indicate that about 20 per cent of primary school teachers come from working-class homes.

TABLE 38

*Advantages of the Teaching Profession for a Woman:
Opinions of Normal School Students*

	No. of Responses
A profession especially fitting for a woman, a future mother	80
Economic security, social position	35
Possibility of being socially useful	23
Possibility to improve oneself as an individual	4
Opportunity to become aware of social problems	1
	143

Note: Information provided by questionnaires from 76 girls in normal schools of Rio de Janeiro.
Source: Josildeth da Silva Gomes, "Escolha de Magistério Público Primeiro como Profissão no Distrito Federal," *Educação e Ciências Sociais*, II, No. 6 (Nov. 1957), 184-243.

Studying a group of girls in two normal schools in Rio de Janeiro, Josildeth da Sílva Gomes asked them, "What advantages does teaching offer a woman?" Seventy-six girls in their middle teens gave 143 answers, which are summarized in Table 38. They thought of themselves primarily as mothers and wives, and saw teaching as suitable both for preparation for these roles and as complementary to them. Some of the girls spoke of the teacher's role as "feminine" and said that they chose teaching rather than some other career to avoid becoming "masculine." The decision to become a teacher, they said, was made while they were in primary school. About two-thirds of the girls had relatives who were teachers.

In a study of a sample of 721 first-year normal school students in the states of São Paulo and Minas Gerais, the girls were asked to indicate, from a list of six statements, the one most important advantage that the normal school could give them. Their choices were as follows:

	Per cent giving this as first choice
Good general culture	35
Preparation for raising my own children	27

Preparation for becoming a primary school teacher	24
A diploma which permits entrance to the university and preparation for an interesting and advantageous career	10
A diploma which promises a career with economic security	3
Association with girls of good social status	1 [2]

These percentages indicate that the normal school course is popular with girls for reasons not entirely or directly connected with the explicit purpose of the course—which is to train teachers for primary schools. In 1960 one-third of all secondary school graduates were girls graduating from normal schools. And since girls make up 50 per cent of secondary school graduates, this means that two-thirds of the girls graduating from secondary schools have taken the normal school course. A comparison of the number of normal school graduates in 1957 with the numbers of normal school graduates who were teaching in primary school in 1957 and 1958 leads to the estimate that 50 per cent of the girls who graduate from a normal school course do not teach during the subsequent year. Some of them enter a university, since the normal school diploma gives its holder the same right to take university entrance examinations that is given to the graduates of the academic secondary school. Some girls take other types of jobs, and some get married. The normal school is in fact the only secondary school available to girls in some of the smaller cities, and in many others it is taught in the same building with the *colégio*, which, with its scientific course and its classical course, is more popular with boys than with girls.

Most primary school teachers have one class for four and one-half hours per day, morning or afternoon. They generally teach five or six days a week, nine months of the year. Where the school is on a three-shift basis, with each shift getting three to three and a half hours of class work, the teacher may teach one or two classes. A few teachers teach two full classes of four and one-half hours each. A study of primary school teachers of the state of Rio de Janeiro, showed that 16 per cent of them had two teaching jobs, while another 6 per cent had another job in addition to teaching.[3]

To be eligible for a job teaching in a state school system a teacher must possess a normal school diploma, but most municipal school systems do not require the diploma. The normal school graduates tend to be concentrated in the states that pay higher salaries, as do the normal school students. Thus in 1958, 74 per cent of Brazil's normal school students were in the four southern states and Minas Gerais, Guanabara, and Espírito Santo, which have 47 per cent of the population of Brazil. The percentages of primary school teachers without a normal school diploma have increased since 1940, when there were 37.6 per cent. This rose to 46.7 per cent in 1950, to 48.3 per cent in 1955, and was 46.6 per cent in 1958.

Salaries of primary school teachers are low in comparison with those of secondary school and university teachers. The average annual salary of a state school teacher in 1957 was 55,200 cruzeiros ($850.00 U. S. at the 1957 value), that of a municipal school teacher, 15,000 cruzeiros ($231.00 U. S.), and that of a private school teacher, 34,000 cruzeiros ($523.00 U. S.). Another way to assess the salary level is to compare it with the government-established minimum wage that is paid the majority of workers for an eight-hour day. The beginning salary of a primary school teacher in the state system in 1960 varied from 250 per cent (Guanabara) of the minimum wage to 122 per cent (São Paulo), 160 (Minas Gerais), 116 (Bahia), 106 (Amazonas), and 44 (Sergipe).

THE ROLE OF THE PRIMARY SCHOOL TEACHER. A study of teachers in the state of Rio de Janeiro summarized the characteristics of the average primary school teacher as follows: a woman between 25 and 43 years old, white, married or single; who contributes to the support of her family but is not alone responsible for it; she comes from a middle-class home, has more formal education than her parents, is not native to the community where she teaches, and does not belong to voluntary or professional associations.[4]

The characteristics of a good teachers, as judged by parents of school children, are shown in Table 39. From this we infer a preference for certain of the possible roles of a teacher in the school: teacher as *instructor*—the teacher is skillful and efficient in organizing the classwork so that the children learn efficiently; teacher as *judge*—the teacher makes impartial judgments about the work of the children and also judges their behavior fairly; teacher as *disciplinarian*—the teacher controls the behavior of the class and keeps them at work, using punishment skillfully

TABLE 39

Characteristics of a Good Teacher:
Opinions of Parents

	% of parents
Efficiency (Explains clearly; is competent; has the ability to make the child learn; pushes children ahead.)	47
Dedication (Interested in children; gives time to her work; works hard with the slow ones; teaches like a missionary.)	39
Authority and energy (Makes the children work; does not tolerate loafing; is energetic; demands respect.)	23
Understanding, affection (is patient; understands children; makes children like her; inspires pupils.)	19
Punctuality (is punctual; never misses school.)	9
Impartiality (Is fair in giving grades and punishments; does not have favorites.)	5
Miscellaneous (Courteous, religious, moral person; experienced and well trained.)	7

Note: The percentages add to more than 100 because some parents named two substantially different attributes.
Source: Aparecida J. Gouveia, "A Escola e o Professor, na Opinão dos Pais," *Educação e Ciências Sociais*, II, No. 5 (Aug. 1957), 179-206. The parents were more or less a random selection from towns and rural areas of the state of Rio de Janeiro. There were 170 parents of primary school children and 44 of secondary school students; 97 men and 117 women; 137 urban and 77 rural.

to cope with aggressive pupils; teacher as *parent-substitute*—the teacher is like a mother, especially to younger children; teacher as *counsellor*—the teacher is a friend and counsellor of the pupil.

On the whole, the parents seem to prefer the more authoritarian roles of the teacher, rather than the softer and more affectionate roles. However, the teacher is seen by them as a parent-substitute as well as an authority external to the home. Some parents, at least, want the teacher to show affection and to win the love as well as the respect of pupils.

The Secondary School Teacher

In 1961 there were about 78,000 teachers in schools of middle level, including about 50,000 in the academic secondary, schools, some of whom taught in two or more schools. Fifty-nine percent were men. As shown in Table 37, there is a tendency for secondary school teachers to come from homes of somewhat higher socioeconomic status than do primary school teachers.

Professor Jayme Abreu comments that "the weakest point in the Brazilian secondary school is located in the teaching force.

When the enrollment increased sharply after 1930, it was necessary to organize an emergency corps of teachers, out of people marginal to other professions and even from people without university training." [5] Although some of these people became first-class teachers, the majority were inadequate. An immediate effort was made through the university faculties of philosophy, science and letters to train secondary school teachers. Enrollment in these faculties increased sharply, and has grown more rapidly than any other category of enrollment. By 1956 there were about 15,000 people who had received licenses to teach from such faculties, but many of them had gone into other kinds of work.

Out of a sample of 1,377 secondary school teachers in public and private schools of the state of Rio de Janeiro in 1951, only 8 per cent had received diplomas for secondary school teaching, and only 50 per cent had a university education (see Table 40).

TABLE 40

The Academic Training of Teachers in Secondary Schools of the State of Rio de Janeiro, 1951

Type of preparation	Number of teachers
Normal school	329
Law school	142
Faculty of Philosophy, Science and Letters	112
Accountant	110
Secondary school (graduate of colégio)	99
Medical school	60
Theological school (priest)	51
Secondary school (graduate of ginasio only)	55
Engineering school	24
Agronomy	14
Dentistry	12
Pharmacy	9
Commercial course in secondary school	8
Chemistry	6
Veterinary Medicine	2
No response	364

Sample: 1,377 secondary school teachers, 711 of whom were men.
Source: Jayme Abreu, *O Sistema Educacional Fluminense* (Rio de Janeiro: Instituto de Estudos Pedagógicos, Ministério de Educação e Cultura, 1955).

The proportion of secondary school teachers who have been explicitly trained in a university for this work was about 20 per cent in 1962, and there are still many people teaching with only a normal school diploma. A person who does not have a license for teaching in secondary school is allowed to take a "proficiency examination" on the basis of which he is given a temporary license to teach. The proficiency examination varies a good deal from time to time and place to place. In the state secondary schools, which are generally more carefully controlled than the private schools, it is sometimes difficult to find sufficient candidates of good quality for vacant positions. For instance, the state of São Paulo in 1955 had 576 vacancies in its public *ginásios* and secured 704 candidates, of whom only 249 were approved. In 1958 nearly 80 per cent of the secondary school teachers in Brazil were teaching on the basis of a proficiency examination.

In a 1959 study of secondary school teachers in the state of Rio de Janeiro, 21 per cent had a nonteaching job in addition to their work as teachers, and half of this group regarded teaching as the minor or secondary activity. Of those who had no work other than teaching, 65 per cent taught twenty-five or more hours of classes a week, and 26 per cent taught thirty-seven or more hours of classes a week. Of the secondary school teachers in this sample, 45 per cent had no more than a secondary school preparation.[8]

Secondary school teachers are much better paid than primary school teachers. In the Rio de Janeiro study, secondary teachers averaged about twice the salaries of primary school teachers. An average salary in 1957 would have been about 90,000 cruzeiros or about $1,350.00 (U. S.) per year. This salary was in payment for teaching twelve classes a week, and could be doubled by a teacher who wanted to teach twenty-five or thirty classes per week.

A teacher enjoys substantial social security benefits, for which a deduction of 5 per cent of his salary is made. He receives medical and hospital insurance and the right to retire on his basic salary after twenty-five to thirty-five years of service.

On the whole, secondary school teachers are a more "professionalized" group than are primary school teachers. More of them teach full time. More of them belong to professional teachers associations. In the Rio de Janeiro study 22 per cent of the secondary school teachers belonged to a teacher's organization, as compared with 6 per cent of the primary school teachers.

The training of a person for secondary school teaching in a faculty of philosophy, science and letters normally takes four years. He specializes in the department in which he will do most of his teaching and his work in this area earns him the degree of Bachelor of Arts. In his fourth year he supplements the studies in his specialty with courses in educational psychology, biological, sociological and philosophical foundations of education, and methods of teaching. He then receives a diploma or teacher's license.

A special fourth year course is offered by the department of education for students who expect to teach in a normal school or to become "technicians of education," in schools or state or federal departments. They spend more time on courses in the field of education, and consequently less in specialized work in other fields.

The role of a secondary school teacher is gradually becoming clearly defined and understood in Brazil, but the continued expansion of secondary schools means that the shortage of teachers will continue for at least another ten years and that large numbers of individuals without university training will continue to teach.

The University Teacher

The university teacher has always had a position of prominence and influence in Brazilian social, economic, and political life. When the first law school professors were appointed early in the nineteenth century, the edict which created schools of law provided that the professor of law should receive the same salary as a judge. The salary at that time was set at 800 milreis (the equivalent of $1,000.00 U. S. of that period) which was fairly substantial for part-time work. The professor was not expected to work full-time at this occupation. Instead he was expected to find his major source of income outside of teaching, and his professorship was counted a mark of distinction in his profession.

The law still classifies the university professorship in the highest level of public officials, and the salary of the *professor catedrático* was fixed in December 1960, at 47,000 cruzeiros a month (the highest federal civil service salary was 36,000 cruzeiros). At the 1960 exchange rate, a salary of 47,000 cruzeiros was equal to about $235.00 (U. S.) a month. And this was not regarded as a full-time position.

The *professor catedrático* is the holder of a *catedra*, or chair, which is the basic unit of the university. He is the chairman of a department. A faculty or a school consists of the teaching activities of a number of *catedras*. The *catedrático* has life tenure of his position—a matter of current criticism and controversy. The question is not whether a university professor should have life tenure of his job, but whether the chairman should have life tenure of that chair, which means that he has control for the remainder of his teaching life of the instruction in his particular department.

The *catedrático* appoints the other members of his department who work under him. He may, and often does, create a highly personal regime. Furthermore, since he may be a part-time teacher, he may not give much time to his administrative duties.

In a small university there may be only one chair to a department; in a larger university there may be several chairs in a department—such as ancient history and modern history, educational psychology and educational administration, sociology and anthropology. That is, there may be two or more subdepartments. The *catedra* is filled by a competition in which the candidates' degrees, publications, and previous experience are examined by a board, and then each candidate must either make a public defense of a piece of research work or undergo a written examination. The board that selects the new *catedrático* from among the candidates consists of some professors within the university and some from outside. This board is chosen by the assembly of *catedráticos* in the faculty.

A teacher prepares to become a *catedrático* by moving up through the ranks as instructor, assistant professor, and lecturer. The first two positions are obtained through direct appointment by a *catedrático*. The lectureship or *livre-docent* position is obtained by passing an exhaustive examination or by publishing a major piece of research or scholarship.

Dissatisfaction with the traditional procedure of choosing *catedráticos* and with the life tenure of a chair has given rise to attempts to bypass the *catedrático* system, which is firmly entrenched in the constitution. The alternative is to give university teachers at various levels contracts that specify their responsibilities. Promotion is then determined more flexibly, on the basis of seniority, teaching effectiveness, and scholarly productivity.

Whatever defects there may be in the system of administering departments of universities, the university professorship has continued to be a position of high social status, with many attractive elements. When it is a part-time position, the professor can give as little as three lectures a week and hold conferences with students and colleagues for perhaps twice that length of time.

He can then devote himself to earning money in his profession, to scholarly work, to politics, or to a second teaching position.

Frequently a man who has had a distinguished career in law, medicine, or engineering will seek a university professorship as a symbol of his success and a token of his high social status. Sometimes a professorial chair is a springboard to a political career in the state or national government. Sometimes it is a safe place in which to wait out a storm of political adversity. The personal freedom of the university teacher has been preserved. He is free to do his scholarship work in his own way, to criticize the government in power, and to worship as he sees fit.

NUMBERS OF UNIVERSITY PROFESSORS. In 1960 there were 19,000 university teachers. This was one teacher to 4.8 students. Since most of the teachers were part-time, and taught about a third as much as a North American university professor, this is equivalent to something like a ratio of one full-time teacher to fifteen students. The ratios vary enormously from one field of scholarship to another. The ratio for teachers of law is about one to twenty, while in schools of engineering it is about one to three, and in schools of medicine about one to seven.

Educators agree that extension of the number of full-time positions is indispensable to any major improvement in higher education, especially if the university seeks to contribute substantially in the fields of research and of creative scholarship—something it has not done in the past. There was a general expansion of full-time appointments after World War II, but the monetary inflation of the 1950's forced the universities in many cases to permit professors to accept other work, since it was not possible to increase salaries as rapidly as inflation decreased the purchasing power of the cruzeiro.

The trend toward full-time professorships has been resumed in the stronger universities. Furthermore, numbers of university teachers hold two teaching positions at the same time, thus making it a de facto full-time position for them.

As university enrollments have grown, the number of young assistant professors and instructors has grown more rapidly than the number of *catedráticos*, and these younger people tend to seek a career in teaching, without another professional job.

THE CONDITIONS OF WORK. There are many disadvantages in the life of the university teacher in Brazil, compared with other countries in Europe and North America. Material equipment is poor. Lecture rooms are not well designed; blackboards and other teaching equipment are often inadequate; libraries and laboratories are very poor by North American and European standards. The professor who is not a *catedrático* seldom gets an office to himself, and almost never has adequate secretarial assistance. Nevertheless, conditions are improving. The *cidades universitárias* (university cities) of São Paulo, Pôrto Alegre, Belo Horizonte, and Rio de Janeiro are supplying new and adequate ly-designed buildings. And the size of Brazil gives a young professor the great advantage of being able to move from one university to another in search of promotion, whereas a small country with a small university system sometimes denies a young man opportunity for promotion simply because he happens to be in a department where there are several good people ahead of him in seniority.

The financial conditions are not as bad as the mere comparison of salaries with those in North America would imply. Full-time teachers get 75 per cent more than the pay of a part-time teacher, and there are increases with added seniority. After thirty-five years of service a professor may retire and receive his basic salary as long as he lives, and this is usually about two-thirds of his salary at the time of retirement. Retirement is mandatory at age seventy, and professors' salaries, by a provision in the constitution, are exempt from income tax.

CONTEMPORARY TRENDS. The trend at present is toward making the professor's career more professional, that is, making it a career in itself, with adequate pay plus rewards for good teaching and productive scholarship. There is also a trend toward making the university more efficient as a teaching institution, by eliminating duplicative courses, stricter admission requirements, and by better vocational guidance of students.

NOTES

1. Hutchinson, *Trabalho, Status e Educação.*

2. Aparecida Joly Gouveia, "Working Paper for a Study of Normal School Students" (unpublished paper, Rio de Janeiro: Centro Brasileiro de Pesquisas Educacionais, INEP, 1961) ; also listed in "Student Teachers in Brazil: A Study of Women's Career Choice" (Ph.D. Dissertation, University of Chicago, 1962) .

3. Aparecida Joly Gouveia, "Professôres do Estado do Rio," *Revista Brasileira de Estudos Pedagógicos,* XXVIII (July-Sept. 1957) , 34.

4. Ibid., p. 33.

5. Jayme Abreu, *A Educação Secundário no Brasil* (Rio de Janeiro: Instituto Nacional de Estudos Pedagógicos, Ministério da Educação e Cultura, 1955) , p. 50.

6. Gouveia, "Professôres do Estado de Rio," p. 36.

13

A
Look to the
Future

BRAZIL is traveling in the same direction that other countries have gone, and if not by exactly the same road, yet by a parallel one. Consequently it is not difficult to foretell some of the things that will happen in the near future. However, the particular changes that occur in Brazil will be different from those in other countries because of differences in size, climate, natural resources, and culture. Assuming that the changes of 1940–60 will continue substantially at the same rate from 1960–80, it should be possible to predict with a good deal of accuracy what is likely to happen in the field of education. The changes that can be foreseen depend on the maintenance of "Order and Progress," the Brazilian national motto, and, indeed, they must occur if there is to be order and progress.

Socioeconomic Changes

The population will continue to grow at nearly the same rate that has been maintained for the last twenty years. From 1950 to 1960—according to the last census—the annual rate of increase was 3.2 per cent. If a rate of 3 per cent is maintained during the next twenty-five years, we may expect a population of about 95 million in 1970 and between 130 and 135 million in 1980.

AREAS OF POPULATION GROWTH. The cities will continue to grow, as will the proportion of the population living in cities. However, this type of growth may be balanced partially by growth in the south central part of the country, through the development of small and medium-sized cities in the states of Goiás, Mato Grosso, western Minas Gerais, São Paulo, and Paraná. The new hydroelectric plants in these areas will provide plentiful power for industry and domestic consumption, and the agricultural production will support an increasing population.

LABOR FORCE. Industrialization and urbanization will increase the proportion of the working force that is active in manufacturing, transportation, commerce, social service, and the professions. Women will increase their participation in the labor force.

STANDARD OF LIVING. The national income will continue to increase more rapidly than the population increases, with a gain in per capita income of 2–3 per cent a year. Therefore the average per capita income will rise about 30 per cent between 1960 and 1970, and an equivalent amount between 1970 and 1980. This is average per capita income. The actual increase of income of the ordinary teacher, construction worker, or farmer will depend on the way the national income is distributed among the various classes of the population, and how much is used for investment in further economic growth.

It may be assumed that agricultural productivity will increase more than it has during the past twenty years. This area of the economy has lagged, but under pressure from the rising demand of a growing population, and especially from the urban element with more money to spend, it appears likely that agriculturists will invest in more machinery and will improve their methods of production. Furthermore, the government assistance projects in the Northeast, the São Francisco valley, and the Amazon should show results in the form of increased production.

Educational Development

As indicated by the trends of the last two decades, Brazil's educational system will continue to expand. There will be more students at every level of education, and the number will grow more rapidly than the population increases. But, of course, quantitative growth needs to be accompanied by qualitative change, and in Brazil's case, for this to come about more extensive reforms than are now in effect are needed. Professor Carlos Correa Mascaro of the University of São Paulo observes that it will be difficult, if not impossible, to maintain for any long period of time a system of education that is so full of quantitative and qualitative defects such as: (1) a primary school system that can only provide space for 50 per cent of the children a few hours a day; (2) a selective system of primary education; (3) secondary education with an academic overemphasis; (4) schools inadequately supplied with the materials necessary for effective teaching; (5) most schools operating on a multiple-shift schedule; (6) a teaching staff without adequate subject-matter preparation and professional training, and one therefore which may blindly oppose the necessary reforms.[1]

Under the present system, however, certain improvements are in sight. Along with the inevitable sheer growth in numbers there will be a greater percentage of students enrolled from the various age groups. Based on the 1940–60 changes, J. Roberto Moreira has projected school enrollments for the next twenty years. His conclusions are printed in Table 41. These larger percentages also indicate an increased literacy rate for Brazil. Since 75 per cent of those who pass the second grade and 97 per cent of those who pass the fourth grade retain the capacity to read and write as adults, the extent of illiteracy among adults in 1980 can be estimated at 20 per cent, less than half of what it was in 1960.

TABLE 41

Projected Growth in School Enrollments in Brazil, 1960-90

	Percentage of each age-group enrolled in school			
Ages	*1960*	*1970*	*1980*	*1990*
7-11	75	87	100	100
11-14	12	18	25	31
7-14	50	57	60	64
15-17	7	12	16	20

Note: Ages are inclusive of the years named.

Source: J. Roberto Morèira, "Perspectivos do Desenvolvimento Educacional no Brasil," *Boletim do Centro Latino-Americano de Pesquisas em Ciências Sociais*, III, No. 3 (1960), 23-37.

Increased enrollment, larger percentages of age groups attending school, and an increased literacy rate are achievements which Brazil can be assured of. But there remain major, and basic, tasks for the school system if even these goals are to be attained successfully, and if other goals, important for the country's development, are to be attained at all.

GENERAL PROBLEMS. The two great tasks of the primary school system in the two decades are to teach lower-class and rural children more efficiently, so as to reduce the present enormous failure rate in the first grade; and add two or three years to the present four or five year course, so that all Brazilian children may have a common school education for six or seven years.

At the secondary school level we may expect the enrollment to double between 1970 and 1980. Two major tasks in this area are to adapt the secondary school system to the greater variety of abilities and expectations which a growing body of students will bring to it; and to make a connection with the primary school so that pupils may pass smoothly from the primary school to the secondary school. If the primary school is extended for two or three years, the secondary school may drop one or two years of its first cycle. Eventually the secondary school system should receive half or more of all youth.

Higher education will also double enrollments during both of the next two decades, so that by 1980 some 8 per cent of young people will enter a university or higher institution. In this area a major problem is to make the teaching more efficient and economical of the time of professors; duplication of instruction needs to be reduced. At the same time, the university teachers need more fulltime teaching positions, and more time and stimulus for their own scholarly and creative work.

TEACHERS. The shortage of trained secondary school teachers will continue, though increasing proportions of new teachers will be university-trained, if adequate salaries are paid.

With primary school teachers the great problem is to get people with adequate training into the rural schools. A solution of this problem will require better salaries and better training, but the salaries must come first.

FINANCE. With enrollments doubling in secondary and higher education, it is a conservative estimate that expenditures on education will be doubled during the decade from 1960 to 1970. While the primary school enrollment will not double, the amount of money spent on it may well double since the present level of expenditures is so far below the expenditure on secondary education. Teacher's salaries must be increased, the school day should be lengthened, and the years of schooling should be extended.

Doubling the educational expenditure will create a problem of national policy. At present slightly less than 2 per cent of the national income is spent by government on education, and private school expenditures bring the total to slightly more than 2 per cent of the national income. But the national income may not double during the next decade. At the 1950–60 rate of increase, it is likely to increase about 60 or 70 per cent between 1960 and 1970. Therefore, it will be necessary to increase the proportion of the national income spent on education from approximately 2.2 per cent to about 2.6 per cent, if the educational expenditure is doubled.

Such an increase could come from government only if the governmental agencies deliberately expanded their educational budgets by about 20 per cent beyond the increase allowed by the growth of national income. They would have to take this money away from some other sector of expenditure, or they would have to raise taxes.

On the other hand, the increase might come from private rather than governmental sources, i.e., parents might pay larger fees for their children in schools and universities. This could take place in several ways. For instance, the government might allow private schools to raise their fees; this has been done in the past, but the government has paid a substantial part of the increase so as to keep the private schools accessible to pupils with low family incomes. At the university level the private universities might raise their fees, and the public universities might commence to charge fees. Such action would be resisted by students, but it might be pointed out that in most other countries the student or his family bears much more of the cost of university education than is the case in Brazil. And, since the vast majority of university students come from middle- or upper-class families, it would not be impossible for them to pay more of the cost of higher education, while an expanded system of scholarships could provide aid to needy students.*

Official Goals for 1970

These estimates of the future growth of education in Brazil are somewhat more conservative than the official government goals for 1970, which were announced at the close of 1962. The Federal Council on Education requested officials of the Ministry to draw up a plan for the expenditure of the three great national funds. Out of the total educational budget arising from the allocation of 12 per cent of tax income to educational programs, 30 per cent goes into the National Fund for Primary Education, and 30 per cent is allotted to each of the funds for secondary and for higher education, leaving 10 per cent for expenses of the Ministry of Education and other purposes.

The Commission for the Planning of Education (COPLED) has drawn up the following statement of goals.

* Anísio Teixeira has discussed this problem of sources of support for an expanded program of education in "A Escola Brasileira e a Estabilidade Social," *Revista Brasileira de Estudos Pedagógicos*, XXVIII, No. 67 (July-Sept. 1957), 3–29.

Quantitative Goals: Enrollment is to be established in primary school of 100 per cent of children between 7 and 11 years of age and of 70 per cent of children aged 11 and 12 in the fifth and sixth grades. In secondary schools the remaining 30 per cent of children aged 11 and 12 are to be accommodated in the first two years of the *ginásio,* and 50 per cent of the 13- and 14-year-olds are to be enrolled in the last two years of the *ginásio.* Then 30 per cent of the group aged 15 to 18 are to be enrolled in the second cycle of secondary school. Finally, the universities are to be expected to enroll half of those who graduate from the secondary school—perhaps 8 or 10 per cent of the age-group. The 1970 goals are supplemented by a more modest set of goals for the three-year period. 1963–66; whether these will be achieved depends largely on the ability of the Brazilian government to pay for the expansion proposed.

Qualitative Goals: In addition, the following qualitative goals are to be achieved by 1970. All primary school teachers are to have some special training—20 per cent in the four-year *ginasial* course, 60 per cent in the three-year normal course of the second cycle of the secondary school, and 20 per cent in courses at the post-secondary level. The last two years (fifth and sixth grades) of the primary school and all the secondary schools are to operate for a full day of six hours, and are to include provision for industrial arts. The university teaching staff is to include at least 30 per cent full-time teachers.

Administration and Organization of Education

Two major unsolved problems involve the organization and administration of the Brazilian educational system.

One is the problem of the relation of the municipal to the state systems of primary schools. While the much cheaper municipal system has been better than nothing, it is not likely that the two systems can exist side by side indefinitely with one spending about three times as much money per pupil as the other. Local community pressures will operate to induce the state to aid the municipal schools and eventually to integrate them into the state system. However, this would be a move toward centralization of responsibility for schools in the state capitals; and many educators believe that decentralization of responsibility and financial support is better for education.

The problem is, then, to find some way of increasing the financial support of municipal schools and at the same time to raise their quality so that they become as good as state schools. In this event, the state school system might decentralize into a system of municipal schools with municipal responsibility and a minimum of state control.

It is not at all clear at this time which way the situation will move in Brazil. It may even move in one direction in certain states and the other direction in other states. Events of the next ten years will probably decide whether the primary schools are to be under centralized or decentralized control from the state government.

The other problem is that of the relation between primary and secondary education. With primary education a responsibility of the states and secondary education a responsibility of the federal government, it is inevitable that the two systems should fail to fit together. The gap between them is one of the great unknowns of Brazilian education today.

One possibility is for the two systems to remain separate, while the primary schools add two or three years to their programs and thus overlap the secondary schools, as has happened in England, where "senior elementary schools" were developed for children up to age 15, and "grammar schools" took children from the elementary schools at age 11, on the basis of an entrance examination. The other possibility is to develop a single-track or unitary system of primary-secondary education, with students passing directly from the primary to the secondary school, generally without an entrance examination. This is the North American system, the Russian system, and that of most of British Commonwealth countries.

The Brazilian solution of the problem will be worked out within the next few years, as secondary education expands and becomes more popular, and the parents ask for a closer integration of the two systems.

Dimensions of Growth

Education will change qualitatively as well as quantitatively, and some idea of the qualitative changes may be gained by a look at the directions of change in structure, functions, and methods of the educational system. To facilitate this way of looking at educational change, we will compare Brazil with the United States. We will note how Brazil stands in relation to the United States on a number of dimensions of change. The several dimensions fall into three main groups, those of structure and organization, social functions of the educational system, and methods of teaching.

STRUCTURE AND ORGANIZATION. The structure and organization of the educational system can be discussed in terms of four dimensions.* Brazil and the United States are far apart on each of the dimensions, but Brazil seems to be moving toward the position of the latter.

Local versus Central Government Responsibility. Brazil's highly centralized form of educational administration seems to be moving away from that pole toward a middle position on the scale. Educational leaders are seeking to place at the level of the *município* more responsibility for the administration and supervision of primary education. In the field of secondary education it is likely that the states will take more responsibility for supervision and eventually for financial support.

Homogeneity versus Heterogeneity. The Brazilian school system is a heterogeneous one, with public and private schools and several types of public schools. At the secondary school level there are a variety of private schools, some run for profit and others not for profit. At the higher education level, there are many small faculties without university affiliation. The United States has more variety than Brazil in higher education. Probably the present degree of heterogeneity will decrease in Brazil, especially at the levels of secondary and higher education.

Social Class Orientation. The tendency of Brazilian education to serve middle- and upper-class people rather than working-class people has been noted. However, the working-class youth is finding his way into secondary schools and universities increasingly, especially in the South. This tendency can be expected to grow, as the system of secondary schools and universities expands. With free tuition in public schools and universities, the entrance of working-class youth into secondary schools will be fostered by improvement in primary schools and a closer liaison between primary and secondary schools.

* We are indebted to Dr. Anthony Leeds for a stimulating exposition of this way of looking at education comparatively, and we have used several of the dimensions defined by him; cf. "Cultural Factors in Education: Some Problems of Applied Anthropology," in *The Social Sciences: Theoretical and Applied*, ed. B. N. Varma (New York, 1961).

The gap between primary and secondary schools will no longer be a formidable barrier to children of working-class families.

Extent of Community Involvement. The Brazilian school tends to be isolated from the local community, which does not pay for it locally, does not supervise it locally, and does not interact with it through parent-teacher or citizens' organization or through efforts by the teachers to use the local community as an object for study. This is the opposite of the situation in the United States. Probably the Brazilian school will move toward greater involvement with the local community, as is evidenced by the fact that the campaign against illiteracy in the rural areas is working through local advisory committees, while the slum schools in Rio de Janeiro are being assisted by the local civic associations that are being formed in these areas.

SOCIAL FUNCTIONS OF THE SCHOOL SYSTEM. In addition to the functions of making people literate and training them for trades and professions, there are a number of other social functions of the educational system which receive various degrees of emphasis in various societies. Several of these functions have been selected to show other directions of change in Brazilian education, as well as to contrast it with that of the United States.

Culture-conserving versus Culture-changing. The Brazilian schools have tended to conserve and transmit the values and the mores of the traditional culture. By teaching the "official" values of a Catholic and Latin culture, the schools and universities have tended to reflect the ways of the older generation in the lives of the younger generation. This contrasts with the tendency in a consciously-changing society such as the United States to teach children to expect and welcome change. However, the Brazilian schools show some signs of treating culture changes more positively, with attention to the industrialization of the country, and with the growth of training for technicians at the secondary-school level and for engineers at the university level.

Political Activism versus Political Passivism. At the secondary and university levels, Brazilian education encourages students to become interested in local and national politics and to take part in political activity. This is a contrast with the general political disinterest which schools and universities of the United States tend to inculcate in their students. It seems likely that interest in local and national politics will continue to be encouraged in Brazil, faced as she is with major social and political problems that must be settled by political processes. *Nationalist versus Internationalist.* The net effect of the formal educative influences in Brazil is to develop nationalist rather than internationalist political interests, even though the schools do not teach extreme forms of nationalism and even though Brazil traditionally has close ties with Europe. However, the trend is toward paying greater attention to international affairs and toward the teaching of attitudes favorable to international cooperation.

Individualist versus Cooperative. In content of the school and university curriculum as well as in methods of teaching, the Brazilian tendency is to create an individualist who acts in his own interest and on his own responsibility. He does not work or learn in and through a group, even though he is a sociable and friendly individual. The group centered quality of education, which is found in the United States, is lacking in Brazilian education. At present there seems to be no sign of change in this respect.

Status-maintaining versus Mobility-promoting. The Brazilian educational system has tended to help people maintain their social status, since secondary and higher education have been largely limited to middle and upper-class people. But the trend is toward the encouragement of social mobility, through expansion of educational opportunity for children of working-class families.

Technician-training versus Generalist-training. The Brazilian tendency has been to give an education devoid of specific "how-to-do-it" training and thus to produce people with a general knowledge that is largely theoretical. Even though higher education tends to be specialized rather than general, the emphasis is on theory rather than practice. This condition is changing, with the growth of technical education at the secondary level and with the growth of engineering schools at the university level.

Activism for Women. A very strong educational trend is leading women in Brazil into a wider range of economic and professional activities. This is seen especially in the growing proportion of women students in the universities, as well as in the commercial secondary schools.

METHODS OF EDUCATION. In methods of teaching there will

certainly be a great deal of change during the next decade or two. Brazilian education is at one end of the scale on most matters of method, where the United States is generally toward the middle of the scale.

Open System versus Closed System. Brazilian education has treated knowledge as a "closed system" in which there are unique answers for every question asked in the school. The multiplication table and the spelling list are the mainstays of this kind of education. However, there is a tendency in Brazil, which is carried further in the United States, to become more concerned with topics and problems that do not permit a simple yes- or no answer. Knowledge is increasingly treated as an "open system" in which the results are to be worked out by pupils and teachers. This implies greater use of discussion rather than question-answer recitation methods, more individual projects, more attention to social studies in the curriculum, and more interest in creativity and originality on the part of students.

Process versus Content. Emphasis upon the acquiring of a body of knowledge is giving way in Brazilian schools to a concern for "process" of thinking. There is a similar trend in the United States, where experimentation with "how to learn" has been a popular form of educational research in the 1960's. This means that more attention will be given to teaching the processes of mathematics and scientific thinking.

General Knowledge versus Specialized Knowledge. The Brazil ian tendency has been to teach for specialized knowledge in a relatively narrow area. This is noticeable especially in the university, with its early specialization in a single department. There is now a trend toward studying a broader field in the university, with courses in several related departments.

Practice and Technique versus Theory. The Brazilian trend is toward training students for a more practical and technical grasp of knowledge, this is related to an increase of interest in the sciences, and especially the applied sciences. More attention is being paid to laboratory and experimental work and to field studies.

Group-centered versus Individual-centered Teaching. It has already been noted that the Brazilian system tends to produce individualists. This result is related to a form of teaching which concentrates on the individual recitation, individual study, individual competition among the students, and individual relations between student and teacher. Now there is beginning to be some attention to the class as a group and to teaching the individual to work in and with a group. However this tendency is not strong.

Permissive versus Authoritative. Perhaps the relation of teacher as authority to pupil as dependent is being supplemented by other forms of teacher-pupil relations which encourage more independence on the part of pupils. While the Brazilian position is far distant from the permissiveness of the American school, it seems to be moving in that direction.

Conclusion

The educational system of Brazil is rapidly taking added responsibility for the rearing of the younger generation in such a way as to make Brazil economically stronger and politically wiser, and socially more democratic. Of the four basic social institutions, the state and the economy are forcing this responsibility on the schools and universities; the Brazilian family is, so to speak, shrugging its shoulders and saying to the schools, "We hope you can do a better job than we have done"; and the church is trying to extend and expand its educational services, hoping to get state support for the process.

There is an urgency about the task of education in Brazil that marks it off from the countries that have evolved their school system gradually in an environment of gradual industrialization and urbanization extending over a century or more. Brazil is in a hurry.

1. Carlos Correa Mascaro, "Custeio de Educação e as Reformas Programadas," *Revista Brasileira de Estudos Pedagógicos*, XXXIV, No. 80 (Oct.-Dec. 1960), 66.

Glossary

Bandeirante: an explorer, frontiersman, and Indian fighter

Caboclo: a hillbilly, a hick—a name first applied to acculturated Indians, then to white-Indian mestizos, and now, generally, to any lower-class rural person.

Cafèzinho: a demitasse of black coffee, generally taken with much sugar

Cafuso: a person of mixed Indian and Negro descent

Caipira: a man or woman who lives in the country and lacks social graces; a lower-class, rural Brazilian

Candomblé: a religious institution, like a church group, which practices an African-American-Catholic syncretistic religion in Bahia

Carioca: a person living in Rio de Janeiro; a cultural trait of that city

Casa grande: the big house or mansion of a large estate during the days of slavery.

Compadre: the name applied to the godparent of a child, and also by him to the child's parent

Compadrio: relationship between parents and the godparents of their children

Colégio: the last three years of the secondary school, normally composed of students aged 16, 17, and 18.

Cortiço: a heavily populated city tenement.

Cruzeiro: the common unit of money in Brazil. Worth about 5 cents U.S. in 1950, 1.5 cents in 1956, 1 cent in 1959, and 0.17 cents in 1963. The cruzeiro was formerly called the milreis (1,000 reis), when the real was the unit of currency in the nineteenth century.

Conto: a unit of money worth 1,000 cruzeiros. At the beginning of the Brazilian Empire in 1832, this was worth about $1,000.00 U.S. Its value in dollars has decreased, due to inflation, and in 1964 it was worth about 75 cents U.S.

Engenho: a sugar mill; sometimes refers to an entire sugar plantation including the mill

259

Favela: a slum in Rio de Janeiro, especially those which dot the hillsides of Rio

Fazenda: a large estate

Fazendeiro: the owner or operator of a fazenda

Gaúcho: a native of Rio Grande do Sul

Ginásio: the first cycle (four years) of the secondary school, normally composed of students aged 12, 13, 14, 15.

IBGE: Instituto Brasileiro de Geográfia e Estatístico (the federal Institute of Geography, Statistics, and Census)

Juventude Universitária Católica: Catholic University Youth

Juventude Operária Católica: Catholic Working Youth

Macumba: the Rio version of the candomble or xango

Maloca: a slum dwelling in the Northeast of Brazil and in Rio Grande do Sul

MEC: Ministério de Educação e Cultura (the federal Ministry of Education and Culture)

Mineiro: a native of Minas Gerais

Moreno: a person with dark complexion

Mucambo: slum in low swampy terrain in Northeastern coastal cities such as Recife

Município: the administrative and government unit in Brazil equivalent to a county in the United States

Nordestino: a native of northeastern Brazil

Pardo: a brown-skinned person or mulatto

Paulista: a native of the state of São Paulo

Prêto: a black-skinned person or Negro

SENAC: Serviço Nacional de Aprendizagem Comercial (National Service of Commercial Apprenticeship)

SENAI: Serviço Nacional de Aprendizagem dos Industriários (National Service of Industrial Apprenticeship)

Sêca: drought

Senzala: the group of slave huts on a plantation or fazenda

Sertão: an isolated place, the backwoods; generally refers to the desert area of the Brazilian Northeast

Sertanejo: the common man who lives in the Sertão

Sobrado: a two-story mansion built in the nineteenth century in the towns and cities

Umbanda: the high priest in an Afro Brazilian cult; sometimes more generally used to refer to this cult

Usina: the modern sugar refinery

Xango: a type of African-Amerindian-Catholic religion practiced mainly by lower-class people in the Northeast

INDEX